Software Development

Building Reliable Systems

Harris Kern's Enterprise Computing Institute

Software Development

Building Reliable Systems

Marc Hamilton

Prentice Hall PTR, Upper Saddle River, NJ 07458
http://www.phptr.com

Editorial/Production Supervision: *Mary Sudul*
Acquisitions Editor: *Greg Doench*
Editorial Assistant: *Mary Treacy*
Marketing Manager: *Miles Williams*
Manufacturing Manager: *Alexis R. Heydt*
Cover Design Direction: *Jerry Votta*
Cover Design: *Talar Agasyan*
Series Design: *Gail Cocker-Bogusz*

Prentice Hall books are widely used by corporations and government agencies for training, marketing, and resale.

The publisher offers discounts on this book when ordered in bulk quantities.
For more information, contact Corporate Sales Department, Phone: 800-382-3419; fax: 201-236-714; email: corpsales@prenhall.com or write Corporate Sales Department, Prentice Hall PTR, One Lake Street, Upper Saddle River, NJ 07458.

Printed in the United States of America

10 9 8 7 6 5 4 3 2 1

ISBN 0-13-081246-3

Prentice-Hall International (UK) Limited, *London*
Prentice-Hall of Australia Pty. Limited, *Sydney*
Prentice-Hall Canada Inc., *Toronto*
Prentice-Hall Hispanoamericana, S.A., *Mexico*
Prentice-Hall of India Private Limited, *New Delhi*
Prentice-Hall of Japan, Inc., *Tokyo*
Simon & Schuster Asia Pte. Ltd., *Singapore*
Editora Prentice-Hall do Brasil, Ltda., *Rio de Janeiro*

Dedication

Having written the equivalent of thousands of pages of code during my career, along with numerous technical articles and other journalistic endeavors, writing a 350 page book on software development did not seem like such a large venture when I began it. Nearly a year later, I must say I greatly underestimated the time and challenges involved. This book, however, is not only a product of my efforts but of the many people who helped me, directly and indirectly, over the last twelve months. The biggest help came from my immediate family who put up with my late nights typing away during winter holidays, summer vacation, weekends, and whenever else a free moment could be found. I therefore dedicate this book to my wife of ten years, Roberta, and our two wonderful children, Camille and Evan.

Acknowledgments

To Harris Kern, who convinced me to write this book in the first place and seemed always available, no matter where in the world he traveled, to review anything from a new paragraph to new drafts of the entire book. Harris worked with me every step of the way, from the first outlines to the final draft, and without his help and support this book would never have been completed.

To Dr. Ray Toal, of Loyola Marymount University. Besides writing the foreword, he edited numerous drafts of the book, contributing greatly to its final form. Dr. Toal, as only a true professor could, scrutinized many of the technical details and examples in the book for accuracy. In addition, he would routinely point out whenever my own work experience introduced some language or vendor bias into the text.

To my staff at Sun Microsystems over the last year, including Steve Ballantine, Carolyn Bumatay, Steven Cheng, David Chu, John Fragalla, Barbara Herr, Anita Jensen, Craig Lehman, Bruce Mathews, Tony Mansour, Neil Parsons, Hamant Patel, Andrew Schmoller, Steve Staso, and Jeff Weiss, for always believing in and supporting me.

To my manager at Sun Microsystems for over four years, Tom Swysgood, not only for supporting my efforts to write this book, but also for providing the drive and innovation to manage the dramatic growth and change at Sun in Los Angeles during that time. Tom may not recall, but it is his forwarded e-mail from Harris that first raised my interest to write this book.

And to all the great people I've had the opportunity to work with over the years at Sun, including:

- Cesar Baray, who taught me how to manage in a sales organization.
- Jae Chung, who taught me the value of never giving up when you really want something.
- Jim Eastman, who took on the challenge of teaching me about sales.
- Dennis Horgan, whose own journalistic endeavors motivated me as I wrote this book and whose immense wealth of IT knowledge added not only to this book but to all the customers he has worked with at Sun.
- Chuck Meyer who finally convinced me to join Sun after five years of trying and has been a mentor and close friend ever since.
- Pete Stafford, who taught me how to break through whatever holds you back.

And finally, to all the great developers at TRW who I've worked with over the years, the people who really taught me about successful software development.

Contents

Part 1
Background 1

Chapter 1

Ten Commandments of Successful Software Development 3

Chapter 2

Software Development Has Always Been Difficult 23

Chapter 6

Organizing for Success 105

Chapter 7

Recruiting The Best Talent 119

Chapter 8

Retaining the Best Talent 127

Chapter 11

Rapid Application Development 161

Chapter 12

Software Productivity, Metrics, and Quality 167

Software Development Tools 211

Chapter 16

Selecting Your Hardware Environment 233

Chapter 17

Component-Based Software Development 261

Chapter 18

Performance Optimization Techniques 267

Chapter 19

Multithreaded Programming 271

Appendix A

Software Development Frequently Asked Questions 311

Appendix B

Java Coding Standard Template 325

Appendix C

Sample Internal Support Agreement (ISA) 345

Figures

Tables

Foreword

Software organizations are looking at a very different world from that of a few short years ago. The whole planet is wired, with shopping and banking done from living rooms as well as from brokerage houses. In the enterprise arena, mainframe applications continue to give way to client/server and multi-tier systems. Desktop PCs are commonplace and practically disposable. Network PCs, the new appliances, will soon be ubiquitous. Soon even our current household appliances will reside on a network.

Fortunately, software developers have many new software tools and technologies on which to thrive in these changing environments. There are new programming languages and modernized versions of old ones. C++ is (finally!) an international standard, with a standard library that makes the old arrays and "char-stars" obsolete except for uses in low-level systems and embedded software. Java's success as a new language is unparalleled due to its safety, portability (write-once run anywhere), and incredibly rich Core APIs. Visual Basic has proven that software *components* really work, and enjoys wide popularity for writing clients and now even middleware business objects. (FORTRAN and COBOL are still with us, and may even persist long enough for a Y10K problem to arise.)

Developers are also working differently. They have builders and visual environments. They are not writing as many "monolithic" applications – instead they are employing frameworks, implementing plug-ins, and writing more and more components. Whether components are JavaBeans or ActiveX controls, or live in a CORBA-wired enterprise, these reusable binaries have had and will continue to have a profound impact on the development, marketing, and sale of software. Componentware takes us beyond object-oriented programming; component-oriented programming has us now paying more attention to reusable architectures and design patterns, using interfaces, and relying less on inheritance and more on composition.

These rapid *technological* advancements have created new, and highly significant, problems in the *people* and *process* domains. In the people domain, new positions, such as Toolsmith, and of course Webmaster, need to be filled. Retention has become a critical issue for many organizations in these days of escalating salaries. Managers need to work in an environment with no small number of arrogant, overpaid and underdressed programmers who take pride in far outperforming and outproducing their co-workers by factors unheard of in other industries.

On the process side, new development methodologies are being created as the rush to move away from mainframes creates real worries about causing a move away from mainframe data-center-oriented disciplines. The basic production challenges still remain: producing software is different from producing other commodities, software is "too flexible" to maximize reuse under tight schedules, and so on. New challenges in verifying massively distributed systems with thin clients are requiring new approaches to the acceptance process. What is clear is that these people and process challenges are not met by applying generic management theories.

Software Development is a book that anyone in the software industry can, should, and would certainly want to read. It provides a unified treatment of people, process, and technology issues without falling into the trap of being too broad and shallow in its coverage. The author has had years of experience in both management and software engineering, and writes with authority in both voices. Managerial types will find useful information on recruiting, organizing and retaining talent, employee profiles, how software quality can be measured, how to use domain experts, and answers to common questions such as "make vs. buy." Developers will no doubt be interested in the technology sections covering programming languages, tools, hardware, multithreading, componentware, distributed architectures and Jini. However, one of the real strengths of the book is how readable the technological sections are to managers and the people and process issues are to developers. Managers need to understand the technology and developers can not be isolated from process and management issues. A pipelined organization where design hands off to development which hands off to QA which hands off to rollout is an organization that will fail; everyone in the organization needs to be involved throughout the entire software life cycle. Developers need to communicate with users while requirements are being gathered; everyone should participate in testing and deployment. This is the book that gives *everyone* the big picture.

We still live in a world where the majority of software development projects are late and over budget. This indicates that making a project successful must be hard (which is no surprise because, as Booch pointed out, software is *inherently* complex). Many people have offered advice to make software success a reality: some with academic theories, some with managerial theories, some with new technologies, some with process model blueprints to follow, some with case studies. *Software Development* tells you what you really need to know with the perfect *mix* of people, process, and technology issues. You will learn what successful organizations do to succeed, what causes projects to fail, how to build and retain a winning team, and get a comprehensive tour of today's brand-new and cutting-edge technologies. You will find solid information that you can put into practice today to make your development efforts successful.

Dr. Ray Toal

Professor of Computer Science

Loyola Marymount University

Los Angeles, California

Introduction

Today, software touches almost every aspect of our lives. From the business critical enterprise applications in the glasshouse data centers of Fortune 500 corporations, to the real-time software in your car's anti-lock brake system, to the web browser on your home PC, software is everywhere. Given the complexity of traditional software development, it is not surprising that estimates show over half of all code in use today was originally designed at least five years ago. Since 1995, however, the widespread use of Internet technologies and the Java platform have fundamentally changed the nature of software development. In the year 2000, besides many never-fixed Y2K bugs, software engineers will be writing code for everything from Enterprise Java-Beans powered application servers to consumer devices capable of spontaneous networking with Jini technology.

There is no doubt companies like Intel and others will be able to continue developing increasingly powerful microprocessors to execute all this new code. Moore's law, stating integrated circuit processing power doubles every twelve to eighteen months, has held true for over thirty years since Intel's co-founder Gordon Moore made his now famous observation in 1965. Many experts, including Moore himself, believe this trend will hold true for at least another two decades. Unfortunately, no such trends have consistently held true for software development.

One of the first authors to write about the difficulty of developing software was Frederick Brooks, whose 1975 book *The Mythical Man Month* describes why adding more people to a software project that is already behind schedule will only make it later. Twelve years later, in his IEEE Computer article *No Silver Bullet: Essence and Accidents of Software Engineering*, Brooks made famous the classic line, "There is no silver bullet in software engineering." In fact, many software projects are modestly successful only because after development delays, hardware speeds increase sufficiently to mask performance problems caused by poor software design. Many other software projects, unfortunately, fail completely because of the lack of mature development processes. In many corporations, software is still for the most part written one line at a time by engineers using text editors and compilers similar to those available twenty years ago. Sure, there are a number of graphical development tools a novice programmer can use to create a simple program. Much more than a fancy development tool, however, will be needed if you are going to successfully complete a major software project.

The most successful software projects are the result of skilled programmers, architects, and other specialists following disciplined processes and aided by modern technology to deliver results on time and under budget. Yet despite the hundreds of books available on the subject of software development, estimates show as many as eighty percent of software projects do not successfully meet their original schedule and budget. The reason for this is that having skilled programmers or powerful development tools, by themselves, does not guarantee successful software development. *Software Development* will concentrate on the attributes of the people, processes, and technology that make the other twenty percent of software projects successful.

Who Should Read This Book

This book is for professional software engineers, software architects, software engineering managers, and MIS managers. The typical reader might be employed in the applications development group of a large company's IT department, work as a developer for a system integrator, or work as an in-house developer for a commercial software vendor. Most of the concepts presented here were developed on mid- to large-size software projects involving five to fifty software engineers. This is not to say these concepts are not useful or applicable if your project is smaller or larger than this. If you are managing a project with more than fifty software engineers, this book is more applicable to your project than ever. It's just that you may be too concerned with higher level management issues to have much time to deal with the actual software engineering process and will focus on the people and process issues. If your project has less than five software engineers, you still should read this book, since all the technology concepts presented remain applicable on even the smallest one-developer projects. Furthermore, once you prove your skills on a small project, you will undoubtedly be called upon to work on larger projects where the people and process issues become more important. Here is what each of you can expect to gain by reading this book.

For software engineers, this book might be best described by starting with what it does not cover. This book is not a basic "how to program" book for novice programmers. Neither is it programming language or hardware specific. We have used both Java and C to illustrate some of the programming examples, simply because of the popularity and familiarity of most programmers with one or both of these two languages. The principles presented, however, are generally applicable to software development in any programming language.

The type of programmer who will benefit from this book is the professional software engineer looking for a broad overview of the latest technologies being used by leading edge companies developing medium to large software projects. This book will also be useful to developers who perhaps have never had the opportunity to work with a group of developers on a large project and want to gain an insight to the skills that will make them successful in such an environment. Much of this book focuses on the design stages of software development and presents concepts and techniques bound to make even the most experienced developers more productive. Because of this book's focus on the design stage of software development, it also provides valuable reading to the software engineer who wants to transition into the role of software architect with additional design responsibility.

Besides providing lessons for the software engineer who wants to become more of a software architect, this book is also valuable reading for experienced software architects. It provides a good update for software architects who want to become familiar with the latest software engineering technologies such as component-based software development, multi-tiered network centric design, object-oriented technologies, and exciting new developments in the Java world such as Jini technology. Given the pace at which such new software technologies evolve, most software architects are likely to find several areas covered in this book in which they do not have hands-on experience. In addition to software technologies, this book provides software architects information on how to design software systems with "best practice" people and process techniques in mind. This will be very useful for architects who have a desire to move into software engineering management.

For software engineering managers, this book provides a unique perspective on the people and process issues surrounding software development. We have included chapters on how to identify, recruit, hire, and retain the best software engineers and architects. Managers new to software development will learn why the experience and skills of their software engineers and software architects will have a bigger impact on the success of their software project than in any other information technology area they might have previously managed. There is not, however, any special "management" chapter in this book. If you are going to be a successful software engineering manager you need to understand all the concepts presented in this book. Many other books concentrate simply on management skills and forget that the best managers not only understand what their software engineers are really doing, they understand what their developers really *want* to do. It follows that productivity is higher when software engineers are doing what, in fact, they really want to be doing. Once you understand these concepts, you will be better able to schedule and budget your software development projects to ensure their success on all levels.

Finally, this book will be useful to MIS managers up through Chief Information Officers (CIOs). While many such managers do not necessarily think of themselves as requiring any software skills, this book provides a unique insight into what is needed for successful software development. For starters, to achieve the greatest productivity, a software development group needs a good software development infrastructure. Software development environments have their own unique requirements for developer desktops, servers, and related network infrastructure. All of this falls under the control of an MIS manager somewhere in the organization. In addition, once software is deployed, which is perhaps the ultimate measuring ground of a project's success, MIS managers need to provide the proper production infrastructure. By understanding basic details about a software project, such as whether it is network-centric or host-based, MIS managers will be better able to provide the proper infrastructure. In turn, by understanding the deployment environment, software architects and developers can make the right design decisions early on and greatly simplify the job of their MIS brethren.

How to Read This Book

Software Development is divided into four parts focusing on the background, people, processes, and technology of successful software development projects. While we hope you read this book from cover to cover, a short, one page or less, introduction is provided at the start of each chapter. Anyone seriously interested in software development, from novice programmers to the most experienced architects and managers, should at least read the introduction to each chapter. In addition, Chapter 1, "The Ten Commandments of Successful Software Development", should be read completely as it summarizes what we believe are the ten most important concepts anyone associated with a software development project should be familiar with. These ten commandments will be referred to again and again throughout the rest of the book. Software architects, developers, and managers will then probably read the various chapters more or less thoroughly depending on their specific interests. The following provides some additional information to help guide you through the four parts of this book.

Part One consists of Chapters 1 through 4 and provides a general background in software development concepts. Software developers and architects can skim through Chapters 2 through 4 as they will probably be familiar with most of this material. Software development managers and MIS managers, especially those without a strong development background, should read through this material and be certain they understand the concepts as they provide a basis for the topics covered in the remainder of the book. Chapters 5 through 9 make up Part Two of the book, focusing on people issues related to software development. This is perhaps the most important section of the book for software development managers. Part Three, Chapters 10 through 13, focuses on software development processes. This part of the book should be of interest to all readers. While it has been said that software development is still more of an art than a science, projects following mature, "best practice" development processes are consistently more successful than those that don't. Chapters 14 through 22 comprise Part Four of the book and cover software development technology. These chapters are more likely to be read thoroughly by a software architect or developer, although managers should at least be familiar with the concepts presented therein.

About the Author

Marc Hamilton started developing software in 1975 while attending high school. Back then, FORTRAN was the language of choice and the school computer was an IBM 1620 with 8K of memory. The text editor was a keypunch and the compiler was a three inch thick deck of computer punchcards. Mr. Hamilton's penchant for software continued at UCLA, where he enrolled as a Computer Science major. UCLA undergrads still used punchcards at the time, although the college's IBM mainframe was substantially more up to date than the IBM 1620. Unfortunately, the mainframe's green screen 3270 terminals and their TSO (IBM's "time sharing option" terminal control software) environment were reserved for graduate student use. As luck would have it, no teaching assistant was available for one of Mr. Hamilton's first programming classes and after volunteering to be the system administrator for the class, he was granted access to one of the vaunted TSO terminals. It was at this point, Hamilton recalls, that he realized his interests in computing were here to stay.

Between his junior and senior years at UCLA, Mr. Hamilton went to work as a summer intern developing software for TRW's Spacecraft Engineering Division. The Southern California aerospace industry was just starting its buildup for the heyday of the Reagan years and he had no trouble finding part-time work at TRW while he finished school. TRW's aerospace group had one of the largest software development organizations in the world, so it was a natural choice for him to continue on there after graduation.

In the early 1980s, software development at TRW generally meant working on a DEC machine. The VAX 11-780 was the workhorse computer of the aerospace industry and VMS was its industrial strength operating system. What the DEC sales representatives probably didn't know, however, was that at 5:00 p.m. each evening, when scheduled production operations ended, new college hires like Hamilton would load disk packs containing the Berkeley Unix operating system (developed by Bill Joy at Berkeley prior to his co-founding Sun Microsystems) and work late into the night on new software prototypes being developed in the C language. The writing was on the wall as new computer companies such as Sun Microsystems in California and Apollo in Massachusetts (Apollo was later purchased by Hewlett Packard) were developing their first workstations.

After a year of full-time work, Mr. Hamilton decided TRW's graduate fellowship program was too good to pass up. It was during graduate school at USC that Hamilton was first exposed to object-oriented programming, with the Symbolics Lisp workstation and its object system called "Flavors." Flavors and another object system, Common Loops, later become the basis for the Common Lisp Object System. Apart from a couple of Symbolics machines, and an occasional project with legacy DEC hardware, Mr. Hamilton spent most of his remaining eleven years at TRW working on a succession of Sun-based software development projects.

At the end of 1993, Mr. Hamilton left TRW to join the system engineering team at Sun Microsystems. Presently, he is a manager of system engineering in Sun's Los Angeles office. At Sun, he continues to be involved with end-user software developers. In addition, he works closely with internal Sun software development organizations, independent software vendors, and developers at commercial system integrators. Over the last five years, he has worked with the software development organizations and IT departments of nearly one hundred different companies, including Xerox PARC, Oracle, Mattel, UCLA, USC, Boeing, TRW, Hughes, Anderson Consulting, Toyota, JPL, and of course Sun Microsystems. In addition, he was one of the founding members of Sun's Java ACES group, responsible for rolling out Java technology and training to Sun's field system engineering force. "I've always had a passion for software," states Hamilton, "and my job at Sun lets me be involved with some of the best software technologists in the world,"

Background

Ten Commandments of Successful Software Development

All great organizations have a vision, a mission, and elemental guidelines for proper behavior that are infused into their people. Perhaps the oldest code of conduct is the Ten Commandments. Since the day Moses stumbled off Mount Sinai, people have applied the idea of condensing their groups' rules into ten, easy to remember, sentences. Following the lead of Moses, we've distilled the successful software development concepts presented in this book into ten commandments of successful software development, as summarized in Figure 1-1. If you want to be consistently successful at software development, be sure you always embrace these ten ideals.

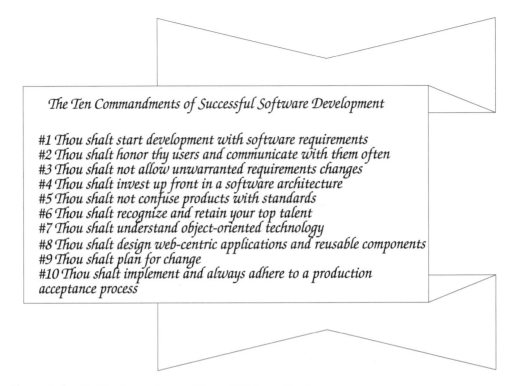

The Ten Commandments of Successful Software Development

#1 Thou shalt start development with software requirements
#2 Thou shalt honor thy users and communicate with them often
#3 Thou shalt not allow unwarranted requirements changes
#4 Thou shalt invest up front in a software architecture
#5 Thou shalt not confuse products with standards
#6 Thou shalt recognize and retain your top talent
#7 Thou shalt understand object-oriented technology
#8 Thou shalt design web-centric applications and reusable components
#9 Thou shalt plan for change
#10 Thou shalt implement and always adhere to a production
acceptance process

Figure 1–1   The Ten Commandments of Successful Software Development

#1 Thou shalt start development with software requirements

Every morning, some software developer wakes up with a great new idea for a software application, utility, or tool. Those who go off and start writing code without first considering the requirements for their program are likely doomed to failure. Invest up front in developing your software requirements and you will be starting down the path to successful software development. A software development organization without any requirements management process in place will not repeatedly achieve development success. Here are some tips as to why and how you should develop and manage software requirements for any project, regardless of size.

For starters, if you can't define the requirements for your software system, you will never be able to measure the success of your development effort. If you were to write a calculator program, would it be successful if it could add two numbers and produce the correct result? What about subtraction, multiplication, and division? Does the calculator need to handle floating point numbers or just integers? How many digits of precision are needed in results? What should the calculator's behavior be if a divide by zero is encountered? Should the results be displayed in a textual or graphical format? How long does the result have to be saved after it is displayed? The list goes on. Even in this trivial example, requirements are extremely important to determining the success of the project.

It is very difficult to write good software requirements. Without good requirements precisely stating what a software program is suppose to accomplish, it is very difficult to judge the application's success, much less complete the project in the first place. One of the main reasons it is so hard to write good software requirements has to do with the nature of human language. English, and for that matter all spoken languages, are very imprecise and leave much to be inferred by the listener or reader. Computers, by their digital nature, are very precise and not easily programmed to infer missing requirements. Therein lies a dichotomy. Think of a requirement statement as simple as "the program shall add the two numbers and display the results." You could raise all the same questions posed in the calculator example in the last paragraph. Even if these questions were answered, more requirements would probably be uncovered during development of the application.

If your software development team is asking questions like those in the previous calculator example, it probably is a good sign. There is no surer failure of a software development project than to have incomplete requirements. Of course the next steps after asking questions and developing requirements are to document them, organize them, and track them. Modern CASE tools (see Chapter 15) include requirements development and tracking functions that help you do this.

Many development projects actually start with a good set of functionality requirements, such as input this, perform this processing, output that. What is often left out are performance and other environmental requirements as summarized in Table 1-1. How quickly does the program have to complete

Table 1–1   Commonly Overlooked Performance and Environmental Requirements

Requirement	Examples
Processing Speed	CPU speed
Memory Capacity	Cache size, RAM size
Network Capacity	Network interface card speed, switch and router bandwidth
Persistent Storage	On-line disk capacity; tape backup capacity

Table 1–1 Commonly Overlooked Performance and Environmental Requirements

Requirement	Examples
Internationalization Support	Will the application be deployed in different countries or in different languages?
Minimum Display	Monitor size and resolution; number of colors supported
Financial	Budget and schedule
Environmental	Power requirements, air conditioning, special temperature or humidity requirements

the required processing? How much RAM or disk space can it use? Does the software have to support internationalization for worldwide use? What is the minimal display size required? Environment related requirements are becoming increasingly important, especially with the advent of cross-platform development environments such as Java. Java truly provides a write-once run anywhere environment ranging from smartcards to workstations to mainframes. A Java applet that looks great on a workstation's 21" color monitor, however, may look much different on the 4" screen of a monochrome personal digital assistant (PDA). Finally, don't forget budget and schedule requirements. In gathering these requirements, the reasons for the second commandment should become very clear to you.

#2 Thou shalt honor thy users and communicate with them often

Most software applications are not used by their own developers; they are intended to be used by the developer's customers, clients, and end-users. This implies that someone in your development organization had better spend a lot of time communicating with users so that their requirements can be correctly understood. In the calculator example from the first commandment, a developer may be perfectly happy with the four basic arithmetic functions while the user would like a square root function or a memory function. What the developer thinks is a complete set of requirements isn't necessarily so.

Moving from a trivial to a real world example, an enterprise-wide IT application may have many types of users, each with their own business requirements. Take a payroll system for example. One type of user is the employee, whose requirements include getting paid the correct amount in a timely fashion. A second type of user is a manager, who wants to be able to administer salary increases and track budgets. A third type of user might be the HR administrator, who wants to compare salary ranges across an entire organization. Each user type will have unique requirements.

The second part of this commandment focuses on the word "often." Frequent communication is required, among other reasons, because English (or any other modern language) is an imprecise language. Communication with users only starts at the requirements definition phase. A developer may have to discuss a requirement with a user several times before the true definition of the requirement is captured. In addition, user requirements are likely to change often, and indeed several requirements may even conflict. Frequent communication with users gives the developer early notice of requirements changes the user is considering.

A successful software development organization has established processes for frequently communicating with users during all stages of the development process. The sooner an incorrect or missing requirement is discovered, the easier it is to fix the problem. Many successful development organizations have made customer advisory teams an integral part of the software development process. Such customer teams participate in all stages of development from initial requirements gathering to production acceptance signoff. The Web-Centric Production Acceptance (WCPA) process presented in Chapter 13 is another vehicle for bringing users and developers together and promoting and instilling good communication practices.

#3 Thou shalt not allow unwarranted requirements changes

While user requirements do often change, it is the job of the development organization to manage these changes in a controlled fashion and assure that requirements do not change or grow unnecessarily. Pity the poor programmer who started off writing a basic arithmetic calculator, agreed to add square roots and a few other user requested functions, then a few more, and even a few more, and soon had the task of developing a sixty-five function scientific calculator. Modifying or adding new requirements can happen for many reasons, not the least of which being the failure to honor Commandments One and Two.

Another reason requirements grow beyond their original scope is simply that software is so easy to change compared to hardware. No one would purchase a calculator at the local electronics store and then expect the manufacturer to add additional transistors to the calculator chip to implement a new function.

If the calculator was a software application, no one would think twice about the ability to add a new function.

Perhaps an even more common reason that requirements change is due to the programmers themselves. Many a programmer has accepted a new user requirement not based on valid business reasons but simply to please a user. Other times the software may be fully functional and pass all unit test requirements, but the programmer just wants to add one more feature to make the application "just a little better." Good developers always want their code to be perfect in their own eyes. The cost of making even simple changes, however, is minor compared to the cost of the retesting and requalifying that may result.

This does not mean to say we are against iterative development. In Chapter 10, *"The Software Life Cycle"*, the use of iterative or spiral development is prominently discussed. Even in a spiral development model, however, new requirements are introduced at the start of each new iteration, not continually during the development process. Since requirement changes impact project budget and schedules, only allowing changes at set points in the software life cycle allows time to trade off the value and validity of each new proposed requirement against its cost. Meanwhile, developers can complete each stage with a frozen set of requirements, speeding the total development cycle.

Object-oriented and component-based software technologies help further isolate the impact of many requirement changes. Still, requirement changes are a constant problem for many software projects. Part of this is the developer's fault. Luckily, managing requirements is mainly a process issue rather than a technical one. Here are some ways to help prevent requirements from constantly expanding beyond their original scope:

- Document all user requirements, allowing the users to review the completed requirements document and agree to its completeness;

- Get users to agree up-front that future requirements changes will only be accepted after being evaluated for schedule and budget impacts;

- Practice iterative development. Get users and developers to understand that the first version is not the final version. That "one last change" can always wait for the next version. Many a software system has suffered unexpected delays because a simple last-minute change rushed through just before release broke huge parts of the system.

#4 Thou shalt invest up front in a software architecture

Every morning, some developer goes to work with software requirements for a new application in hand and starts writing code. Those who go off and start writing code without first developing a software architecture for their program are likely doomed to failure. Invest up front in your software architecture and you will be starting down the path to successful software development.

Developing an architecture for an industrial-strength software system prior to its construction is as essential as having a blueprint for a large building. The architecture becomes the blueprint, or model, for the design of your software system. We build models of complex systems because we cannot comprehend any such system in its entirety. As the complexity of systems increases, so does the importance of good modeling techniques. There are many additional factors to a project's success, but starting with a software architecture backed by rigorous models is one essential factor.

In the face of increasingly complex systems, visualization and modeling become essential tools in defining a software architecture. If you invest the time and effort up front to correctly define and communicate a software architecture, you will reap many benefits including:

- accelerated development, by improved communication among various team members;
- improved quality, by mapping business processes to software architecture;
- increased visibility and predictability, by making critical design decisions explicit.

Here are some tips on how and why to always start your software development project with a software architecture.

Start with a minimum yet sufficient software architecture to define the logical and physical structure of your system. Some sample activities performed are summarized in Table 1-2.

A software architecture is the top level blueprint for designing a software system. To develop a good software architecture requires knowledge of the system's end users, the business domain, and the production environment, including hardware and the other software programs the system will interface with. Knowledge of programming languages, operating systems, development tools, and programming frameworks is also necessary to develop a good software architecture. As software systems grow more and more com-

Table 1–2 Software Architecture Activities

Activity	Example	Architecture Level
Gather user requirements	Generate use-case examples	Logical architecture
	Document sample user activities	
Perform domain analysis	Create class diagrams	
	Create state diagrams	
	Create sequence diagrams	
	Create collaboration diagrams	
Start design and production acceptance	Define packages and components	Physical architecture
	Define deployment environment	

plex, ever more knowledge is required of the software architect. Object-oriented and component-based technologies may simplify individual programs, but the complexity typically remains at the architectural level as more objects or components and their interaction must be understood.

There are no shortcuts to designing a good software architecture. It all starts with a small number, perhaps one to three, of software architects. If you have more than three architects working on a single program's software architecture, they probably are not working at the right level of detail. When a software architecture delves too deeply into detailed design, it becomes impossible to see the whole architecture at a top level and properly design from it.

Most software applications are much more complex than the makers of GUI development tools would sometimes like you to believe. Every application should be built around a software architecture that defines the overall structure, main components, internal and external interfaces, and logic of the application. Applications that work together in a common subsystem should adhere to an architecture that defines the data flow and event triggers between applications. Finally, applications that run across your entire organization need to follow some set of minimal guidelines to assure interoperability and consistency between applications and maximize opportunities for reuse of components.

Software architectures should always be designed from the top down. If you are going to implement a multi-tier software architecture across your IT organization, its nice to do this before you have lots of components written which can only communicate with other applications on the same host. Start by developing your organization's overall application architecture. Next, you should define the system architecture for the major systems that will be deployed in your organization. Finally, each application in every system needs to have its own internal software architecture. All of these architectures should be developed up front before you develop any production code or invest in any purchased software packages. The notion of completing a software architecture up front does not contradict the spiral model of software development that utilizes prototyping and iterative refinement of software. Rather, prototyping should be acknowledged as an essential step in defining many parts of your architecture.

Trying to design a global set of every reusable component you think you might ever need is a losing proposition. You only know which components will be useful with lots of real experience delivering systems. If you don't prototype, you don't know if what you're building is useful, tractable, and feasible, or not.

#5 Thou shalt not confuse products with standards

A common mistake made by IT organizations is to confuse products with standards. Standards are open specifications such as TCP/IP or HTML. Standards can either be *de facto* or official. *De facto* standards, while not endorsed by any standards body, are widely accepted throughout an industry. Official standards are controlled by standards bodies such as the IEEE or ISO. Products can implement specific standards or they may be based on proprietary protocols or designs. Standards, because they are typically supported by many vendors, tend to outlive specific products. For instance, in the early 1990s, Banyan Vines was one of the top two network operating systems for PCs. Today, suffering from its own proprietary protocol, Banyan Vines has been relegated to a niche player in the network operating system market.

If your IT organization chooses to standardize on a product, say Cisco routers for network connectivity, you should not do so until you first standardize on a standard protocol for network connectivity, such as TCP/IP. Here are some common mistakes IT organizations make when defining their application, system, and software architectures.

- The application architecture is defined at too high a level. Some CIOs make the mistake of declaring Windows NT (or Unix, or Mainframes) their corporate application architecture. NT is an operating system, not an application architecture for an IT organization. Even the various third party programs designed for NT, or any other operating system, do not define all the characteristics of how to run a business. This is not to say that a corporation might not standardize on NT and use it wherever possible in its IT infrastructure, only that an application architecture requires a finer granularity of detail. In general, application architectures should not be so specific as to be tied to particular products.

- The application architecture is defined at too low a level. Oracle Version 8 is not an application architecture – it is a specific version of a vendor's database product. Once again, application architectures should not be product specific. A better architecture phrase would be, "relational databases that implement the SQL standard." Once again, this may not preclude a company from deciding to purchase only SQL DBMS systems from Oracle, but specific product choices should be made only after the underlying standards decision has been made.

- A system architecture does not address how the system is going to be tested. Many software projects have wonderfully elegant (from a computer science perspective) architectures that result in projects that fail miserably because no attention was ever paid to how the system was going to be tested. One of the most commonly overlooked test factors is performance testing. A system architecture must take into account how a system is going to be fully exercised and tested. This is especially relevant when designing multi-tier applications. For instance, in a three-tiered system, the architecture may allow for individual testing of components in each of the three tiers, but may not allow for end-to-end system testing to verify the correct interoperation between all three tiers. An equally bad architecture allows for end-to-end testing without allowing for testing of components in each individual tier. There is no worse plight to know that your whole system isn't operating successfully and have no way to isolate what component is causing the problem.

- A software architecture does not consider production rollout of the application. Besides taking into account how an application will be tested, the process of rolling out an application into production needs to be considered in your software architecture. Many great systems have been designed that were never fielded because the infrastructure to support their widespread use was not available. Chapter 13 presents our Web-Centric Production Acceptance process, which specifically addresses the production rollout process for web-centric applications.

#6 Thou shalt recognize and retain your top talent

Too many software development books concentrate on technology or management practices. At the end of the day, a lot of your success in software development will come down to who you have working for you and how happy they are in their work. You can have the best technology and organize your team in the best way possible, but if you have the wrong team it won't do you much good. Another surprise, given the effort so many organizations put into recruiting talent, is their failure to recognize and *retain* that talent after they join the organization.

Organizations that are successful at retaining their top talent start by recognizing their top talent. There are plenty of metrics that can be gathered around a developer's productivity and quality. Don't forget, however, more subjective criteria as summarized in Table 1-3. Who are the developers who

Table 1–3   Traits of Successful Developers

Skill Dimension	Trait	Example
Technical	Operating system knowledge	Understands operating system principles and the impact of OS on code design choices
	Networking knowledge	Understands networking infrastructure and matches application network demands to available infrastructure
	Data management	Understands how and when to use databases, transaction monitors, and other middleware components
	Hardware	Knows the limits of what can be accomplished by the software application on various hardware configurations
Business	Understands the business	Can differentiate between "nice to have" requirements and those that are essential to the function of the application
	Market knowledge	Keeps up-to-date on developer tools, frameworks, and hardware

Table 1–3 Traits of Successful Developers

Skill Dimension	Trait	Example
Professional	Written and verbal communication	Effective presenter at code reviews; documentation is easy to read and understand
	Teamwork	Participates actively in other's code reviews
	Flexibility	Can work well on a wide variety of coding assignments
	Reliability	Always completes assignments on time; strong work ethic
	Problem solving skills	Viewed as a "goto" person for help in solving difficult software bugs

always show up at other code reviews and make constructive comments? Who is known as the "goto" person when you have a tough bug to find? Which developers really understand the business you are in? Who has the best contacts with your customers? Be sure not to concentrate 100% on hard metrics and overlook such factors as these. Once you know who you want to keep around, go about thinking of ways to make it happen.

Throughout most of the 1990s, demand for skilled high technology workers has far exceeded the supply. It is easy to throw software developers into this general category and assume good developers are no harder to find than other high tech workers. Based on our experiences, we believe good software developers are even more scarce than good IT personnel in general. Just consider some of the numbers. The Java language was introduced as a new programming language in 1995. By late 1997, IDC estimated that there was a worldwide demand for 400,000 Java programmers and that this would grow to a need for 700,000 Java programmers by the year 1999. While much of this demand has been filled by retraining existing developers to program in the Java language, it still represents a tremendous outstripping of the supply of knowledgeable Java programmers.

Developer skill, more than any other factor, is the largest single determinant to the outcome of successful software projects. This is reflected in software costing and scheduling models, most of which place higher weighting factors on developer skill than all other factors, including even project complexity. In other words, skilled developers working on a complex software development project are more likely to produce a successful application than lesser skilled developers working on a simpler project. It is no accident, therefore, that this book devotes a large part of its text to describing what makes a good developer (Chapter 5), how to hire one (Chapter 7), and how to retain your developers after they are hired (Chapter 8). Studies have shown that top developers can be two to three times more productive than average developers and up to one hundred times more productive than poor developers. This wide range of productivity and its standard deviation is higher than for any other profession. Good developers not only produce more lines of code, their code has fewer errors, and the code they produce is of higher general quality (i.e., it performs better, is more readable, is more maintainable, and exceeds in other subjective and objective factors) than code produced by average or poor developers.

One false belief we have heard from many software development managers, especially those without a development background, is the notion that as development tools become more advanced, they "level the playing field" between average and great developers. Anyone who has ever attended a software development-related convention has seen slick demonstrations showing how "non-programmers" can use a development tool to quickly build an application from scratch. Modern development tools, especially Integrated Development Environments (IDEs) addressing everything from requirements definition to testing, certainly help developer productivity. This is especially true in the area of graphical user interface code. Even with the best of IDEs, however, there remains a highly intellectual component to software development. The best software requirements, the best software architectures, and the most error free code continues to come from the best software developers and software architects.

Rather than leveling the playing field, our experiences have shown that good IDEs, used as part of the development process, increase rather than decrease the difference between average and great developers. There is often a compounding effect as an unskilled developer misuses a built-in function of the IDE, introducing bugs into the program, while never gaining the experience of thinking out the complete solution. We are not, of course, by any means against the use of good IDEs or the concept of code reuse. It's just that neither of these are a substitute for developer skill.

#7 Thou shalt understand object-oriented technology

Every key software developer, architect, and manager should clearly understand object-oriented technology. We use the term "object-oriented technology" versus "object-oriented programming" because one does not necessarily imply the other. There are many C++ and Java programmers who are developing in an object-oriented programming language without any in-depth knowledge of object-oriented technology. Their code, apart from the syntax differences, probably looks very much like previous applications they have written in FORTRAN, C, or COBOL.

While object-oriented technology is not a panacea for software developers, it is an important enough technology that the key engineers in every development organization should understand it. Even if your organization does not currently have any ongoing object-oriented development projects, you should have people who understand this technology. For starters, without understanding the technology you will never know if it is appropriate to use on your next project or not. Secondly, due to the long learning curves associated with object-oriented technology, organizations need to invest in it long before they undertake their first major project. While object-oriented programming syntax can be learned in a few weeks, becoming skilled in architecting object-oriented solutions usually takes six to eighteen months or more, depending on the initial skillset of the software engineer.

#8 Thou shalt design web-centric applications and reusable components

As in the case of object-oriented programming, not all software architectures will be web-centric. With the explosion of the public Internet, corporate intranets and extranets, however, web-centric software is becoming more and more universal. This changes not only the way you design software, but also some of the very basic infrastructure requirements as well. Here are some of the infrastructure components needed for a typical web-centric application:

- Database server. A web-centric application will typically access one or more corporate databases. Unlike a two-tiered client-server application, however, a web-centric application is less likely to access a database directly. More commonly, a web-centric application would access some sort of middle-tier *application server* containing the business rules of the application. The middle-tier application would then communicate with the database server on behalf of the web-centric client. There are many advantages to such a multi-tiered approach, including greater application scalability, security, and flexibility.

- Application servers. In a web-centric architecture, application servers implement the business logic of the application. In many cases, this is programmed using the Java language. From a Java program, the Java Database Connectivity (JDBC) API is most often used to connect back to the central database. Specialized application servers may offer services such as DBMS data caching or transactions. A single business function is often broken down into components that execute across many application servers.

- Web servers. Web servers are used to store and distribute both Java applications and web pages containing text and graphics. Many advanced applications will generate web pages dynamically to provide a customized look and feel.

- Caching proxy servers. These servers, while not explicitly part of the application, are typically located strategically across the network to cut down on network bandwidth and provide faster access times to web-based data and applications.

- Reverse proxy servers. A reverse proxy server is typically used to provide remote users secure access over the Internet back to their corporate Intranet.

- Web clients. Until recently, a web client meant either Netscape's Communicator (or Navigator) browser or Microsoft's Internet Explorer browser. Today, a web client could still be one of these browsers, or it could be any of the following:

  - An HTML rendering JavaBean component in your application

  - An applet viewer built into a Java Development Kit (JDK)

  - A Java application

  - A collection of functions built directly into the operating system

One of the main advantages of web-centric design is that it starts taking IT out of the business of supporting heavyweight clients. In fact, most newer operating systems ship with one or more bundled web browsers so no additional client installation is required for a web-centric application. Even if you are deploying to older desktops without a bundled web browser, the popular browsers are available for free and easily installed. If a web-centric application is designed correctly, the end-user client really doesn't matter, as long as an HTML rendering component and Java Virtual Machine (JVM) are present.

If there is any disservice that the web has brought to software development, it is that inexperienced managers may believe that the web has trivialized web-centric software development. True, almost any word processor today can spit out HTML code and dozens of development tools promise "point and click" generation of Java code while the web makes software distribution a non-issue. All of this has allowed web-savvy organizations to develop new applications on "Internet time," several times faster than using traditional client-server environments. Its has not, however, by any means, trivialized software development. From requirements definition through production acceptance, the same disciplines that apply to client-server development hold true for web-centric development. We remind developers of this continually throughout our Web-Centric Production Acceptance (WCPA) process, presented in Chapter 13.

While embracing web-centric design does not necessarily require using reusable components, it certainly is a good time to start. More and more development organizations every day are investing in the design and development of reusable components. Chapter 17 of this book discusses component-based software development in greater detail, along with several of the more popular component frameworks. It is such frameworks that have fostered the popularity of reusable components. Consider some of the reasons why more and more people are investing in reusable component-based design.

It can take longer and be more expensive to design and implement a given function as a reusable component than as a non-reusable one. The savings only come when the component is reused. Especially with web-centric design, however, you will find your developers reusing well-designed components more and more. This reuse is facilitated by component standards such as JavaBeans and the wide range of development tools that support JavaBeans component integration. The cost trade off, therefore, is to compare the overhead of reusable design with the average number of times a component is expected to be reused. A reusable component, on average, might cost from 10% to 25% more to develop. Few development managers today could justify a 25% cost and schedule overrun just to save the next project money. However, properly implemented, reusable components can begin saving a project money today.

- If you invest in the design of reusable components and an accompanying framework, you will undoubtedly find components you can reuse from elsewhere in place of some of the code you would otherwise develop.
- It is likely components developed on your own project can be reused elsewhere in the organization.

- You can buy and sell components (either externally, or by exchanging with other development groups inside your company).
- Well built components are much easier to swap out and upgrade.

#9 Thou shalt plan for change

The best developers and architects plan for change during all phases of the software life cycle. During the course of an average one year development cycle, not only will the design be subject to change, so too will the user requirements, the development tools, the third party software libraries, the DBMS system, the operating system, the hardware, the network, the programmers, and many other aspects of the application that cannot possibly be foreseen or otherwise planned for. Some aspects of change, such as a new release of the operating system, can certainly be planned for by discussing schedules with the vendor and making a decision whether a new release should be installed or not. Sometime during the application's life, however, the underlying operating system will probably have to be upgraded so it's really just a matter of when changes such as these are done. In either case, you still have to plan for the changes.

The longer the expected project lifetime, the more important it is to plan for change. The Cassini mission to Saturn, operated by JPL, was launched in October of 1997. With any luck, the spacecraft will enter orbit around Saturn in 2004. The JPL engineers running the Cassini ground station definitely must plan for changes in hardware and software prior to the spacecraft's encounter with Saturn in 2004. Any company that designs a long lifetime product with an embedded hardware or software component must pay careful attention to planning for change. Back down on earth, for instance, every high-end Xerox printer contains an embedded workstation controller. Typically these workstations are commercial off-the-shelf products with an average lifespan of eighteen months. Xerox high-end printers are designed for five to ten or more years of continuous operation. Xerox must plan for change in the embedded workstation component for each of its printer lines.

There are many ways to plan for change. For starters, allow extra budget and schedule in your project for unforeseen changes. At the start of the project, work to clearly identify all risk items that could lead to a possible change somewhere in the future. During the design, look for ways to mitigate the risk of a change further downstream. At the coding level, look for ways to quickly and easily set up code to be adapted to new situations and events within your business. For instance, use tabular definitions whenever possible versus "hardcoding" these parameters into your code. Here is a real life example of two companies that implemented the same application, and how they did (or didn't) plan for change.

We worked with two companies of about the same size that implemented the Oracle Financials application package in early 1997. In both companies, various business units wanted to modify the standard financials applications to meet some unique need of the business unit. Much of Oracle Financials operation is table driven with those tables residing in a DBMS. The IT department thus entertained each business unit's request as most of the changes could be done by a database administrator with little or no coding. The first company went ahead, approved, and implemented the customizations for each business unit. In the second company, they planned ahead for change and considered what the impact of making the customizations would be the next time Oracle Financials came out with a major upgrade. The latter company decided the marginal business benefits of providing the customization was outweighed by the future costs to maintain these upgrades.

Well, as you might guess, in 1998, Oracle Financials released a major revision, based on their Network Computing Architecture (NCA). With NCA, the Oracle Financials client could be deployed via a web browser, versus loading client software on each desktop requiring access to the application. NCA offers tremendous business advantages to corporations through reduced application administration costs along with the improved functionality that is bundled into the release. The company who did the customization is still evaluating how to roll out Oracle's NCA as the customization they performed prevents a simple upgrade and the DBAs who did the initial customization are not yet trained on NCA. By contrast, the second company, with no extensive customization, was able to complete the upgrade to NCA in a single weekend. They have been enjoying the added functionality and client administration cost savings ever since.

#10 Thou shalt implement and always adhere to a production acceptance process

Mentioned several times already in the first nine commandments, our last commandment centers around the use of the Web-Centric Production Acceptance (WCPA) process presented in Chapter 13. In our book we focus on the WCPA as tailored for web-centric applications. The WCPA is really a superset of the Client-Server Production Acceptance (CSPA) process presented in *Managing the New Enterprise*. Most of the WCPA will be useful even if you are not yet designing web-centric applications. Production acceptance takes an application from the early stages of development and into a production status. However, planning for WCPA really begins at the first stages of the software development process. This is where we first start getting users involved, and keeping them involved throughout the development process through the use of customer project teams. At the same time, the development team needs to start getting IT operations involved. The WCPA shows that it is never too early to start getting both users and operations involved.

One of the reasons we developed the WCPA is to serve as a communications vehicle. All too often, development organizations are isolated from the business groups who will use their application and the operations group that will run and maintain them. Proper use of the WCPA will help promote and instill good communication practices. Just as iterative development is a key software development process, so to is iterative and ongoing communications with operations and with users.

This commandment is important because, without a closely followed WCPA, your business may lose valuable revenue or even customers because your web-centric application does not function as expected. Perhaps one of the earliest examples of a WCPA can be traced to Netscape's web server when they first opened for business in mid-1994. When designing their web site, Netscape engineers studied the web server load of their competitor at the time, the Mosaic web site at the National Center for Supercomputer Applications (NCSA). The NCSA site was receiving approximately 1.5 million web "hits" a day at the time. Netscape engineers thus sized their web site to initially handle 5 million hits a day, over three times the NCSA site's capacity. Even that aggressive sizing, it turned out, was not sufficient as the site exceeded 5 million hits a day during its first week of operation. Luckily, Netscape had planned their web site architecture to be scalable, and were able to add additional hardware capacity to handle the load.

The success of the WCPA process is also related to the robustness of your software system's architecture. An even greater percentage growth than Netscape's occurred at AT&T when they first offered their customer Internet service, AT&T Worldnet. AT&T had expected to sign up 40,000 customers for their Worldnet Internet service during its first month of operation and had designed the site accordingly. During its first month of operation, Worldnet registered 400,000 new subscribers, ten times the expected amount. Luckily for AT&T, they had architected the system for growth and put in place the equivalent of a WCPA process. As a result, all new subscribers were able to start receiving service with few complaints of busy signals on dial-in attempts (in contrast to some other well-known Internet services).

A great example of what happens when you don't follow a complete WCPA process occurred at a major U.S. bank during 1998. The bank was planning an upgrade to its Internet home banking service. Prior to the upgrade, the bank used a load balancing scheme to distribute users to a number of front-end web servers, all of which connected to the bank's mainframe back-end systems. As part of the upgrade process, the bank was planning to let all users change their login ID and password, thus allowing more individual flexibility than the previous bank-generated login ID scheme. The first time a customer logged in after the upgrade, he would be required to select a new login ID and password or confirm keeping the old login ID. This process was delegated to a separate new web server in order to not interfere with any of the software on the existing load-sharing servers. The bank, of course, did have some production acceptance processes in place and tested the entire process completely prior to deploying the upgrade. Unfortunately, they did not adequately test the performance of the entire web-centric system. On the first day of production, users started to complain of extremely long access times. Unfortunately, the bank had not taken into account the potential bottleneck of funneling all users through the single server while they were queried for potential login ID changes.

While no process can guarantee a new production system will function 100% correctly, web-centric applications require new kinds of planning like that covered in the WCPA. Not only are user loads on the Internet much more unpredictable, web-centric applications typically involve the interaction of a much larger number of software and hardware systems.

2

Software Development Has Always Been Difficult

In Chapter 1, we defined our own ten commandments for successful software development. In this chapter, we present some of the reasons why successful software development has always been so difficult in the past. The answer lies in the unique combination of people, processes, and technology that need to come together for a software development project to succeed. If you understand the dynamics of this combination, you will start to understand why there has never been, and never will be, any "silver bullets" in software development. This is a necessary starting point in understanding the difficulty surrounding successful software development. Only by learning from lessons of the past can we hope to avoid making the same mistakes in the future. Let's take a brief look at the history of modern software development and identify some of the difficulties surrounding successful software development it.

In the 1970s, development backlogs for corporate IT departments averaged eighteen months or longer. Since IT was usually the only department with the necessary resources to develop software, it owned the monopoly and wasn't often concerned about service levels or prices. In the 1980s, developers struggled with PCs, DOS, and 64K memory limitations. In the 1990s, just as many software developers thought they were starting to understand client-server software, widespread use of the Web set expectations for point and click access to any piece of corporate data. Software and network infrastructures struggled to catch up with web technology that obsoleted, literally overnight, many of even the newest client-server software architectures. One thing, however, has remained constant over time: there are no silver bullets in software development.

Successful software development starts with good requirements and a good software architecture, long before the first line of code is ever written. Even then, since software is easy to modify, compared to hardware, it often is all too easy for users to change the requirements. The impact of changing a single line of code, however, can wreak havoc on a program, especially a poorly designed one. On the people side, you'll need more than just a few good software developers for a successful project. Besides good developers, you'll also need system administrators and other support staff, such as database administrators in your development organization. As you schedule and budget a project, remember to make programmer skills the largest weighting factor, more so than the language, development tool, OS, and hardware choices you will also have to make. Finally, start planning for testing, production rollout, and maintenance of your software early in the project life cycle, or you'll never catch up. If COBOL programmers in the 1970s would have planned for users accessing their programs through a web-based front end in the year 2001, imagine where we would be today!

Software's Difficult Past

In the 1970s, IT departments running large mainframes controlled most of the corporate software development projects. The mainframe was the infrastructure for the enterprise computing environment. COBOL was the language of choice and any department with adequate budget willing to wait for the average IT department programming backlog of eighteen months could have the application they wanted developed or modified. Software was difficult to develop if for no other reason than because development was so tightly controlled by a small group of people with the necessary skills and access to expensive computers. In reality, much of the perceived unresponsiveness of centralized IT organizations was not due to any lack of software development skills or organizational structure, it was simply a result of the software architectures imposed by COBOL and mainframes.

Mainframe-based enterprise software applications, such as payroll processing, were typically large monolithic programs in which even simple changes were difficult to implement. The complicated structure of such programs usually limited the number of people who could modify them to their original developers. It was cost-prohibitive to have a new developer learn enough about a large mainframe program to modify it. This is painfully obvious today as many organizations return to 1970s era code and try to update it to be year 2000 compliant. For this reason, development managers would instead simply wait for the original developers to finish their current task and then assign them to go back and modify their earlier work. COBOL technology was well understood by those developers who programmed in it. Even in the rather simplified model of centralized mainframe development organizations, however, people and process issues already played equal weight to technology issues in their impact on the success of software development.

In the 1980s, inexpensive PCs and the popularity of simpler computer programming languages such as BASIC led to the start of IT decentralization. Even small departments with no formal IT staff could purchase a PC, figure out the details of DOS configuration files, and get a department member with a technical background to learn BASIC. There was no longer always a requirement to wait eighteen months or more for a centralized IT organization to develop your software program. All of a sudden large companies had dozens or perhaps even hundreds of "unofficial" IT departments springing up, with no backlog to complete, who could immediately start developing stand-alone applications. The only infrastructure they needed was a PC and plenty of floppy disks for backing up their programs. Software seemed easy for a moment, at least until a program grew larger than 64K or needed more than a single floppy drive's worth of storage. Even the year 2000 was only a far-off concern that crossed few developers minds. Most PC applications couldn't access mainframe data, but most developers were too concerned about installing the latest OS upgrade to worry. Software development was still difficult, we were just too busy learning about PCs to worry about it.

One result of the 1980s PC boom on software development was the creation of "islands of automation." While the software program on a stand-alone PC might have been very useful to its user, such programs often led to duplicated work and lower productivity for the organization as a whole. One of the biggest productivity losses suffered by organizations was probably duplicate data entry because a stand-alone system could not communicate with a centralized system and the same data was required by both systems. Many organizations still suffer from the "multiple data entry" problem today and it continues to be a challenge to software developers who must reconcile different formats or different input errors when trying to collect and merge data. This process, referred to as "data cleansing", is especially true in one of the hottest new fields of software, data warehousing. Data cleansing is a well- known problem to anyone trying to build a large data warehouse from multiple sources. Electronically connecting "islands of automation," rather than resolving the problem, simply increases the volumes of data that must be combined from various systems. As with many software development-related problems, the answer lies not in simply interconnecting diverse systems, but in doing so with a common software architecture that prevents such problems in the first place.

In the 1990s, corporations started to worry about centralized software development again. Microsoft Windows replaced DOS and brought a graphical user interface to stand-alone applications, along with a whole new level of programming complexity. Business managers realized that stand-alone PC applications might solve the need of one department, but did little to solve enterprise-wide business and information flow problems. At the same time, Unix finally matured to the point that it brought mainframe level reliability to client-server systems. This helped connect some of those PC islands of automation, but at a cost. MIS directors often found themselves supporting three separate development staffs: for mainframes, Unix, and PCs.

In the second half of the 1990s, our kids suddenly started teaching us about the World Wide Web and the Internet. Almost overnight, network infrastructure went from connecting to the laser printer down the hall to downloading multi-megabyte files from the web server halfway across the world. All it takes is a few clicks and anyone who can figure out how to use a mouse can get stock quotes and Java-enabled stock graphs on a web browser. A few more clicks to register on the site and you can be completing e-commerce transactions to sell or purchase that same stock. With the explosion of the Internet and its inherent ease of use, the same expectations for accessing corporate data, upwards of 80 percent of which is still stored on mainframes, were instantly set. Fewer computer users than ever before understand or even care about software development and its accompanying infrastructure. Software development, however, continues to be very difficult, and mostly for the same reasons.

The Year 2000 and Other Similar Problems

Software has always been very difficult to develop and even more difficult to modify. Witness the billions of dollars being spent by corporations worldwide to upgrade or replace approximately 36 million applications so they will function correctly in the year 2000 (Y2K) and beyond. Those unfamiliar with software development struggle to understand why something as simple as the representation of the year, a four digit number comprehended by most kindergarten children, can wreak such havoc on software. Given software's difficulty in handling the Y2K issue, it is even more amazing that brand new computer programming languages like Java can help accomplish such feats as bringing color images back from a small toy-like rover on Mars and allow them to be displayed on our PCs at home a few minutes later.

Many people think the Y2K problem is a one-time occurrence in the history of software. This is not at all so. Some other similar software problems include:

- Around the year 2015, the phone system is projected to run out of three-digit area codes, requiring changes to approximately 25 million applications
- In 1999, European countries switched over to a new universal currency, the euro, for non-cash transactions. By mid-2002, the use of the euro will be expanded to include cash transactions. These changes will impact approximately 10 million applications.
- On August 21, 1999, the Global Positioning System (GPS) week-counter will rollover. GPS keeps track of dates by recording the number of weeks from midnight on January 5, 1980 using a modulo 1024 approach. This will impact approximately 250,000 applications.
- Around the year 2075, United States social security numbers, based on a nine digit number, are expected to run out. Approximately 15 million applications use social security numbers and would be impacted by this.

It Is Hard to Structure Development Organizations for Success

There are certainly more wrong ways to structure a software development organization than there are correct ways. No single organizational structure, however, will meet every company's needs. Centralized development organizations are often too big to be responsive to departmental concerns. Decentralized organizations may not have enough staff to provide needed specialty skills. Nevertheless, certain organizational concepts apply no matter how you structure your developers. For instance, integrated software development teams, where software architects, developers, testers, and other specialists are teamed together, almost always have fewer barriers to success than more traditional "silo" organizations. In the latter, software architects, developers, and testers are divided into separate teams and hand over the project from one step of its life cycle to another. There are several problems with this type of organization. First, it is not conducive to iterative development processes. Secondly, since no group has ownership in the other's products, there is a natural tendency to blame problems on the work of another group. Chapter 6 focuses on organizing your software development organization for success and provides more information on these and other organizational topics.

It Is Hard to Schedule and Budget Correctly

While entire books have been devoted to software development scheduling and budgeting, it remains rare to find a software development project completed under budget and on schedule. One reason is that software schedules and budgets are often set by development managers early in a project's life cycle with little or no buy-in from the actual developers. Another reason is that many software development projects begin with pre-set budget or schedule limitations and then try to back-into the eventual end-product. The best single piece of advice we have is to avoid using historical "magic numbers" from other projects when developing your budget or schedule. Accurate software development scheduling and budgeting requires that you understand the project, know the developers, development environments, and other factors that will impact your schedule and budget. These issues are addressed in Chapter 12.

It Is Hard to Select the Right Language and Development Tools

Language choice continues to have a major impact on software development projects, starting with the software architecture. For a given project, the software architecture will look quite different if FORTRAN is chosen as the development language than if the Java language was chosen. Chapter 14 discusses some of the features and benefits of today's most widely used programming languages. Combined with other information in this book, the reader should be able to quickly narrow the language choice for any single project to one or two languages. Once a language is chosen, you will also need to select one or more development tools. Many development tools start by having you design the user interface and thus focus on that task. Mapping the user interface to the back-end database and adding business logic is left as an exercise to the developer. Other tools start with the database design, and use this to derive the user interface and structure the business logic. In both cases, the developer is forced to trade off one design for the other. A better approach, although supported by fewer development tools, is to start by defining your business logic. Once the business logic of an application is designed, it is then much easier to derive an appropriate user interface along with the required back-end database structure. Chapter 15 discusses the features to look for in a development tool and describes the various kinds of development tools available.

It Is Hard to Select the Right OS and Hardware Platform

In the future, platform independent languages like Java might make OS and hardware issues irrelevant. Today, however, the OS and hardware platform chosen continues to have an impact on software development. Chapter 16 discusses general requirements for hardware environments, including developer desktops, servers, and production hardware. Also discussed in this chapter are hardware architecture issues, such as SMP versus MPP, and their impact on software architecture.

It Is Hard to Accomplish a Production Rollout

One of the most overlooked reasons for the failure of software projects is the difficulty associated with a successful production rollout. From bringing on-line a new corporate-wide financial system to upgrading a simple software application, successful production rollout does not happen without careful planning and execution. Some of the best designed and developed software applications never see production use because they did not take into account some important factor of the production environment. Chapter 13 presents our solution to the production rollout problem, the Web-Centric Production

Acceptance process. As with many software development issues, planning for production operations needs to begin early in the software life cycle as the software architecture is being defined. Many chapters in this book, therefore, will contain information related to helping you accomplish a successful production rollout of your software project.

Software Development Defined

This chapter provides some basic background on software development concepts and terminology. A wide range of concepts, from software life cycle to programming paradigms to software architectures, are defined. Everyone on your software development team, from junior system administrators to senior project managers, should be familiar with the concepts presented in this chapter. This will provide a "common vocabulary" for everyone on your team to communicate with. If you are starting a new project, or have a large number of new team members, you might want to hold a "Software Development 101" training day, covering some of the basic concepts discussed in this chapter. Besides using such a training day to build a common vocabulary, it also provides a great chance for team building. If you do have a training day, be sure to give everyone the opportunity for hands-on activities. You might want to start with projects using the sample programs contained in this chapter or perform other simple activities such as having everyone build their own web page.

If you are a manager or other non-developer who has never written code before, this chapter may seem very long and difficult to get through. We have kept it as simple as possible but did want to include sufficient background in one chapter to allow you to complete the rest of the book. For experienced developers, this chapter may contain a lot of basic information that can be safely skipped over. As this chapter is intended to be only an overview, all the concepts introduced, plus many more, are covered further in either the Process or Technology sections of this book.

31

Software Life Cycle Overview

Many people unfamiliar with large-scale software development view it as a one-step process. Sit down and write the code. This may work for a simple program developed by one person, but such a process quickly breaks down when any level of complexity is introduced. A more typical software life cycle includes at least seven well defined stages:

- requirements specification
- functional specification
- design
- implementation
- integration
- validation and verification
- maintenance

Early software development life cycles followed a "waterfall" model, as illustrated in Figure 3-1, where one stage followed another sequentially in time. Winston Royce first described the waterfall model in his 1970 paper, *Managing the Development of Large Software Systems*. At the time of its development, the waterfall model was a large step forward in software development. For the first time, it added a formal structure to the overall software development process and identified key steps such as requirements definition, system design, coding, and testing. As software development organizations adopted the waterfall model, software development tasks such as requirements analysis, system design, and coding were each done by separate groups of people. For instance, when system design was completed, the system designers would hand over the design to the developers who would write the actual code. Some of the reasoning behind such models was based on the notion that each phase was independent and needed to be fully completed before moving onto the next phase.

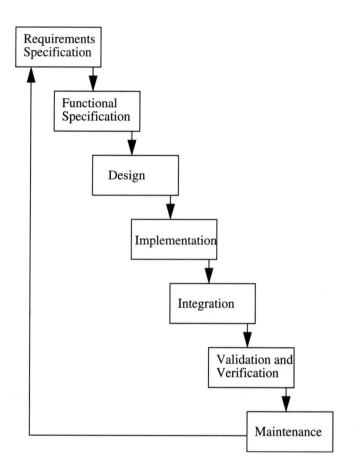

Figure 3–1   Waterfall Development Model

Over time, such practices brought their own shortcomings to the waterfall model. In large organizations, such a model did not foster communication between groups and in fact often prevented it. As separate requirements, design, and coding groups developed, so to did specialists in each area who did not necessarily understand the technologies employed by other project groups. Requirements engineers often came up with requirements that were impossible to implement given current technology. Design engineers, in turn, would often misunderstand requirements and develop system designs that did not meet user needs. Developers who misunderstood or did not like the designs handed to them by the design engineers made further modifications during the coding phase. Finally, the test team would test items in the software they believed to be important, without necessarily benefiting from the knowledge gained in earlier phases of the development process.

Today, just as car companies place manufacturing engineers in the same office as their design engineers to improve the engineering process, most software development is done using some sort of iterative or "spiral" development process. The spiral development model is illustrated in Figure 3-2. Dr. Barry Boehm, then of TRW, first developed the spiral development model, publishing his model in the 1988 IEEE Computer article, *A Spiral Model of Software Development and Enhancement*. In a spiral model, not only does each development phase overlap, the development phases also have feedback loops into previous phases allowing for continual improvement in the software process. Chapter 10 of this book spends more time defining and discussing software development life cycles and how to improve them.

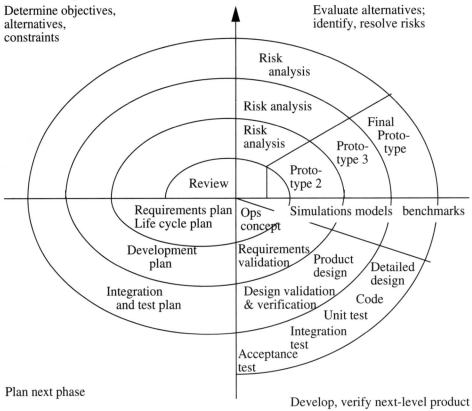

Figure 3–2   Spiral Development Model

The spiral model is a refinement of the traditional waterfall model, explicitly recognizing the development cycles in a large software project. This model incorporates risk analysis into the process and allows developers, as well as clients, to stop the process, depending on expected returns from new requirements. Basically, the idea is incremental development, using the waterfall model for each step; it's intended to help manage risks. The idea is to not define in detail the entire system at first. The developers should only define the highest priority features and then implement those. With this knowledge, they can then go back to define and implement more features in smaller chunks.

The spiral model defines four major activities within its life cycle:

- Planning: The determining of project objectives, alternatives, and constraints.

- Risk analysis: The analysis of alternatives and the identification and solution of risks.

- Engineering: The development and testing of the product.

- Customer evaluation: The assessment of the results of the engineering.

The model is represented by a spiral divided into four quadrants, each representing one of the above activities. The spiral model uses iterative development with the first iteration beginning at the center of the circle and working outward. Successive iterations follow as more complete versions of the software are built. At the beginning of each iteration of the life cycle a risk analysis is undertaken and a review of the project is taken at the end of the iteration. Actions are to be taken to counteract any observed risks, at any time.

Programming Paradigms

Several distinct programming paradigms are recognized by the software industry. The two primary ones are procedural and object-oriented programming. This section provides a brief introduction to these and several other programming paradigms that are in common use today.

Procedural Software

The procedural software paradigm is the most basic of programming models. A procedural program consists of one or more procedures or functions. Every program has a main function which is its starting point. The program hello_world1 is a very simple C program consisting of a single main function that prints out the message "hello world." Since C is a common procedural language, all the examples in this section will be given using actual C code. Unless your program is very simple like the "hello world" example, however, it will have additional functions, alternatively called procedures or subroutines in some languages. These functions can be called from the main function or from other functions. Following is the hello_world1 sample program.

```
/* Program hello_world1 */
#include <stdio.h>


int main()


{
 printf("Hello World");
 return(0);


}
```

For those unfamiliar with C, the line

```
#include <stdio.h>
```

instructs the compiler to include the standard input/output (stdio) include file within the program. This include file contains definitions that are needed to use C's built-in input/output functions. The most basic output function is the "print formatted" (printf) function, which in the above example is printing a simple string.

Now lets look at the same program utilizing a separate function. This program, called hello_world2, is shown below. Modularizing code into separate functions is one of the key techniques used in structured programming models. Before reviewing this code, it will help to tell you that in C, code comments are delimited by the "/*" and "*/" characters. Anything between these character strings is considered a comment and not processed by the compiler.

```
/* Program hello_world2 */

#include <stdio.h>

int main()

{


 /*
 ** This is the main function
 ** It calls the print_message function to do its work
 */

 print_message();
 return(0);

}

/***************************
** Function print_message **
*************************/

void print_message()

{

 printf("Hello World");

}
```

While the hello_world2 program is a trivial example of function calls, it still illustrates one of the basic advantages of structured programming gained when you factor your code into separate functions, code reuse. Now that the print_message() function is separated from the main program, it can be reused in other applications. Structured programming has been widely used in the software development industry since Dijkstra first wrote about the harmful effects of "goto" statements in 1968.

Most programs will also use one or more variables. A variable stores data that is used by the program. Variables commonly have a name, a type such as integer or floating point, and a scope. The scope of a variable defines where in the program the variable will be known and accessible. Computer languages handle variable scope in different ways but typically some combination of local and global variables are supported. A local variable is only known within some well defined section of code, such as a block of code or a function. Global variables are typically known throughout the program. For instance, consider the program simple_variables1, shown below. In this program, the variable total is a global variable and is accessible in both the main function and the function add20. In the function add20, the local variable x is local only to the function. Their value is independent of the local variable of the same name in the main function.

```
/* Program simple_variables1 */

#include <stdio.h>

int total;        /* a global variable */


int main()

{

  int x;          /* a local variable */
  int status;     /* function return status */

  /* Initialize global variables */
  total = 0;

  /* Initialize local variables */
  x = 10;


  /* Call function add20 */
  status = add20();

  /* Add x to the global variable total */
  total = total + x;

  printf("The total is %d\n", total);
  return(0);

}

/*****************
** Function add20 **
*****************/

int add20()

{

  int x = 20;            /* initialize local variable */

  /* Add x to the global variable total */
  total = total + x;
  return(0);

}
```

The use of global variables, as illustrated in the above example, is often considered a poor programming practice because it impedes reusability. The function add20, for instance, could not be used by another program because it relies on the global variable total to store its results. Another approach to coding this function is presented in the next section on Modular Software.

In the simple example programs shown so far, all functions were kept in a single file. As a program grows in size, you will most certainly want to break up the functions so that each file contains only a single function or a group of closely related functions. For further ease of packaging, the functions in a group of files can be collected into a library. Purely procedural libraries are stateless. A stateless library, or function, does not retain any information from one invocation to another.

Modular Software

Modular software is very similar to procedural software but adds the concept of state to libraries. For instance, a function could be written to add a number to a running total, where the total would be kept in-between invocations of the function. In a procedural language such as C, modular software must either use global variables or some sort of other persistent storage. Initialization of global variables must normally be done outside the function, either in the main function or another initialization function.

When writing modular software using global variables to maintain state it is not possible to write *reentrant* code. In reentrant code, functions can be called multiple times, possibly from different functions, without concern for losing state. The program modular1, shown below, modifies the previous example program, sample_variables1, by passing total into the function add20 as a parameter instead of using a global variable. The updated total is then passed back to the calling program in the function's return value. In this example, it is up to the calling function to maintain the state of the variable total.

```
/* Program modular1 */

#include <stdio.h>

int main()

{

  int total;      /* local variable, used to maintain state */
                  /* for the add20 function */
  int x;          /* a local variable */

  /* Initialize local variables */
  total = 0;
  x = 10;

  /* Call function add20 */
  total = add20(total);

  /* Add x to the local variable total */
  total = total + x;

  /* Call function add20 again */
  total = add20(total);

  printf("The total is %d\n", total);

}

/******************
** Function add20 **
******************/

int add20(int my_total)

{

  int x = 20;          /* initialize local variable */

  /* Add x to my_total */
  my_total = my_total + x;

  /* Return the new total */

  return(my_total);

}
```

From the example above, we start to see some reasons why programmers appreciate object-oriented languages. For instance, when variables and variable names are shared between functions, the code becomes difficult to read. There is no explicit concept of encapsulation or data hiding. The next section introduces the reader to some simple object-oriented programming concepts and starts to explain some of the benefits of object-oriented programming.

Object-Oriented Software

Object-oriented software is a major departure from procedural software. In procedural software, programming modules are based around specific tasks or functions. For instance, a procedural software model of a coffee machine would have functions for filling it with water, adding coffee, brewing the coffee, and so on. The coffee machine would be represented either by global variables shared among all functions or by variables defined in the main function and passed as parameters to lower level functions. In contrast, an object-oriented software program would be designed around a model of the basic object: the coffee machine. Objects, simply put, are just software models of things in everyday life, such as a coffee machine, a car, a tree, and so on. In theory, object-oriented software can be developed using any programming language. Usually, however, someone wanting to develop object-oriented software would use an object-oriented programming language such as C++ or Java that has language level support for objects.

To be considered object-oriented, a programming language should support three minimum characteristics: encapsulation, inheritance, and dynamic binding. Encapsulation is used to implement information hiding and modularity. Inheritance provides a particular mechanism for code reuse and code organization. Dynamic binding allows applications to be programmed to the interface of general classes of objects so that they need not even be recompiled when new kinds of specific objects are added to the system. These characteristics will be further defined as this section continues. First however, some basics characteristics of objects will be discussed.

At this point, some readers may still be confused about the difference between objects and procedures or functions. One of the subtle but most distinguishing characteristic of objects is that an object can have a lifetime greater than the object that created it. For instance, a coffee machine object might create a cup of coffee object. A programmer can delete the coffee machine object in the program and the cup of coffee object can still live on.

In a procedural world, when one function calls a second function, the second function only exists within the scope and lifespan of the first function.

In procedural programming, the two basic constructs used to create programs are functions and data structures. As we have seen, data structures may be contained within functions or may be represented by stand-alone global variables. In object-oriented programming, the basic construct is a *class*. A class contains both function definitions, called *methods* in object-oriented parlance, and data structures, referred to as *fields*. To understand object-oriented programming, it is important to understand the difference between classes and objects. A class is the blueprint for creating a certain type of object. Now think of your application program as a factory. Using your blueprint, or class, the factory can create one or more instances of the object. The methods are operations that manipulate the fields to query or change the state of the object.

In the implementation of an object, the object's state is defined by class fields, or instance variables. Instance variables are variables local to the object. An object's behavior is defined by its methods. A method is similar to a function in a procedural language with one big difference. While procedural functions stand alone, methods are always defined as part of a class. A class is a collection of fields and methods which define a particular object. Methods manipulate the instance variables to create a new state. Unless specifically made public and shared, instance variables cannot be accessed directly by other objects. Instead, if another object wants to set or get an instance variable, it must do so by calling methods provided by the object.

Below is a simple example of a class written in the Java language. This code is actually a complete Java application that you can compile and run with any Java compiler. In this example, the class name is CoffeePot, it contains one method called `startCoffeePot`, and this method has several fields such as `capacity` and `cupsRemaining`. In reviewing this example, it may be helpful to refer to the Java language section in Chapter 14. In addition, one of the best tutorial references on object-oriented programming is the Java tutorial available at http://java.sun.com/docs/.

```
public class CoffeePot{

    /* The method startCoffeePot brews the coffee */

    public static void startCoffeePot() {
        /* Initialize local variables */
        int capacity = 10;
        int cupsRemaining = 0;
        boolean full = false;
        boolean empty = true;

        /* Start brewing the coffee */
        System.out.println("Brewing " + capacity +
                        " cups of coffee...");

        /* Coffee ready! */
        full = true;
        empty = false;
        cupsRemaining = 10;
    }

    /* Here is the main method */
    public static void main(String[] args){
        System.out.println("Starting to brew the coffee.");
        startCoffeePot();
        System.out.println("The coffee pot is now full!");
    }

}
```

In addition to fields and methods, many languages also directly support the concept of superclasses and subclasses. For instance, one might define a car class, with subclasses of sports car and family car. Information about the class is maintained in its instance variables. For instance, a car class might have instance fields for max speed, current speed, number of passengers, and color.

As introduced above, classes differ from procedural structures because classes contain methods defining the operations that can be invoked on the object. By contrast, procedural structures contain data structures only and all operations are left to be implemented in functions. By example, a car might have a "set speed" method. Separating an object's interfaces from its implementation make it much simpler to change the implementation without changing the interface. This makes large projects much easier to develop. For instance, suppose ten different subsystems in a car's software had the ability to set the speed of the car. Each would do so by calling the "set speed" method. Now if the developer wants to rename the current speed variable inside the object, no change is necessary in the ten subsystems that call "set speed." In a procedural language, "current speed" might have been stored as a global variable and each of the ten subsystems might have set the variable directly. Thus any change to the variable name or type would require changes everywhere.

Another way object-oriented languages gain functionality is through the concept of inheritance. There are two basic types of inheritance supported by object-oriented languages: implementation inheritance and interface inheritance. The difference between the two is subtle to grasp but very important to understand so we will explain it in detail. An object's "interface" is a contract that states what functionality will be supported by the object. This is the simpler of the two concepts to understand and therefore use. For instance, consider a language that supports interface inheritance. If the sports car class is a subclass of the car class, it would inherit the interfaces of the car class, including the "set speed" method. This makes sense because if a sports car is a type of car, then you should be able to set the speed of a sports car.

On the other hand, consider implementation inheritance. Some object-oriented languages also support implementation inheritance. This is when a subclass can inherit not only its parent's interfaces but also the implementation of those interfaces. This often does not make sense. For instance, the car method for "max speed" may implement a 65 mile per hour max speed. A sports car max speed may be 100 miles per hour and thus implementation inheritance makes no sense in this case. Languages that support implementation inheritance typically allow for conditional inheritance or overriding of default inheritance. This now starts to lead to complicated language syntax and sometimes difficult to read programs. More importantly, it complicates the architecture of your program.

Distributed and Concurrent Software

A program executing on your computer typically consists of a single process. Most modern operating systems are capable of multi-processing and can run more than one program at a time. The operating system contains special privileged processes that controls access to system resources such as the CPU, memory, file system, and network. User applications access these system resources by making function calls to the appropriate operating system libraries. The relationship between the CPU, OS, and user processes is illustrated in Figure 3-3. So far, all the program examples we have discussed ran as a single process on a single host computer. Whether you are programming simple procedural C code or the latest object-oriented Java components, there will probably come a time when your project will require the use of distributed and/or concurrent programming techniques.

Distributed development breaks up a process so that different parts of the process can execute on separate distributed hosts. Chapter 21 discusses several popular methods of distributed programming included CORBA, JavaBeans, and ActiveX. In concurrent or multithreaded programming, a software process is divided into multiple threads that can execute independently and concurrently. Multithreaded programs thus can take advantage of more than one CPU on a multi-CPU host. Even on a single CPU machine, multithreaded programs can benefit from the asynchronous nature of most applications. Chapter 19 discusses multithreaded programming in greater detail.

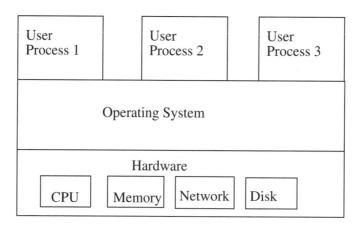

Figure 3–3 H/W, OS, and User Processes

Distributed development breaks up a process so that different parts of the process can execute on separate distributed hosts. Chapter 21 discusses several popular methods of distributed programming included CORBA, JavaBeans, and ActiveX. In concurrent or multithreaded programming, a software process is divided into multiple threads that can execute independently and concurrently. Multithreaded programs thus can take advantage of more than one CPU on a multi-CPU host. Even on a single CPU machine, multithreaded programs can benefit from the asynchronous nature of most applications. Chapter 19 discusses multithreaded programming in greater detail.

Development Environments

Compilers turn source code instructions into architecture specific executable code. For instance, C compilers are typically named cc. To compile the program hello_world1.c, a developer could enter the command:

```
cc hello_world1.c
```

On most systems, this would create an object code file named hello_world1.o and executable file called hello_world1. Creating the executable file from the object code file is also referred to as "linking" the program. Many compilers also perform the linking step automatically unless instructed not to. Most modern development environments do not require the typing of any commands to invoke the compiler or linker. Rather, these commands are automatically invoked through a simple button-click on the development tool's user interface.

After compiling a program, a programmer will debug the program to find and correct any errors. While simple debugging can be done by such primitive techniques as inserting print statements into the code, most developers would rather use some sort of graphical source code debugger. A modern debugger lets a developer step through the execution of code one line or one function at a time. At each step, the value of program variables can be examined, and if necessary, set to new values. Most debuggers also allow developers to set breakpoints at arbitrary lines of code or at specified functions. Debuggers will also catch most fatal errors and allow the developer to examine the state of the program at the time of the error.

Modern development environments combine editors, compilers, and debuggers into a single graphical tool that simplifies the edit-compile-debug cycle where programmers spend so much of their time. In addition, a good development environment will include other tools such as:

- a graphical editor for creating user interface code
- context sensitive editors and search tools
- class browsers for object-oriented code and call tree browsers
- performance analysis tools
- source code control tools

System Modeling Tools

Today, a software architect almost always uses some sort of system modeling tool to graphically represent the architecture of a software system. One of the more common modeling languages in use today is the Unified Modeling Language, or UML. UML is an industry-standard language for specifying, visualizing, constructing, and documenting a software system. With UML, a system architect creates a "blueprint" for construction (design and coding) of the system. UML was created by Grady Booch, Ivar Jacobson, and Jim Rumbaugh of Rational Software. UML represents a collection of "best engineering practices" that have proven successful in the modeling of large and complex systems.

Just as good blueprints are important for constructing an office building, having a model of your software system before you actually start writing code is equally important. For starters, having a good model written in a common modeling language helps foster communication among the project team. Having a model helps you decompose complex software systems into individual pieces that are easier to comprehend. The importance of your software model thus becomes more important as the complexity of your system increases.

The UML consists of:

- Model elements — fundamental modeling concepts and semantics
- Notation — visual rendering of model elements
- Guidelines — idioms of usage within the trade

In designing UML, its developers consolidated a set of core modeling concepts that were used across many existing methods and modeling tools.

These concepts are needed in most large projects. In addition, UML provides extensibility and specialization mechanisms to extend its core concepts.

UML is programming language and development tool independent. Many vendors besides Rational Software provide UML tools. Rational's UML modeling tool, discussed in Chapter 15, is called Rational Rose. UML includes a set of high-level development concepts such as collaborations, frameworks, patterns, and components which allow easy exchange of UML models between compliant tools. UML is also software process independent. While UML was certainly designed with object-oriented software architecture in mind, in can also be used to model non object-oriented applications.

In terms of the views of a model, the UML defines the following graphical diagrams:

- use case
- class
- statechart
- activity
- sequence
- collaboration
- component
- deployment

For a complete set of example diagrams see: http://www.rational.com/products/rose/features.html.

These diagrams provide multiple perspectives of the system under analysis or development. The underlying model integrates these perspectives so that a self-consistent system can be analyzed and built. These diagrams, along with supporting documentation, are the primary artifacts that a modeler sees, although the UML and supporting tools will provide for a number of derivative views.

UML includes features to support modeling of a wide range of modern software techniques, including extensibility mechanisms: stereotypes, tagged values, and constraints; threads and processes; distribution and concurrency (e.g., for modeling ActiveX/DCOM and CORBA); patterns and collaborations; activity diagrams (for business process modeling); refinement (to handle relationships between levels of abstraction); interfaces and components; and a constraint language. Any software architect today who is designing large, complex systems must use a modeling language like UML.

Software Architectures

Once you decide what programming paradigm, language, and development tool you are going to use, you are ready to gather requirements and develop a software architecture. At a very high level, a software architecture defines how different parts of the project are going to be mapped to different hardware components. Some of the more common software architecture types are introduced below.

A host-based software architecture, also referred to as a one-tier or single-tier architecture, consists of one or more software processes executing on a single host computer. A one-tier architecture could run on as small a computer as a PC or as large a computer as a mainframe. One-tier architectures can simplify a project as all inter-process communication is limited to a single machine. However, not all host-based software architectures are small simple programs. Some of the largest, most complicated software programs ever written are mainframe applications with one-tier architectures.

PC-based one-tier software architectures are typically single user. Mainframe one-tier software architectures typically have hundreds or even thousands of users. In a one-tier architecture, users would run an application via some sort of terminal. One type of IBM terminal is the well-known 3270 terminal with its green screen. The "3270" designates not only the terminal type but also the communication protocol. One-tier mainframe applications that were once accessed exclusively by 3270 terminals may now be accessed by a variety of devices, including PCs and network computers running 3270 terminal emulators.

As PCs and workstations proliferated in the 1980s, software architects started to develop client-server based software architectures. In a client-server architecture, a software application is broken up into two parts consisting of a client and a server. The "server" part of the application provides services that are utilized by the "client" portion of the application. One common allocation of functionality in client-server architectures is to have the server provide data storage and business logic functionality while the user interface is provided by the client. Of course there are many other possible types of client-server applications. Sun's Network File System (NFS) protocol was an early example of a client-server application implementing a network based file system. In NFS, files are physically stored on a server while the interface provided by the NFS client has all the appearances of a local file system. Even today's common web browser gains much of its functionality from a client-server architecture with the browser being the client to one of the many web servers on the Internet.

Most new software being developed today is based on some sort of client-server or multi-tier architecture. Modern client-server software is often further categorized into one of the architectures described below. A client-server architecture is an example of a two-tier architecture where one tier is the server and one tier is the client. In many two-tier architectures, the relationship between client and server is not always well defined. Both tiers may alternate being both a client and a server to the other. A two-tier architecture where neither tier is purely a client or a server is often referred to as a peer-to-peer architecture. As two-tier architectures evolved, they gave way to three-tier and other multi-tiered software architectures.

A three-tier software architecture is simply one in which the application is broken down into three layers, typically executing on three different computers. A common three tier architecture, illustrated in Figure 3-4, contains the data storage on one tier, the business logic in a second tier, and the user interface in a third. The main advantage of a three-tier architecture is that it becomes simpler to modify the user interface, business logic, or data storage components without affecting the other components. Another advantage is scalability. Since the data storage and business logic are separated, they can each be hosted on their own server. Furthermore, while many systems are architected such that their database cannot be divided among two servers, application logic typically can. For instance, a company's financial system may require a single database server but accounts payable and order entry, two business logic modules that would use the database, could be separated onto separate servers.

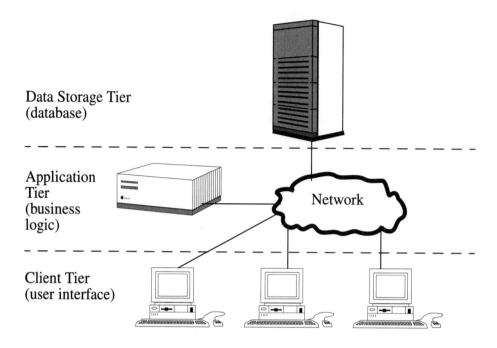

Data Storage Tier
(database)

Application
Tier
(business
logic)

Network

Client Tier
(user interface)

Figure 3–4   Three-Tier Software Architecture

If a three-tier software architecture is good, then is a multi-tier (more than three tiers) one better? As useful computing power is available on smaller and smaller devices and as cross-platform interoperability becomes easier, architectures such as the multi-tier shopping example shown in Figure 3-5 will become more common. The top tier is still the database or data storage tier. Business logic is also separated onto a second tier, as in the three-tier example. What changes is that the user interface is now separated into three additional tiers. Tier 3 would be a web server providing product information such as pricing and availability. Tier 4 would be a point-of-sale device for recording the transaction. Tier 5 would be a Java smartcard used to identify the purchaser and perhaps also carry electronic cash. The promise of cross-platform languages such as Java is that they can run on all tiers of a multi-tier architecture. This makes it simple to move functionality from one tier to another as may become necessary for performance or other reasons.

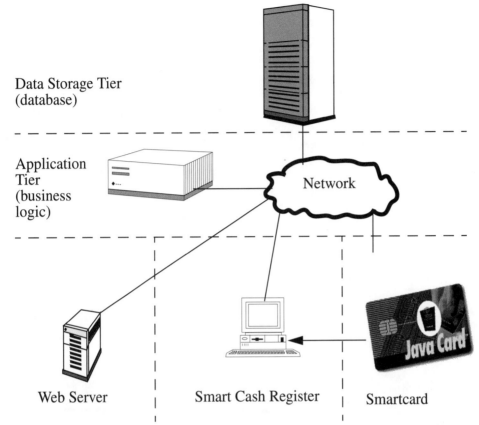

Data Storage Tier
(database)

Application
Tier
(business
logic)

Network

Web Server   Smart Cash Register   Smartcard

Figure 3–5   Multi-Tier Software Architecture

The ultimate refinement of the client-server architecture is the network-centric architecture. Two, three, or multi-tier architectures may all be used to implement a network-centric design. In a pure network centric architecture, data, business logic, and user interfaces travel from many sources on the network and are ultimately presented to the user in a web browser or "webtop" environment. While a web browser sits on top of a traditional window system and desktop environment, a webtop actually uses the web browser as the primary desktop interface. The ultimate goal of network-centric webtop computing is to provide access to information

- to anyone (who is authorized)
- anytime
- anywhere
- on any computing device.

Just as today's, "dialtone" is a universal metaphor for availability and accessibility of the phone system, network-centric architectures aim to provide "webtone" for computer users.

One disadvantage of multi-tier architectures is they are often more difficult to debug when problems arise. If a three-tier architecture is performing poorly, is it a result of database, middle-tier, or user interface loading issues? Alternately, it could simply be a bottleneck in the network connecting any two of the tiers. Anyone who has waited patiently for a web page to download knows that network-centric architectures don't necessarily solve all their performance problems.

Trends in Software Development

Many of the basic concepts behind software development have remained the same for five, ten, twenty years or more. This chapter discusses some of the major trends affecting software development in the late 1990s. Many software projects contain a database component, typically a relational database (RDBMS). Given sufficient processing power and correct database design, a good RDBMS can easily handle databases hundreds of gigabytes or even several terabytes in size. Object-oriented data and the expanded use of multimedia data types, however, place a huge strain on RDBMS systems developed to hold relatively small records with simple field types. Object-oriented databases have existed for some time, but often lacked the performance, administration tools, and robustness of the mainstream RDBMS products. Today, every major RDBMS vendor has announced plans or is actually shipping "Universal" DBMS products that expand their RDBMS functionality with object-oriented and multimedia capabilities.

One of the biggest users of RDBMS products are the so-called packaged software vendors such as SAP, PeopleSoft, and Baan. Some database companies such as Oracle actually have their own packaged applications for financial, manufacturing, and other domains. Ten years ago, eighty percent of Fortune 500 companies used some sort of in-house developed financial or manufacturing software. Today, over eighty percent of the same companies are implementing packaged software solutions. Perhaps only the use of "Webtop Computing" with its potential for platform independence has been a faster growing trend. In a true web-centric environment, a "webtop" replaces the user's traditional desktop window system with a web browser and web browser based applications. However, since any webtop application can also run in a web browser running on top of a traditional desktop window system, the transition to webtop computing can be a simple and incremental one. If Internet standards for webtop applications such as HTML and Java are followed, then the webtop becomes platform independent. Content and access to data now become more important than hardware and operating system concerns.

As the shortage of skilled programmers in the United States grows, along with increasing programmer salaries, there is growing motivation to ship development overseas where skilled programmers can be hired for substantially lower salaries. The benefits and risks of such practices are discussed further in this chapter. Another way to potentially lower costs is to streamline your software development infrastructure. Where should you cut back on infrastructure, how can tasks be automated, and how can bureaucracy be reduced? These issues and others are discussed further below.

The Universal DBMS

Database Management Systems began life as tools to store, index, and access large numbers of relatively short and simply structured records. Hierarchical, network, and other data organization schemes were used by mainframe databases in the 1970s. In the 1980s, relational database management systems (RDBMS) became popular on midrange and even workstation class systems. RDBMS systems were optimized for relatively small records with simple field types such as integers or characters. In part, this was a performance and capacity issue. Large multimedia data types, such as images or video, were less common and typically only managed with customized hardware and software. Production use of object-oriented software was still uncommon and therefore there was little need for huge object-oriented database systems. Today, in large part because of the explosive growth of the web, multimedia data is common and new languages such as Java have greatly simplified object-oriented programming. As a result, the leading RDBMS vendors have re-architected their database products to provide universal DBMS capabilities designed to handle any data type effectively.

Multimedia data, such as video or even large images, are a good example of a data type that was not handled well by earlier RDBMS systems. While most RDBMS systems could store an image or even a video clip as a binary large object (BLOB), that was all they could do. They did not provide any operators to index or search BLOB data types. In addition, maximum RDBMS record sizes often were not sufficient for storing larger images or video clips. RDBMS performance, with I/O optimized for smaller records, did not store multimedia data types well even when maximum record sizes were not an issue. Large image data and video data was thus traditionally stored in regular flat data files, with the RDBMS being used, if at all, only to store ancillary information, or metadata, about the images.

Another example of a specialized data type not handled well by traditional RDBMS systems is geographically encoded data with latitude-longitude pairs. In this case, while a RDBMS can easily store latitude-longitude pairs in a record, many do not provide any effective method to spacially index or search on such data types. For instance, consider a RDBMS table storing rectangular area data defined by four latitude-longitude pairs. To answer a user query of the type, "is the point (x, y) inside the rectangular area defined by (x1, y1), (x2, y2), (x3, y3), (x4, y4)?" would be very time-consuming with a pure RDBMS. As shown in Figure 4-1, this is a very simple problem to solve visually. Since this type of data is not relational, however, the RDBMS would have to do a sequential search through each record in the table searching for a record where

- $x1 < x < x4$
- $y1 < y < y4$

This type of search is a very time consuming computational problem for a traditional database to solve. In part because of limitations like these, geographic information system (GIS) vendors typically implemented their own data storage programs for spacial data, using non-relational indexing and search mechanisms such as R-Tree representations.

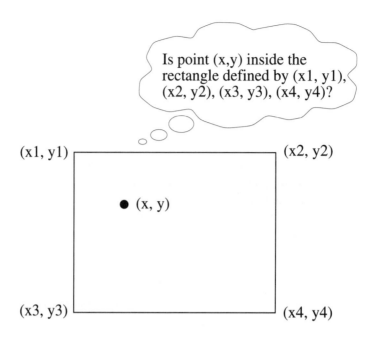

Figure 4–1 Spacial Data Record Query

DBMS vendors have taken three approaches to developing universal DBMS systems:

1. adding "bolt-on" data types and operators to an existing RDBMS;
2. integrating new data types and operators into the kernel of an existing RDBMS; or
3. adding more traditional RDBMS data types and operators into an object-oriented DBMS. For each new data type, a DBMS must also implement storage, indexing, and searching functions. Each approach has its own pros and cons.

Implementing new data types and operators via "bolt-on" software has the advantage of being easier to implement as the new functionality can often be implemented with very little knowledge of or impact to the DBMS kernel. This method of implementing new data types has been called both "Data Blades" and "Data Cartridges" by RDBMS vendors. In addition, if RDBMS vendors publish the interface they are using for bolting-on new data types, third parties may develop their own bolt-on data types leading to more choices and functionality for the software developer. One of the disadvantages to this approach is that since the bolt-ons typically modify key RDBMS kernel data structures, possible corruption in a bolt-on may lead to corruption or malfunctioning of the RDBMS. It is thus imperative to test each piece of bolt-on software as carefully and thoroughly as the kernel itself is tested. This however, becomes difficult to do as the bolt-on code base grows in size or starts being implemented by third parties other than the RDBMS vendor.

The second method, integrating new data types and operators into the RDBMS kernel, is often more difficult and time consuming to implement, mainly because it can involve significant changes to the core kernel of the RDBMS. Each change to the kernel must be carefully architected and designed so as to not increase functionality and performance in one area at the detriment of another. By their very nature, such modifications can only be completed by the RDBMS vendor who thus controls the availability of each new data type, versus leaving the process open to third party implementations. On the positive side, quality and performance of the RDBMS can be more tightly controlled using this type of approach. In practice, many RDBMS vendors have taken the approach of providing new data types via some combination of these first two approaches.

The third way to develop a universal database is to start with an object-oriented DBMS (OODBMS) and add relational data types and operators. In theory, this is much easier to do than visa-versa. However, in practice, the RDBMS vendors have a long history of providing the scalability and performance required by the mainstream DBMS marketplace. OODBMS vendors may be able to provide similar functionality, but not performance against relational data types. For the most part, therefore, usage of OODBMS systems has stayed confined to relatively niche, low volume applications.

Packaged ERP Software and its Customization

The *term enterprise resource planning software*, or *ERP software*, describes the enterprise-wide applications commonly deployed by leading manufacturers and other large companies in a widening array of markets. The most common ERP software "packages" come from companies such as SAP, Peoplesoft, Oracle, and Baan. Unlike the word processor or spreadsheet software package you buy at the local computer store, ERP software packages do require customization during the design and deployment process that can last from six to eighteen months or more. Significant amounts of software development may be required during this process. In addition, your lead software architects will require not only detailed knowledge of the customization being done, but familiarity with the ERP package itself. The use of ERP software packages, as you will see, presents both significant challenges as well as opportunities for a company's software development organization.

In the past, most companies developed their own enterprise-wide applications. While "packaged" software applications have always existed, they often did not have enough functionality when compared to custom-developed code. In the 1970s and 1980s, most large companies owned one or more mainframes and had a resident mainframe application development staff. Many companies did purchase basic financial software packages for their mainframes, and large manufacturing companies sometimes used mainframe-based manufacturing resource planning, or MRP systems (the precursor to today's ERP software packages). Still, the limited, by today's standards, functionality of these systems meant large in-house application development staffs needed to be maintained.

In the 1990s several trends led to the widespread use of "prepackaged" application software for general ledger, order entry, billing systems, accounts payable, accounts receivable, manufacturing, marketing, sales force automation, human relations, and other business functions. First, many companies replaced mainframes with client-server systems, or at least deployed PCs to a much wider percentage of their employees. This not only placed a much higher demand on the amount of business software needed but it also introduced a much higher degree of heterogeneity to the average computing environment. At about the same time, business process re-engineering, or BPR, was nearing its heyday as the cure for everything from excessive middle-management bloat to quality issues. At the same time, advances in software development made it easier for larger ERP suites to provide a greater degree of the functionality needed across a wider range of industries. As a result, most Fortune 500 corporations have now switched from custom development of ERP solutions to acquiring and customizing packaged ERP software applications.

Most ERP initiatives today are driven by three types of business objectives:

1. Gaining greater efficiency at the heart of the enterprise
2. Improving integration of functions across the enterprise
3. Extending integration outside the organization, i.e. through improved supply chain management

This has driven the growth of the ERP market from $5.2 billion in 1996 to $10.0 billion in 1998 and onward to an estimated $19.0 billion in 2001, according to research by AMR and BT Alex Brown. The yearly growth figures are shown in Table 4-1.

Table 4–1   Current and Projected ERP Market Growth

Year	Market Size ($billion)
1996	5.2
1997	7.2
1998	10
1999	13
2000	15.6
2001	19.0

The continued demand for ERP software is being driven by six key factors.

1. *The continued move to distributed computing.* All of the major ERP players have adopted some type of multi-tier distributed computing model for their architecture. This makes these solutions ideal candidates for corporations trying to replace their older, mainframe based systems.

2. *Industry specific solutions.* All of the major ERP players tailor their content and capabilities for specific vertical markets. This is expanding the market for ERP vendors beyond their initial target of large manufacturing companies. As a result, new growth opportunities are being found in many service industries. An excellent example of such growth is in the utility industry, where new deregulation mandates have companies struggling to revamp their infrastructure to become newly competitive.

3. *The middle market opportunity.* According to Forrester Research, over half of the ERP license revenues will come from the small to middle market by the year 2000. This market is growing at nearly twice the rate, 37 percent versus 18 percent, as large companies. The move of packaged ERP solutions to small and middle sized companies is aided by two additional trends. First, the base of software

architects and engineers with ERP package experience continues to grow. Secondly, as vendor offerings become more robust in functionality, less customization is required.

4. *Expanding geographic markets.* Once again, according to Forrester Research, the North American ERP market share will shrink from 60 percent as recently as 1996 to 40 percent by the year 2000. ERP vendors that provide the best support for simultaneous use of multiple languages and currencies will benefit most as multinational corporations expand their ERP usage.

5. *The Year 2000 (Y2K) and European Monetary Union (EMU) imperatives.* Many corporations adopted ERP systems as a means of solving the Y2K compliance issues of older mainframe MRP systems or custom developed code. A similar imperative affected any corporation doing business in countries within the European Monetary Union, starting in 1999.

6. *The buy versus build preference.* Most CIOs today lean toward packaged applications as opposed to custom programming initiatives. Even in cases where an ERP package must be highly customized, the software development required is significantly less than would be required to implement a custom solution. Given the scarcity of good software development talent, it is no wonder most CIOs would rather save their development resources for other projects.

In the future, ERP solutions are likely to become less monolithic and more specialized and componentized. More and more, CIOs expect any business function to be delivered across an n-tier architecture to a standard web browser platform. Just like today's ERP solutions are distinct software applications from the underlying DBMSs, CIOs in the future may pick best of breed ERP applications from multiple vendors without worrying about the added integration burden this would incur today.

Webtop Computing and Platform Independence

Today, more and more companies are making a web browser part of the standard desktop environment. Whether for internal usage only, or with access to the entire Internet, it is hard to find a corporate desktop today without some sort of web browser. A webtop is no more than a network computing architecture that allows all of a user's functionality to be delivered via their web browser. While today most pure "webtop" environments are deployed in single function, "heads down" environments like a call center, more and more functionality is being deployed via the webtop every day. This is an evolutionary versus revolutionary process. Since most corporate desktops already have a web browser today, IT departments can start deploying webtop applications at any time using existing desktop PCs. Once all the applications required by a particular user are available on the webtop, the IT organization can evaluate moving to Network Computer clients and further reduce the desktop administration overhead.

A company's adoption of web technologies typically follows four stages as shown in Figure 4-2.

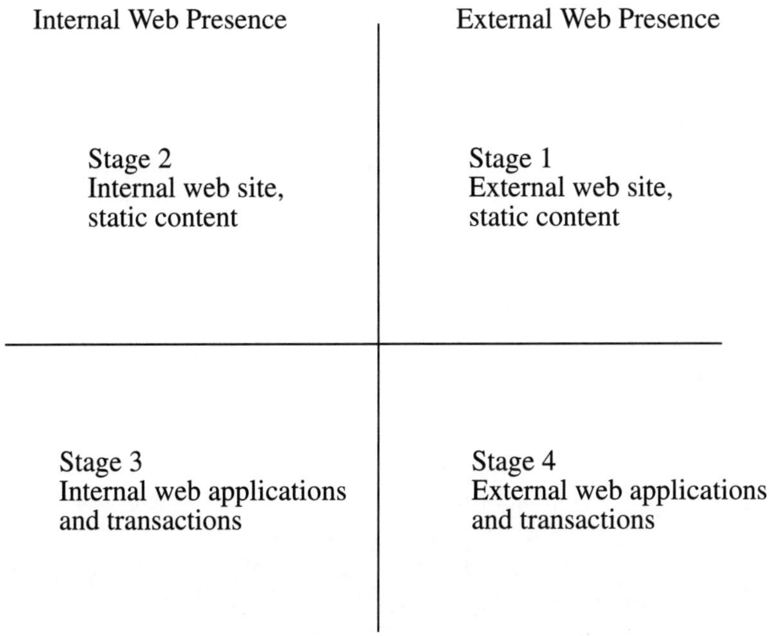

Internal Web Presence	External Web Presence
Stage 2 Internal web site, static content	Stage 1 External web site, static content
Stage 3 Internal web applications and transactions	Stage 4 External web applications and transactions

Figure 4–2   Adoption of Web Technologies

In stage one, corporations begin by having an external web presence consisting of static content. Often the web page design is developed by the marketing division and corporate IT has no involvement or control other than perhaps supplying the telecommunications infrastructure. In other cases, the entire web site is hosted at an Internet Service Provider (ISP) and corporate IT has absolutely no involvement.

In stage two, corporations establish an internal web presence or Intranet. Typically, corporate IT has a greater involvement at this point, at least in providing web browsers and IP connectivity to the desktop. The IT organization at this stage may or may not provide centralized web hosting services, proxy/caching servers, and content development and management. Today, nearly all servers ship with some type of bundled web server software and virtually every desktop comes with a web browser, allowing many Intranets to develop from grass roots movements without much oversight from IT. Since the real power of an Intranet is in its content, IT organizations should probably focus at this stage on providing centralized indexing and search servers rather than on developing content.

In stage three, corporations actually start to conduct transactions and deploy applications over their Intranet. At this stage, IT organizations are typically heavily involved in developing and supporting the applications infrastructure. This is also the stage at which significant administration cost savings start to be realized.

In stage four, corporations extend transactions and application deployment out to external users. Typically, this is first done via an extranet, linking internal corporate systems with those of a few key suppliers. After gaining experience with conducting transactions via an extranet, this functionality is often extended to the corporation's entire end-user base via the Internet. Many of the first-generation external transaction capabilities were front-ended by simple HTML forms interfaces. However today, additional functionality is being provided not only by providing external transactions, but by front-ending these transactions with more functional Java technologies.

Offshore Development

The shortage of skilled software developers in the United States, coupled with their high salaries, has led many development organizations to consider moving some or all of their software development overseas. Countries as diverse as India and Russia have an excess of well-educated and trained software developers that can be hired for a fraction of the salary of their equivalently experienced counterparts in the United States. Here are some guidelines for companies thinking about offshore development:

- Don't move your architecture offshore. Unless you are moving 100% of your development overseas, keep your software architects local. Software architecture is the most crucial part of software development and you should keep this function as close to your business as possible.

- Use existing foreign employees to recruit overseas. In a large development organization, chances are you have someone in your group from the country or region you are considering to move part of your development to. That person may very well still have ties to that region. This person might not only be able to provide you with first-hand references on overseas schools and firms, but a recruiting trip home may be an added incentive.

- Separate out well defined, modular components with a limited number of interfaces for offshore development. Having your software developed halfway around the world will certainly limit iterative development. You should identify software modules that have few dependencies and can be tested without requiring local resources.

- Apply the same standards to software developed overseas as you would to locally developed software. Don't simply accept a finished product and assume it will work correctly. Remember, good software processes are crucial to successful software development. You have to be concerned that the software processes you have defined for your organization are being followed overseas. If you don't already have these processes in place, moving development overseas will not necessarily buy you any benefits. Similarly, if your processes are too bureaucratic, don't just rely on moving development to someplace where the bureaucracy doesn't exist. Instead, you should concentrate on streamlining your IT infrastructure.

Similar guidelines should be followed if you are planning to outsource your software development to a company that sends work overseas. This can often be a much easier way to take advantage of overseas software development resources.

Streamlining IT Infrastructure

One company we worked with had a six month wait for endusers who requested a new desktop PC. Furthermore, users never seemed able to obtain the latest PC models until they had been shipping for six months or more. These complaints mystified the account sales representative of the PC supplier as the company seemed to have an adequate PC procurement budget and routinely purchased the latest PC models. Not until we had spent some time with the IT organization did we identify the problem. Each PC purchased by the IT group was delivered to a main warehouse. As capital equipment, the PC needed to receive a property tag before it could be delivered to the end user. Property tags were the responsibility of the finance department and finance had only one worker responsible for placing property tags on PCs and all other office furniture. IT was well aware the company had long suffered from a five month backlog to tag property, but did not consider it their responsibility or problem.

Streamlining IT and related infrastructure is the responsibility of every member of your software development organization. This doesn't mean getting rid of mainframe production disciplines just because you are moving to a client server environment. Modern software development needs more infrastructure and processes than ever before. Much of this infrastructure can be automated or otherwise streamlined. This does, however, take initial resources to accomplish. For instance, mainframe programmers never gave backups a thought – the operator always took care of that. How many PC developers, on the other hand, have lost work because someone, usually themselves, forgot to backup their disk drive. The solution, of course, is not to stop work ten minutes early and force everyone to do backups, it is to install a network-wide backup application. However, someone has to purchase and install the backup utility which is an initial cost. In the long run, however, a good backup program will pay for itself many times over.

Another area where IT infrastructure must be streamlined without sacrificing robustness is in production acceptance. Ten years ago, an application might be upgraded every twelve to eighteen months. Production rollout meant taking the mainframe down over the weekend to install the new application. Today, network-centric architectures make it possible to roll out application upgrades over a worldwide network on an as-needed basis. In these environments production acceptance testing and rollout procedures need to be more complete than ever. You do need to worry about what happens when a user executes a Java applet out of their browser's cache after its been updated on the server or how to recover from a partial database update if a network link is severed. Furthermore, given the larger audience of users that these incidents could affect, automated rollback and recover procedures are even more important.

Today, everyone in a software development organization has to take responsibility for every aspect of quality. From gathering the first requirements to rolling out the deployment hardware, quality needs to be inbred into the DNA of every development organization. Quality, however, cannot come about by chairing yet another committee to decide what next year's quality goals should be, as depicted in Figure 4-3. Successful software projects, those of high quality, come about from organizations that have a streamlined IT infrastructure where everyone is concerned everyday about what will make their project successful. More often than not, a developer or other team member may not even use the name quality to refer to a process they are following. It just becomes part of what they set as their personal minimum bar of performance.

Figure 4–3 How Not To Define Software Quality

Part 2

People

Building a Winning Software Development Team

In the mainframe world of the 1970s, CIOs had an easy time building their software development teams. You hired some COBOL programmers, a few system analysts, and some operators, gave them a manager, and you were set. Eighteen-month backlogs for application changes were common but CIOs didn't worry much because users had nowhere else to turn. In the PC world of the 1980s building a software development team was even easier. Unfortunately, this lead to many CIOs losing control over the application development process. Any department with a PC, a BASIC programmer, or maybe even just someone good at spreadsheet macros, could be in the software development business. When IT department backlogs were too long, many departments went off and implemented their own applications. This of course worked fairly well, at least until all those separate applications developed by different groups had to communicate or share data. What resulted, in many organizations, were islands of automation with little or no communication between them.

The Developer Shortage

In the early 1990s, many CIOs looked to client-server solutions to try to decrease development time and application backlogs. Many attempts at deploying client-server solutions, however, failed in part because no central group controlled all those distributed desktops that the "client" part of the application had to be deployed on. One of the reasons that so many CIOs in the late 1990s have looked to solutions based on network computing architectures is because they allow organizations to combine the best of the mainframe and PC paradigms. Corporate data can once again be centralized and applications deployed over Intranets with web and Java technologies. The new technologies associated with network computing architectures, such as object-oriented computing and the Internet, however, come at a price. Building a winning software development team is now much more difficult as IT staffs must be retrained or experienced talent hired from the outside (or both). Besides the traditional software development positions, there is a whole new range of specialists needed: webmaster, toolsmith, graphic artist, CORBA and Java developers, and the list goes on. Most of these positions didn't even exist five years ago.

The U.S. Bureau of Labor Statistics' projections list computer and data processing services, including software development, as the industry with the fastest employment growth from 1996 to 2006. A projected 108% growth rate equates to 1.3 million new jobs. It is estimated that as many as a third of these jobs will be related to software development. The Information Technology Association of America (ITAA), in 1997, surveyed large and mid-sized U.S. companies and estimated they had 191,000 unfilled IT positions, again with up to a third of these related to software development. In 1998, a Newsweek study[1] estimated there were 478,000 unfilled information technology jobs. Whatever number you believe, there is no doubt that recruiting, retraining, and retaining skilled IT professionals is the number one management challenge faced today by CIOs worldwide. This chapter examines some of the key staff positions needed in a modern software development organization. While not all development teams will need full-time dedicated individuals for each position identified in this chapter, successful software projects probably will require most of the technical, managerial, and relationship skills discussed in this chapter at some point in the project lifecycle.

It is no wonder that two of the most common concerns of CIOs today are (not necessarily in this order):

1. The three R's, or how will they Recruit, Retrain, and Retain a skilled software development team (and other IT professionals); and
2. How long will they be able to retain their own job.

---

1.   Newsweek, July 20, 1998.

In Chapter 6, we discuss different ways to organize a software development organization to increase your chances of successful software development. First, however, some of the different skill sets you will need to recruit, retrain, and retain skilled engineers for your software development team will be described in this chapter. The information presented here will enable you to write complete job descriptions and serve as a guide for interviewing candidates. While the jobs described are typical of what one might find in a Fortune 500 organization, exact job descriptions will, of course, vary from company to company. You should use these job descriptions as a template and modify them to meet the requirements of your own organization.

For each development role, this chapter lists typical education, experience, and skills required. A typical top level organization chart is shown in Figure 5-1. This organization chart is for illustrative purposes only. A complete set of more specific organization charts for different sizes and types of software development organizations is included in Chapter 6. Jobs described in this chapter include general software development positions such as:

- Director of Software Development
- Chief Software Architect
- Software Development Manager
- Senior Software Engineer
- Software Engineer II
- Software Engineer I

We also cover a number of specialty positions. Not every software development organization will have these specialty positions as they may report to some other group within the information technology organization. We cover these positions here because of their large impact on the success of many software development projects. The specialty positions discussed include:

- Toolsmith
- Webmaster
- Database Administrator
- Server System Administrator

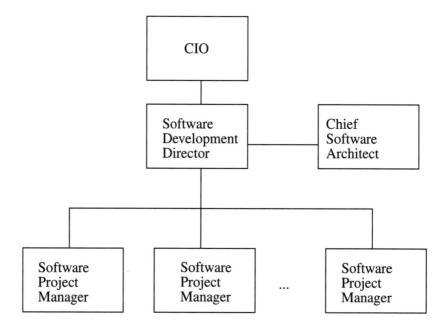

Figure 5–1   Sample Organization Chart

Software Development Job Descriptions

Director of Software Development

Nature of Work

The Director of Software Development is a highly responsible senior manager with responsibility for all software development activities within the organization. This position typically reports directly to the Chief Information Officer (CIO). In all but the smallest development organizations, this will be at least a second level management job.

Education and Experience Profile

A typical candidate for this position will have at least fifteen years work experience in software development or a closely related engineering field. Recommended education for this position is an advanced degree, either in computer science, engineering, or business with a concentration in management information systems. At least five years of first level management experience is also recommended along with five or more years experience as an individual contributor in a software development role. Even though this is a second level manager position, we have seen few individuals succeed in such a role if they do not have "hands on" development experience.

Management, Leadership, and Personal Skills

- Thorough understanding of the company's vision and goals, business operations, and markets.
- Thorough knowledge of the theories and principles of management and administration.
- Thorough knowledge of planning, project management, budgeting, and quality assurance as it relates to software development projects.
- Thorough knowledge of developing RFIs and RFPs along with the criteria for evaluating vendor proposals, products, and services.
- Excellent oral and written communication skills.
- The ability to formulate, present, and support budget estimates and financial plans concerning software development activities along with the related hardware and software acquisition costs.
- The ability to manage feasibility studies and economic analyses designed to improve effectiveness and efficiency of software development applications, tools, and processes.
- The ability to establish and maintain effective working relationships at all levels.
- A passion for software development.
- The ability to inspire and lead through others.
- The ability to train and mentor software development project managers.
- The ability to coordinate and prioritize customer requests with the assistance of other managers to ensure the highest level of service possible to the customer.

- The ability to direct the setting of performance standards, write performance evaluations, issue counseling forms and disciplinary actions, handle employee complaints and grievances, and recommend the hiring, termination, and promotion of staff.

Technical Skills

- Knowledge of current technological trends in the software development industry, such as object-oriented programming, multi-tier software development, component architectures, design patterns, and web-based software.
- Knowledge of computer languages, operating systems, application packages, database management systems, networks, and hardware capabilities.
- Knowledge of system integration issues between diverse platforms (PCs, Unix, mainframes).
- The ability to gather and analyze data and draw logical conclusions.

Chief Software Architect

Nature of Work

The Chief Software Architect is the most senior technical position within a software development organization. This individual is responsible for the overall application architecture of the organization. The chief software architect also sets directions for enterprise-wide standards in the area of languages, tools, and processes for software development. This position typically reports to the director of software development, and perhaps occasionally to the CIO within the corporation.

Education and Experience Profile

A typical candidate for this position will have at least fifteen years work experience in software development across a wide variety of development projects. Recommended education for this position is an advanced degree, either in computer science, engineering, mathematics or a closely related field with a concentration in software engineering.

Management, Leadership, and Personal Skills

- Understands the company's vision and goals, business operations, and markets.
- Has knowledge of planning, project management, budgeting, and quality assurance as it relates to software development projects.
- Has knowledge of developing RFIs and RFPs along with the criteria for evaluating vendor proposals, products, and services.
- Has excellent oral and written communication skills.
- Has the ability to lead feasibility studies and economic analyses designed to improve effectiveness and efficiency of software development applications, tools, and processes.
- Has the ability to establish and maintain effective working relationships at all levels.
- Has a strong passion for software development.
- Has the ability to inspire and lead software developers throughout the organization.
- Has the ability to train and mentor senior software engineers.

Technical Skills

- Has thorough knowledge of current technological trends in the software development industry, such as object-oriented programming, multi-tier software development, component architectures, and web-based software.
- Has thorough knowledge of computer languages, operating systems, application packages, database management systems, networks, and hardware capabilities.
- Has thorough knowledge of system integration issues between diverse platforms (PCs, Unix, mainframes).
- Has the ability to gather and analyze data and draw logical conclusions.
- Routinely writes and publishes technical articles, papers, reports, journals, or books on software engineering.
- Has the ability to direct software and hardware benchmarks.
- Has thorough knowledge of enterprise and system modeling.
- Has thorough knowledge of object-oriented analysis.

- Has fluency with object-oriented modeling tools (including UML) and languages.

Software Development Manager

Nature of Work

The Software Development Manager is the individual with ultimate responsibility for delivering a high quality software project meeting all required functionality within schedule and on budget. This individual directs the successful design, implementation, and delivery of one or more projects, depending on the project size and management experience. This position typically reports directly to the director of software development and is typically a first level manager position with seven to ten direct reports. However, on a large project, this may be a second level management position.

While specific software development management responsibilities will vary widely based on organization structure and project size, certain criteria are shared by the manager responsible for a 3 developer 3 month project and an 80 developer multi-year project. This section describes the typical skills shared by successful project managers. Our focus in this chapter is on skills unique or critical to the management of software development projects.

Education and Experience Profile

A typical candidate for this position will have at least ten years work experience in software development or a closely related engineering field. Recommended education for this position is an advanced degree, either in computer science, engineering, or business with a concentration in management information systems. At least five years of experience as an individual contributor in a software development role is recommended.

It is very difficult to manage a software development team without having a development background. Depending on the project size and complexity, between five and ten years development experience is desirable for a first level software development manager. Without hands-on development experience, it is not only too difficult to understand the technology, it is also difficult to understand how to manage and motivate developers. This in turn means a technical degree is a good minimum education to require for development managers. An MBA degree is typically not required of first level managers as long as they have basic business and management training, often gained through in-house courses. An in-house course can be more closely tailored to the business needs of the organization than a general university level course. Likewise, an advanced technical degree is not a typical requirement as development managers should concentrate on people and management skills and rely on the software architect for the heavy technical work.

The above should not be construed to imply that every senior developer with five to ten years experience should be considered a candidate for management. An all too common mistake of organizations is to thrust their best developers into management roles without proper management or business training and without any consideration of the developer's desires. An almost equally bad mistake is to drive your best developers into management roles by not providing equally attractive technical career paths. Providing equal management and technical career paths lets you retain the best developers and avoids driving them to take management positions simply because they have hit an artificial barrier in their technical career path. It is interesting to note that many VPs or director level managers in development organizations actually have criss-crossed career paths, having transitioned between technical and management roles several times or more during their career.

Management, Leadership, and Personal Skills

- Understands the company's vision and goals, business operations, and markets.

- Understands theories and principles of management and administration.

- Has knowledge of planning, project management, budgeting, and quality assurance as it relates to software development projects.

- Has excellent oral and written communication skills.

- Has the ability to establish and maintain effective working relationships.

- Has a passion for software development.

- Has the ability to inspire and lead other software developers.

- Has the ability to train and mentor software engineers.

- Has the ability to coordinate and prioritize customer requests with the assistance of other managers to ensure the highest level of service possible to the customer.
- Writes performance evaluations, issues counseling forms and disciplinary actions, handles employee complaints and grievances, recommends the hiring, termination, and promotion of staff.

Technical Skills

- Has knowledge of current technological trends in the software development industry, such as object-oriented programming, multi-tier software development, component architectures, and web-based software.
- Has knowledge of computer languages, operating systems, application packages, database management systems, networks, and hardware capabilities.
- Has knowledge of system integration issues between diverse platforms (PCs, Unix, mainframes).
- Has the ability to gather and analyze data and draw logical conclusions.

Senior Software Engineer

Nature of Work

A Senior Software Engineer is one who can take responsibility for the analysis, design, and implementation of software systems. This individual will stand out as the most experienced and knowledgeable software engineer on the projects to which he/she is assigned. The senior software engineer will typically report to a software development manager.

Education and Experience Profile

A typical candidate for this position will have at least ten years work experience in software development across a wide variety of development projects, or an advanced degree and at least eight years experience. Recommended education for this position is an advanced degree, either in computer science, engineering, mathematics, or a closely related field with a concentration in software engineering.

Management, Leadership, and Personal Skills

- Understands the company's vision and goals, business operations, and markets.
- Communicates clearly and concisely, both verbally and in writing.
- Establishes and maintains effective working relationships at all levels.
- Has a strong passion for software development.
- Inspires and leads other software engineers on their project and on other projects within their organization.
- Has the ability to train and mentor more junior software engineers.

Technical Skills

- Has thorough knowledge of current technological trends in the software development industry, such as object-oriented programming, multi-tier software development, component architectures, and web-based software.
- Has thorough knowledge of computer languages, operating systems, hardware capabilities, and two or more software specialty areas such as application packages, database management systems, middleware products, or networks.
- Has thorough knowledge of system integration issues between diverse platforms (PCs, Unix, mainframes).
- Has the ability to perform system integration of software systems across heterogeneous platforms.
- Has knowledge of GUI design.
- Has the ability to gather and analyze data and draw logical conclusions.
- Occasionally writes and publishes technical articles, papers, or reports.
- Has the ability to perform software and hardware benchmarks.
- Has knowledge of enterprise and system modeling.
- Has knowledge of object-oriented analysis.

Software Engineer III

Nature of Work

A Software Engineer III is one who can participate as a team member in all phases of the software lifecycle, including the analysis, design, and implementation of software systems. The position will typically report to a software development manager.

Education and Experience Profile

A typical candidate for this position will have at least six years work experience in software development across a wide variety of development projects, or an advanced degree and at least four years experience. Recommended education for this position is a degree, either in computer science, engineering, mathematics, or a closely related field with a concentration in software engineering.

Management, Leadership, and Personal Skills

- Understands the company's vision and goals, business operations, and markets.
- Communicates clearly and concisely, both verbally and in writing.
- Establishes and maintains effective working relationships at all levels.
- Has a strong passion for software development.
- Has the ability to train and mentor more junior software engineers.

Technical Skills

- Has knowledge of current technological trends in the software development industry, such as object-oriented programming, multi-tier software development, component architectures, and web-based software.
- Has thorough knowledge of computer languages, operating systems, hardware capabilities, and one or more software specialty areas such as application packages, database management systems, middleware products, or networks.

- Has thorough knowledge of system integration issues between diverse platforms (PCs, Unix, mainframes).

- Has knowledge of GUI design.

- Has the ability to gather and analyze data and draw logical conclusions.

- Occasionally writes technical articles and reports.

- Has knowledge of object-oriented analysis.

Software Engineer II

Nature of Work

A Software Engineer II is one who can participate as a team member in all phases of the software lifecycle, including the analysis, design, and implementation of software systems. The position will typically report to a software development manager.

Education and Experience Profile

A typical candidate for this position will have at least three years work experience in software development or an advanced degree and at least one year work experience. Recommended education for this position is a degree, either in computer science, engineering, mathematics or a closely related field with a concentration in software engineering.

Management, Leadership, and Personal Skills

- Understands the company's vision and goals, business operations, and markets.

- Communicates clearly and concisely, both verbally and in writing.

- Establishes and maintains effective working relationships at all levels.

- Has a strong passion for software development.

Technical Skills

- Has knowledge of current technological trends in the software development industry, such as object-oriented programming, multi-tier software development, component architectures, and web-based software.

- Has thorough knowledge of computer languages, operating systems, hardware capabilities, and one or more software specialty areas such as application packages, database management systems, middleware products, or networks.

- Has the ability to gather and analyze data and draw logical conclusions.

Software Engineer I

Nature of Work

A Software Engineer I is an entry level software development position. This individual will participate in detailed level design, coding, and unit test of software modules. While it is tempting to place entry level software engineers directly into coding assignments, we find getting them involved in the detailed design process of a task is important. The software engineer who does his own detailed design is more likely to do the coding correctly because he understands the reasons behind each detailed design decision.

Besides working on their own code, entry level programmers also participate in code walk-throughs for other programmers. What separates entry level programmers from more senior ones is their expected productivity levels and the amount of mentoring and training they require. We try to place entry level programmers on teams with more senior programmers and provide plenty of opportunities for informal mentoring and training. While all new programmers receive training on internal software standards, development tools, and policies, there is no substitute for having someone nearby to ask a question of when the need arises.

In many organizations, entry level software engineers might not be expected to provide any training to more senior members of the programming team. However, with technology changing so quickly, new college hires often have experience in areas other members of the team do not. After they have been working on a project for a month or two, we ask all entry level software engineers to select a topic they studied in school or have a keen interest in and present a training session on it to the rest of the project team. At the very least, this serves to develop presentation skills that will be useful later in design and code reviews. Often, however, we find new hires actually come up with meaningful topics to present which later get incorporated into some aspect or another of the project.

The position will typically report to a software development manager. Working in an entry level position, this individual will typically be assigned a mentor who is a more senior software engineer.

Education and Experience Profile

A typical candidate for this position will have zero to three years work experience in software development. Recommended education for this position is a technical degree, either in computer science, engineering, mathematics, or a closely related field with a concentration in software engineering.

Management, Leadership, and Personal Skills

- Understands the company's vision and goals, business operations, and markets.
- Communicates clearly and concisely, both verbally and in writing.
- Establishes and maintains effective working relationships at all levels.
- Has a strong passion for software development.

Technical Skills

- Has knowledge of two or more computer languages, including one object-oriented language such as Java or C++.
- Has knowledge of operating system principles and basic hardware capabilities.
- Has basic knowledge of current technological trends in the software development industry, such as object-oriented programming, multi-tier software development, component architectures, and web-based software.

- Has the ability to gather and analyze data and draw logical conclusions.

Toolsmith

Nature of Work

The position of Toolsmith is a new one that has appeared over the last several years on software development projects using a very large number of third party development tools and utilities. The need for a toolsmith role is being driven by the ever increasing number of commercial off the shelf (COTS) packages. Since object-oriented languages like Java and C++ and component architectures like JavaBeans and ActiveX drive the market for more and more commercial off the shelf (COTS) packages, we expect more and more software development projects will have someone in a toolsmith role.

The toolsmith is a senior software engineer whose responsibilities include analyzing project requirements to select appropriate COTS tools, working with the software architect to integrate COTS tools into the overall design of the application, training other software engineers on proper use of COTS tools in the project environment, and being an overall project resource in the use of COTS tools. The toolsmith also works closely with the chief software architect to assure that the use of COTS tools for software development is standardized as much as possible across the organization. The toolsmith typically reports directly to a software development manager.

Education and Experience Profile

A typical candidate for this position will have at least ten years work experience in software development across a wide variety of development projects, or an advanced degree and at least eight years experience. Recommended education for this position is an advanced degree, either in computer science, engineering, mathematics, or a closely related field with a concentration in software engineering. The individual will have a broad experience base working with COTS design and analysis tools, class libraries, integrated development environments (IDEs), graphics user interface (GUI) design tools, configuration management tools, testing tools, middleware packages, DBMS packages, and other general development tools and utilities.

Chapter **5** | Building a Winning Software Development Team

Management, Leadership, and Personal Skills

- Understands the company's vision and goals, business operations, and markets.
- Communicates clearly and concisely, both verbally and in writing.
- Establishes and maintains effective working relationships at all levels.
- Has a strong passion for software development.
- Inspires and leads other software engineers on their project and on other projects within their organization.
- Has the ability to train and mentor other software engineers in the use of COTS tools.

Technical Skills

- Has thorough knowledge of current technological trends in the software development industry, especially in the use of COTS tools for object-oriented programming, multi-tier software development, component architectures, and web-based software.
- Has thorough knowledge of computer languages, operating systems, hardware capabilities, and COTS tools such as application packages, database management systems, and middleware products.
- Has thorough knowledge of system integration issues between diverse platforms (PCs, Unix, mainframes), especially as it relates to the integration of COTS components with in-house developed software and integration across different COTS components.
- Has the ability to perform system integration of software systems containing COTS components across heterogeneous platforms.
- Has knowledge of GUI design using COTS tools.
- Has the ability to gather and analyze data and draw logical conclusions.
- Has the ability to write and publish technical articles, papers, or reports on the use of COTS tools in the project environment.
- Has the ability to perform software and hardware benchmarks to evaluate different COTS tools.
- Has knowledge of COTS tools for enterprise and system modeling.
- Has knowledge of COTS tools for object-oriented analysis.

- Has thorough knowledge of writing plugins for COTS products (i.e., plugins for Netscape Navigator, Photoshop, etc.).

Webmaster

Nature of Work

Over the last five years, the position of Webmaster has grown from non-existent to one typically performed part time after hours by some forward thinking engineer, to a highly respected position overseeing everything from graphics design to electronic commerce to high volume transaction systems. It is estimated that over fifty percent of new software being written today will be involved, in some way or another, with a web-based application. Many software development organizations, however, still contain little or no experience base with web-based applications. All too often, new applications are simply "thrown over the fence" with web site integration left to the webmaster and his deployment team. Even if your software project has nothing to do with the web, it may be useful to have an internal webmaster to run a project web server. Many development organizations find a project web page quickly becomes the focal point for everything from fostering sharing and reuse of software components to scheduling review meetings to tracking bugs.

Within a software development organization, the webmaster is typically a senior engineer with at least Software Engineer III or equivalent experience. While on a small project the internal webmaster may still be a part-time position; on larger projects the webmaster can easily be a full time position. This position reports to the software development manager. Many software development organizations actually have a webmaster and perhaps an entire web team at the top level of the organization, reporting directly to the director of software development.

Education and Experience Profile

A typical candidate for this position will have at least six years work experience in software development across a wide variety of development projects, or an advanced degree and at least four years experience. The webmaster should also have two or more years experience running a web server environment. Recommended education for this position is a technical degree, either in computer science, engineering, mathematics, or a closely related field with a concentration in software engineering. The individual will have a broad experience base working with different web server packages, middleware, back-end DBMS systems, web server DBMS integration, and Java technology.

Management, Leadership, and Personal Skills

- Understands the company's vision and goals, business operations, and markets.
- Communicates clearly and concisely, both verbally and in writing.
- Establishes and maintains effective working relationships at all levels.
- Has a strong passion for software development.
- Has the ability to train and mentor other software engineers in creating their own web pages.

Technical Skills

- Has thorough knowledge of current technological trends in web server, web client, and middleware software.
- Has thorough knowledge of multiple web client platforms including Netscape Communicator and Microsoft Internet Explorer.
- Has thorough knowledge of the Java platform, including Java servlets, Java applets, Java applications, JDBC (for DBMS connectivity), and Java middleware platforms.
- Has thorough knowledge of CGI protocol including its strengths and limitations.
- Has thorough knowledge of two or more scripting languages such as Perl or Tcl.
- Has thorough knowledge of web server and web client integration issues between diverse platforms (PCs, Unix, mainframes).
- Has knowledge of Java Server Pages and Active Server Pages.
- Has thorough knowledge of web site maintenance tools.
- Has thorough knowledge of web site monitoring and performance analysis tools.

- Has the ability to perform software and hardware benchmarks to evaluate different web-based applications and tools.

- Has thorough knowledge of web site security issues, including setting up secure web servers using the SSL (secure socket layer) protocol, password protecting web pages, and web server configuration issues related to site security.

- Has knowledge of writing plugins for COTS products (i.e., plugins for Netscape Navigator, Photoshop, etc.)

Database Administrator

Nature of Work

The Database Administrator (DBA) works with commercial DBMS packages and tools to design logical data models, translate logical models into physical models (database schema), implement data storage, data integrity, data consistency, and data security, manage database backup and recovery, and manage available database space. Within a software development organization, the DBA will typically be responsible for one or more DBMS packages used as part of the development environment as well as any DBMS packages that are part of the actual software application being developed and thus required for application testing. This position will typically report to a software development manager but may also report to a separate operations department.

Education and Experience Profile

Depending on the number, size, and complexity of project databases involved, the DBA position may range from a junior to a senior one. A junior DBA position typically requires one to three years related work experience and a degree in computer science or related field. A senior DBA position typically requires seven years related work experience, four or more as a DBA, or an advanced degree in computer science or related field and four years related work experience.

Management, Leadership, and Personal Skills

- Understands the company's vision and goals, business operations, and markets.
- Communicates clearly and concisely, both verbally and in writing.
- Establishes and maintains effective working relationships at all levels.
- Has the ability to train and mentor other software engineers in creating efficient SQL queries.
- Has a strong passion for database administration.

Technical Skills

A senior level DBA position would be targeted at an engineer who is thoroughly capable in all of these areas. A junior level DBA position would be targeted at an engineer who is capable in a subset of these areas.

- Evaluates project-wide database infrastructures, develops detailed analysis reports and recommendations for database systems. Defines logical data model.
- Plans, designs, and implements databases on a variety of platforms. Proficient at translating logical data models into physical data models (schema).
- Understands features and performance limitations of different database platforms.
- Understands and has experience implementing database cluster systems, including high-availability failover and parallel database options.
- Plans and implements database backup and recovery procedures. Understands optimal database backup strategies and is experienced at integrating database backup procedures into general purpose backup tools such, as Legato or Veritas.
- Has knowledge of database monitoring, tuning, and capacity management tools and utilities.
- Has knowledge of database connectivity APIs, including JDBC and ODBC.
- Has knowledge of database software installation and maintenance, database creation, startup, and database shutdown.

- Has knowledge of database I/O and memory allocation characteristics and in tuning I/O and memory for optimal database performance.

- Has knowledge of database locking, transaction, and concurrency controls.

- Has knowledge of referential integrity and its enforcement using foreign keys and primary keys.

- Has knowledge of two phase commit protocols used by different DBMS packages.

- Has knowledge of distributed database concepts, including database replication.

- Has experience in optimizing single and multi-table queries through the correct use of indices.

- Participates in quality audits of database systems to ensure consistency throughout the software development organization.

- Has knowledge of database benchmarking techniques.

- Evaluates vendors' DBMS product offerings and helps select the best suited DBMS for project applications.

System Administrator

Nature of Work

The System Administrator is an advanced technical position with responsibility for technical consulting, server design, network design, planning, implementation, management, and operational support for all computer hardware platforms. Because most software engineers are likely to be able (and want) to administer their own desktops, we will concentrate in this section on the server system administrator. This individual will be responsible for administering all file, DBMS, application, and other servers used within the software development organization. Many times this individual will report up through an operations group rather than through the software development organization. Nevertheless, we cover this position here because of its importance to any software development organization.

Education and Experience Profile

- A server system administrator generally has a technical degree and at least two to five years experience working as a desktop system administrator.

Management, Leadership, and Personal Skills

- Understands the company's vision and goals, business operations, and markets.
- Communicates clearly and concisely, both verbally and in writing.
- Establishes and maintains effective working relationships at all levels.
- Has a strong passion for supporting software development organizations.

Technical Skills

- Evaluates, installs, monitors, debugs, audits, and maintains server software on a variety of hardware platforms.
- Maintains a "run book" of server configurations and operational procedures.
- Acts as the main liaison to the hardware and operating system vendors for all server maintenance and support activities.
- Writes user documentation as appropriate.
- Installs, tests, and implements server operating system upgrades and enhancements.
- Prepares specifications for server hardware and software environments that adhere to technical standards and ensures interoperability with other servers in the organization.
- Responds to emergency calls relating to server performance, diagnosis of problems, and repairing problems.
- Maintains data integrity and security of server software.
- Monitors server performance including DASD, CPU, network, and memory utilization.
- Responsible for creating and maintaining user accounts and associated databases such as NIS, LDAP, and Automounter.

- Responsible for creating and maintaining host and system databases, including DNS.
- Has knowledge of cross-platform server backup packages such as Legato or Veritas and their implementation.
- Has knowledge of server Reliability, Availability, and Serviceability (RAS) features and the ability to properly configure a system to take advantage of all available RAS features.
- Has knowledge of RAID configurations including striping and mirroring and the ability to correctly configure DASD to optimally meet all business requirements including cost and performance.
- Has knowledge of server clustering techniques.

Skills Tracking

We recommend you automate your organization's skills tracking process. This makes it easier for developers to keep their skill profiles updated as well as allows for creation of a searchable database. Tracking the skills of your software developers serves many purposes. For a developer, it provides an opportunity for self-evaluation, allows them to track their skills versus others in the organization, and helps in setting development goals. For managers, tracking provides a metric to evaluate their organization's strengths and weaknesses in order to help establish training and hiring priorities. A searchable skills database also allows one to locate needed skills across a large organization. We also use a portion of the skills tracking evaluation during the interview process to help judge the technical expertise of candidates.

We have included sample self-evaluation templates for object-oriented programming skills in C++ and Java. The Java self-evaluation was patterned after the earlier C++ template. In both cases, these evaluations attempt to differentiate those who simply know the syntax of the language and those who truly understand object-oriented programming.

Sample C++ Programming Self-Evaluation

Rating 0: No Skill

- I have no experience programming with an object-oriented language such as C++.
- I would require guidance, mentoring, and training in order to become a productive object-oriented programmer.

Rating 1: Beginner

- I have knowledge of how basic object-oriented concepts such as encapsulation, identity, and inheritance are implemented in an object-oriented language such as C++.
- I can program a basic abstract data type such as a linked list using classes.
- I have taken a basic course in object-oriented programming using C++.

Rating 2: Intermediate

- I know the difference between just using C++ syntax as a better form of C versus object-oriented programming in C++.
- I have a good grasp of the C++ language and am comfortable in a minimum of 7 out of 10 C++ programming constructs.
- I understand the concept of references and pointers.
- I know that the concept of the array in C++ is messy and avoid arrays in favor of vectors from the standard library.

Rating 3: Accomplished

- I can write efficient C++ code with an understanding of the intricacies of C++ memory management.
- I can conduct code reviews. I can mentor others on basic concepts of C++.
- I have 1 to 2 years of everyday relevant experience involving C++.

- I know the difference between assignment and initialization and how the difference between them gets reflected by the difference between an assignment operator and a copy constructor.
- I understand conversions, including implicit conversion and explicit conversion.
- I can explain how a constructor is different from member functions.

Rating 4: Expert

- I have a good grasp of all concepts of the C++ programming languages including some of the less well known concepts such as virtual base classes, namespaces, exceptions, and templates.
- I have written at least one class library that is fully object-oriented. I can render an object model into C++ without missing any intrinsics.
- I can teach concepts to others and can troubleshoot their tasks. I stay on top of major commercial C++ class libraries as well as IDE tools.
- I have more than 2 years of everyday relevant experience with object-oriented implementations of C++.
- I bring extra value through innovative approaches to all situations that require knowledge of C++.
- I am able to troubleshoot the tasks of others involving this skill.
- I am versed in newer features of C++ such as templates, exception handling, and namespaces.
- I know the strengths and weakness of C++ as an object-oriented language. I can compare it to other languages such as Java.
- I am familiar with the standard C++ library and can use functionals and iterators efficiently.
- I have knowledge and some experience in object persistence and distributed objects.

Rating 5: Master

- Given my accomplishments in C++, I could be recognized as an industry expert in C++.
- I could or do contribute to the public body of knowledge on object-oriented implementations of C++ through publishing papers and books.

- I know the evolution of the C++ language as well as its future direction.
- I have solid knowledge and experience in object persistence and distributed objects.

Sample Java Programming Self-Evaluation

Rating 0: No Skill

- I have no experience programming with an object-oriented language such as Java.
- I would require guidance, mentoring, and training in order to become a productive object-oriented programmer.

Rating 1: Beginner

- I have knowledge of how basic object-oriented concepts such as encapsulation, identity, and inheritance are implemented in an object-oriented language such as Java.
- I can program a basic abstract data type such as a priority queue or B-tree using Java classes.
- I have taken a basic course in object-oriented programming using Java.

Rating 2: Intermediate

- I write true object-oriented Java code versus simply using Java syntax to write code that could be written in C.
- I can explain the differences between interface and implementation inheritance and can give an example of how you would use Java interface inheritance.
- I have a good grasp of the Java language and APIs and am comfortable in a minimum of 7 out of 10 Java programming constructs.
- I understand the concept of object references and can explain how it differs from pointers in C++.

- I understand all the basic Java class libraries such as AWT, java.net, and java.io.

Rating 3: Accomplished

- I can write efficient Java code with an understanding of the intricacies of the Java virtual machine memory management.
- I can conduct code reviews. I can mentor others on basic concepts of Java.
- I have 1 to 2 years of everyday relevant experience involving Java.
- I understand how to write JavaBeans.
- I know the difference between abstract classes and interfaces.

Rating 4: Expert

- I have a good grasp of all concepts of the Java programming language APIs including some of the less well known concepts such as serialization, reflection, and low-level event handling for creating custom components.
- I have written at least one class library that is fully object-oriented. I can render an object model into Java without missing any intrinsics.
- I can teach concepts to others and can troubleshoot their tasks. I stay on top of major commercial Java class libraries as well as IDE tools.
- I have more than 2 years of everyday relevant experience with object-oriented implementations of Java.
- I bring extra value through innovative approaches to all situations that require knowledge of Java.
- I am able to troubleshoot the tasks of others involving this skill.
- I am versed in newer features of developing Java APIs.
- I know the strengths and weakness of Java as an object-oriented language and can compare it to other languages such as C++.
- I have knowledge and some experience in object persistence and distributed objects.
- I can explain the differences between the JDBC, RMI, Java IDL APIs and explain when each should be used.
- I can explain the differences between the Java Card, Embedded Java, Personal Java, and Java API sets.

Chapter 5 | Building a Winning Software Development Team

Rating 5: Master

- Given my accomplishments in Java, I could be recognized as an industry expert in Java.

- I could or do contribute to the public body of knowledge on object-oriented implementations of Java through publishing papers, books, and/or at conferences.

- I know the evolution of the Java language as well as its future direction.

- I have solid knowledge and experience in object persistence and distributed objects.

Behavioral Value Assessment Interview

Using behavioral based interviewing techniques to help judge a candidate's core values is not unique to software development. Every company tries to hire individuals with strong values that reflect those of the organization. Here are eight simple questions you can ask to help judge a candidate's values. For each group of questions, corresponding behaviors and traits of people to look for are listed. Each candidate should be given a score for each trait listed.

If you have not practiced behavioral based interviewing before, it may be very enlightening for you to do so. The general concept behind this technique is to ask a candidate questions that will invoke a specific response describing a previous situation. By drilling down and getting a candidate to discuss specific actions they took in response to different situations in the past, you can usually gain a better understanding of how that person will behave in an actual work environment.

The questions are divided into four value areas.

Value #1: Initiative

Here are two sample questions that can be used to measure a candidate's initiative.

1. Tell me about something you did recently that gave you a personal sense of accomplishment.
2. Tell me something you really wanted to do recently.

Some sample behaviors of people who take initiative include:

- Knows how to ask questions
- Knows how to deal with uncertainty
- Exudes confidence
- Surfaces issues
- Requests opportunities
- Seeks out work beyond what is expected
- Takes advantage of opportunities to learn
- Sees value in even mundane tasks
- Finds ways to stay motivated

Table 5–1 Initiative Value Rating

Trait/Rating	Poor	Fair	Average	Good	Excellent
Competence					
Quick Learner					
Problem Solving					
Proactive					
Risk Taker					
Enthusiastic					
Hard Worker					
Work Ethic					
Self Motivation					

Value #2: Dedication

Here are two sample questions that can be used to measure a candidate's dedication.

1. Tell me about a time you were under pressure to get something done.
2. Tell me about a difficult problem you recently had to solve.

Some sample behaviors of people who exhibit dedication include:

- Does what it takes to get the job done
- Shows commitment

Table 5–2   Dedication Value Rating

Trait/Rating	Poor	Fair	Average	Good	Excellent
Self Confidence					
Goal Oriented					
Focused					
Driven					
Sense of Conviction					

Value #3: Flexibility

Here are two sample questions that can be used to measure a candidate's flexibility.

1. Tell me about a time when you worked as part of a team to complete a project, including your role on the team and the outcome of the project.
2. Tell me about a time when you had to do something you never had to do before.

Some sample behaviors of flexible people include:

- Ability to tolerate ambiguity

- Leverages others to help solve problems
- Willingness to learn new things
- Makes personal sacrifices to learn

Table 5–3 Flexibility Value Rating

Trait/Rating	Poor	Fair	Average	Good	Excellent
Flexible					
Creative					
Innovative					
Team Player					
Facilitator					
Unselfish					
Adaptable					

Value #4: Respect

Here are two sample questions that can be used to measure a candidate's respect for others.

1. Tell me about a situation where you had to work with someone who saw things differently than you did.
2. Tell me about a situation where you were the new person on a project or where there were more experienced people than you.

Some sample behaviors of people with respect include:

- Established rapport
- Willingness to compromise
- Listens to the ideas of others
- Learns from others with more experience

Table 5–4 Respect Value Rating

Trait/Rating	Poor	Fair	Average	Good	Excellent
Communicative					
Listening Skills					
Professional					
Responsive					
Well thought of by peers					

Your Software Development Partners

In the 1970s, many large software development organizations were run entirely with in-house staff with little or no purchased software other than the operating system and compiler. While this trend started to reverse itself in the 1980s, software development organizations still remained notorious for having the "not invented here" syndrome. Such organizations will often write their own versions of common tools and utilities when perfectly suitable ones are available for purchase or reuse from other sources. Those with not invented here syndrome, of course, believe that any software their own group did not create could not possibly be as good as something written in-house.

Even in the 199's, these trends still exist and are not necessarily isolated to one-off situations. A large tape backup software vendor estimates that ninety percent of system backups are still done with homegrown backup scripts. With all the different tape backup products on the market today, there is undoubtedly more than one package that would fit the needs of almost any organization. Sometimes, however, the problem is not the lack of available applications but the overwhelming number of them. Several Unix vendors claim to have more than 10,000 third party software applications available on their platform. Unfortunately, few IT organizations can afford to train their staff to use even one percent of this number of applications. The complexity and the diversity of today's software offerings is one reason some CIOs have decided to outsource some or all of their infrastructure.

Outsourcing is certainly the other end of the spectrum from "not invented here." Outsourcing, however, is not a cure all for all the support woes of a software development organization. If the outsourcer continues to use the same homegrown backup scripts, you are not solving your problems but simply making them more difficult to control. In general, you should outsource functions that are well understood by your organization yet not considered to be part of your core competency. When used appropriately, however, system integrators and outsourcers can be beneficial partners to your software development organization.

While many software development organizations consider other software vendors to be their partners, they often take a different approach when it comes to hardware vendors. Too often, project teams bring in the usual host of vendors when they are ready to make a hardware purchase and perform an evaluation highly tied to whoever has the best price/performance ratio that given month. As vendors tend to continually leap-frog each other in performance, this can be a very short-sighted way of making hardware decisions. By contrast, if you partner with one or two hardware vendors, they will be much more willing to share information with you about trends, future products, capacity planning, and provide other value-added services for your development team.

Finally, and all too often overlooked, the most important partners to your development organization are the internal or external customers of the software you are developing. They are the ones that ultimately pay for the system and decide your fate. Involving your customers early and often in the software development process is crucial to achieving the best software quality.

Organizing for Success

Many CIOs recognize that the organizational structure of their software development group has an impact on the success of their application development efforts. Unfortunately, there is not always the same level of consensus among CIOs on what the correct organizational structure should be. This chapter starts by defining the organizational structure and examining its importance to successful software development. Different types of organizational structures, along with their pros and cons are discussed. Sample organization charts are given for small, medium, and large software development organizations. This chapter also contains discussions on centralized versus decentralized organizations and the use of virtual project teams.

The Dimensions of an Organization

An organization is defined by much more than boxes containing job titles and names connected by lines representing a reporting structure. Besides organizational structure, an organization is defined by the multiple dimensions spanning the people, processes, and technology represented within it. Some of these dimensions include:

- *People Dimensions*: Each individual in an organization has certain skills, and these skills are typically measured against formal or informal performance metrics leading to rewards (compensation) as incentives for future performance. The people in an organization establish its culture, those behavior patterns and values that are generally recognized as being adopted.

- *Process Dimensions:* The procedures and methodologies used by people in the organization. Almost all organizations define their own internal economies through processes for budgeting, priority settings, and project approval.

- *Technology Dimensions:* The specific skills and tools people in the organization use to carry out the business function of the organization.

The Importance of Organizational Structure

Of the different people, process, and technology dimensions of an organization, structure is by far the most fundamental. Without a sound structure, people in the organization lose their culture and compete for individual rewards rather than for the good of the organization. Without structure, processes have no home and internal economies collapse because of conflicting objectives. Without structure, technology is no longer pursued for business reasons and either languishes or is simply pursued as a research interest rather than for the good of the organization. While these concepts hold true for any information technology organization, they are especially true for software development organizations, no matter what their size.

Many a small software startup begins life with no more than a couple of developers working out of a garage. Not much organizational structure is required at this point in a company's history, however organizational structure still exists. For instance, in 1977, when Bill Gates and Paul Allen formed their partnership and officially named it Microsoft, the company had minimal organizational structure. Less than a dozen employees worked at Microsoft's first office in Albuquerque, New Mexico, and everyone knew who was in charge. No complicated organization charts were needed to figure out everyone's reporting structure. At the same time, all employees knew what their role was in the company and what they were trying to accomplish. This was because any organizational structure that was needed could be informally communicated among each of the employees.

At the other end of the spectrum are IT departments of Fortune 500 companies, large independent software vendors, and commercial system integrators. An entry level programmer at Microsoft today probably needs several different organization charts to show the reporting structure among 20,000+ employees and up to Bill Gates. Having organization charts alone, unfortunately, is no guarantee of a healthy corporate structure. In any large organization, there are many dimensions to measuring the success of the corporation's structure. While no organizational model fits all development departments, certain traits stand out among companies that routinely produce successful software products.

Streamlining Bureaucracy

One of the side effects many development organizations have suffered as they grew has been increased bureaucracy. While over half of this book is devoted to people and process issues, the aim is to help streamline bureaucracies, not develop new ones. For instance, at some companies, a standard operating procedure is that, with few exceptions, no document shall ever require more than two approvals, one from the person who authored the document and one from the final approver. Besides empowering employees, this makes it very simple to place blame when an incorrect decision is made. In addition, this removes the possibility for two superiors to reject a document and send it back to the original author with conflicting modifications.

Sample Organizational Structures

The next four sections describe alternative organization schemes commonly found in software development departments:

- Project centered organizations
- Department centered organizations
- Matrix organizations
- Product line organizations

While none of the above will be perfect for every software development group, they each offer useful ideas for coming up with your organization scheme.

Project Centered Organizations

Organizations centered around project teams are typically found in smaller or newly formed groups. A project centered organization approach is suitable for groups of about 5 to 40 people supporting 1 to 8 projects of small to medium duration, perhaps up to a year each. In such an organization, each group is primarily self-sufficient and is staffed by enough skilled developers to address every stage of the development life cycle. This in turn means most individuals will have responsibility for some facet of development other than just programming, such as requirements, architecture, configuration management, or testing.

As development organizations grow larger, project centered organizations become less desirable. At one level, the number of projects grows to outstrip the needed specialty skills so you cannot provide a developer with the needed skills to each project. Another problem is specialist knowledge and even general skills tend to not be shared between individual projects that are operating in their own microcosms. As organizations outgrow project centered organizations they often reorganize into department centered organizations.

Department Centered Organizations

Department centered development organizations start to become practical as a group grows above 25 developers or 5 projects. At these staffing levels, there are sufficient people to form multiple departments centered around particular software skills or life cycle areas. For instance, a 40 person group might have departments for:

- system and database administrators
- user interface programmers
- application programmers
- configuration management, test, and quality assurance

A common mistake in department centered organizations is to break software architects into a separate department or group. We have found this can lead to elitism and be very counterproductive. First, it starts to separate the architects from the developers who are doing the actual implementation. Architects thus become more quickly out-of-touch with the latest development methodologies actually being used. Also, while every developer does not want to be an architect, every developer likes to have some say in the design. If developers are too separated from architects, they may have a built-in incentive to prove the architect's design was wrong by not working their hardest to implement it. When this happens the architect will most likely blame the problem on developer incompetence than on any architectural flaws. The whole iterative development process becomes harder to implement smoothly.

Matrix Organizations

When your development organization grows to several hundred people or more, you may want to consider a matrix organization. Matrix organizations are sometimes used in companies with a large number of software developers working on a broad array of software projects. One side of the matrix is organized along skill sets while the other side of the matrix is organized across projects. In a matrix organization, every developer has two managers. One manager is from the department or skill set matrix and one manager is from the project matrix. A developer typically stays in a single department for as long as he or she continues working in that skill area. A developer would only stay on a project for the length of time his or her particular skill was needed and then return to his or her department for another assignment. Table 6-1 shows how employees might be assigned from different departments to several different projects. As shown in the table, not all departments necessarily have employees working on all projects.

Table 6-1   Sample Personnel Assignments

Department	Project 1	Project 2	Project 3
Requirements Analysis	John	Kevin	Betty
Business Systems	Steve, Nancy	Carol	Bruce
Web Development	David		Barbara
Operating Systems	Charlie	Jeff	
Realtime Processing			Lisa
Configuration Management	Brian	Peter	Frank
Integration and Test	Joe, Henry	Dan, Tim	Leslie

Individual departments are responsible for hiring and training developers and supplying them to projects as needed. Department managers work with project managers to properly forecast requirements and equitably assign developers to projects considering the best interests of the corporation.

A matrix organization obviously requires a certain minimum size to sustain the overhead of two management chains. One challenge with such an organization is to develop the right number and mix of departments. Another challenge is to sustain developer loyalty to projects when their long term management lies in the department organization. Because of these issues, a product line organization is often better suited.

Product Line Organizations

In a product line organization, developers are organized into projects based on business product lines as opposed to skill set departments. A product line organization is responsible for staffing the skill sets required for its project mix. For instance, one product line might have requirements analysts, OS experts, some web developers, and configuration management. Another product line might have requirements analysts, real-time coding experts, and configuration management. This works if product line organizations are sufficiently large that enough developers exist to staff duplicated functions throughout departments. The downside is that software projects will most often require different sets of skill levels at different times in the software life cycle. Each product line must always have sufficient resources to staff for peak periods while worrying about the lulls in-between.

Recurring Organizational Themes

When choosing how to organize your software development organization, these recurring themes and concepts are ones you should address:

- creating a software process team
- balancing centralized versus decentralized organization
- managing virtual teams

Creating a Software Process Team

Regardless of organization, every development organization should have a software process team. This team, made up of representatives from each software skill area, should be tasked with developing standard processes used throughout the organization. These individuals can thus become process "experts" that help train the rest of the organization.

Balancing Centralized versus Decentralized Organization

Most IT groups have experimented with different mixes of centralized versus decentralized organizations. The arguments on both sides are well-known. Centralized organizations generate economies of scale and provide developers the most opportunity to specialize. A development group of 50 people can probably have several specialists in user interface development. Break that same organization down into 10 groups of five and no group may be able to afford a dedicated user interface or other specialist. The down side of centralized organizations are they often are not responsive to individual business unit demands, especially to smaller business units. In theory, a decentralized development group dedicated to an individual business unit can be more responsive to local needs.

Our suggestion is to keep a small centralized development organization for enterprise-wide systems and for company-wide architecture issues. Individual business units should be responsible for developing their own local applications.

Managing Virtual Teams

Static software development organizations worked well when software was limited to a small, well-defined, and static set of functions within an organization. Today, business requirements often may call for the creation of virtual teams that span across all aspects of a company, not just its development organization. The classic example is the marketing department that decides the company needs to have an electronic commerce web site. Besides the IT and marketing departments, this might involve the legal department, the sales department, product departments, and the art department. Today's business drivers mean such teams need to be able to come together, perform their function, turn over a product for maintenance, and disband to go off to other jobs, perhaps several times a year or more.

Figures 6-1 through 6-3 show sample software development organization charts for different sized software development organizations. There are many different types of development organization structures you could come up with besides those illustrated below. Following the concepts presented in this chapter, you should tailor one of these organization charts to best suit the requirements of your group.

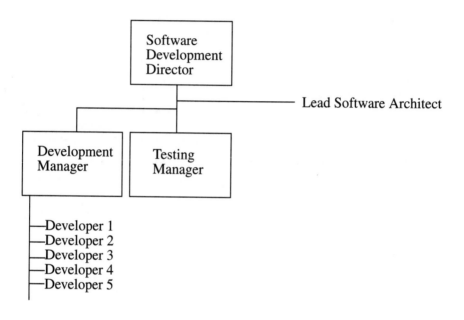

Figure 6–1   Small Corporate Software Development Department

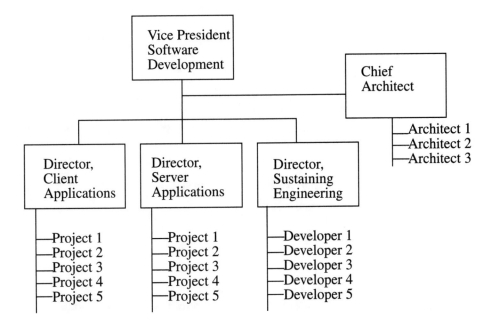

Figure 6–2   Medium Corporate Software Development Department

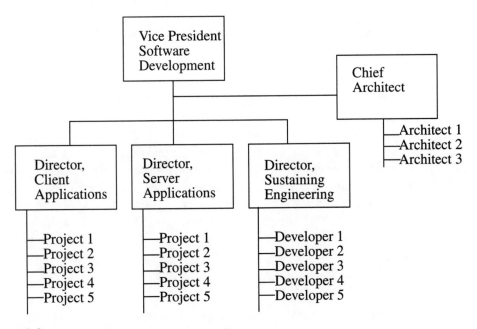

Figure 6–3   Large Corporate Software Development Department

Thirteen Organizational Structure Mistakes

No matter the size of your software development organization, there are certain mistakes you want to avoid. Many cultures consider thirteen to be an unlucky number, so we have drawn from other developers mistakes to list the thirteen organizational structures that frequently fail, no matter how lucky the manager feels. Good organizational structure is a matter of management theory, science, and experience, not luck. So here are our "unlucky thirteen" mistakes to avoid.

#1 Combining software development and operations into a single organization.

The job of operations is to keep applications up and running. The easiest way to do this is to never change anything. Combining development and operations into a single organization has the natural tendency to stifle innovation. Software development organizations should be separated from operations to allow new and modified applications to be developed as required to support the business needs of the company.

#2 Organizing software technology specialists by project.

A modern day software development project requires a wide range of software specialists during different times in the software life cycle. If you have a small organization with only one specialist and two projects, it is clear the specialist needs to work on both projects, perhaps at different times. As your organization grows and develops more specialists, you still want to have specialists work across projects wherever and whenever they are most needed. What happens if you assign technology specialists by project and each project ends up having a small number of specialists that must act as generalists while doing the work of another specialist assigned to a different project? The result is your organization as a whole cannot take advantage of all its specialists where they are most needed and fails to take advantage of the synergies of being one integrated development organization.

#3 Organizing software technology specialists by application domain (i.e., financial, manufacturing, etc.).

This results in the same problem as mistake number 2, above. Given a fixed headcount, each application domain receives a smaller group of specialists who therefore are driven to become more generalists. There is no room for software technology specialists that span across application domains, for instance a GUI design specialist.

#4 Organizing software developers by delivery platform (i.e., Windows, Unix, and mainframe).

Developers tend to naturally develop biases in favor of their assigned platform. As a result, there tends to be little or no innovation in new platforms (for instance, network computers) or cross-platform approaches (for instance, webtop computing or client-server systems).

#5 Separating software development and software maintenance groups.

When you separate software development and software maintenance groups, you end up requiring the same types of software specialists for each group. This means you either have to double headcount in your organization for specialists or force one group to reduce specialization. In addition, it becomes harder to create incentives for software developers to do things right the first time as they know another group will ultimately be responsible for fixing any mistakes. In addition, such an organization tends to develop two classes of software developers, leading to morale problems.

#6 Representing projects in the formal organizational structure versus defining project teams that cut across organizational boundaries.

This leads to a reorganization whenever a major project ends. As a result, software developers spend an inordinate amount of time looking for their next job or find unnecessary reasons to prolong their existing project.

#7 Organizing software developers into long-term and short-term development groups.

Once again, this type of organization requires two of every software specialist and builds unnecessary competition between the two groups. In addition, this organization often encourages point solutions that may be quicker to implement but cost more in the long term because of higher maintenance costs and difficulties in integrating with enterprise-wide applications.

#8 Designing organizations that need "super-developers" to succeed.

In today's complex software development environments, no single developer can be a specialist in all fields. The organization should allow and reward developers who become true specialists in a single field. Also, the workload should be managed to allow software developers to lead balanced lives. No one can work eighteen hours a day forever and be expected to maintain his or her work quality and personal satisfaction.

#9 Designing organizations that tolerate underachievers.

This is the corollary of mistake number 8. A healthy organization employs everyone's complete range of talents to their fullest. Software developers who are allowed to underachieve will become bored with their work, which will only lead to poorer quality and further underperformance.

#10 Designing organizations that reward empire building.

Organizational structures should eliminate all incentives for empire building. This means providing equal career paths for both senior level software engineers and software development managers. Along the same lines, career paths should be provided both for software generalists and software specialists, as both are needed in a healthy organization.

#11 Setting organizational goals that compete against each other for customer satisfaction.

Customer satisfaction should be the ultimate goal of all software development organizations. One organization should not have goals whose achievement effects the customer satisfaction of another organization. For instance, if two development groups are working on applications for the same customer that must ultimately be integrated together, one organization should not be rewarded for meeting its timelines if this was only done at the expense of creating a more difficult integration task for the second group.

#12 Organizing around individuals versus personality types.

Every experienced software development manager recognizes the importance of matching a developer's job to their personality. However, even in the most stable of organizations, individuals come and go. You should not therefore, design organizations around individual personalities. Instead, organize them around more general personality types. This allows them to recognize the value of individual diversity without having to reorganize every time someone comes and goes.

#13 Mandating organizational changes from the top down.

There comes a time when all software development organizations must change to adopt to new business models, technologies, or clients. However, mandating a structural change has little or no effect if it is not accompanied by cultural and process changes. The best way to assure successful change is to manage it via a participative process where all developers are given a chance to effect the final outcome.

Recruiting The Best Talent

While this book covers recruiting in Chapter 7 and retention in Chapter 8, successful software development organizations know the two are closely linked. The same attributes of a successful development organization that attracts top software talent are the same attributes that will help you retain your staff and reduce turnover. Furthermore, the best retention practices start with careful recruitment and hiring. If you want to have low turnover, it is not sufficient to simply hire skilled software professionals; you must hire engineers that will fit the specific requirements and culture of your organization. This chapter presents some of the best practices in recruitment for the software industry, with the following chapter focusing on the retention part of the recruitment and retention equation.

Unless you have a fully staffed software development organization and are expecting no growth or turnover, you should be concerned about recruiting and hiring the best talent. The best software developers will produce significantly better code than their average counterparts. The top software architects will produce designs that are much more likely to be successfully completed. So how can you find and hire the best developers and architects? One key attribute of organizations that successfully staff for growth is constant recruitment to keep a full pipeline of candidates, even if they currently have no open positions. Another key attribute of successful organizations is hiring from internal referrals. Most companies find there is no better way to recruit qualified software development candidates than through personal referrals.

This of course brings up a key point. If your software development team member is not happy in the job, he or she is not likely to refer others to the organization. After reading the next two chapters, it should become very clear why recruiting and retention are so closely tied. Many of the best retention practices double as things that can help recruit top talent to your organization.

In addition to discussing ways to recruit software development talent, this chapter also describes what to look for in successful developers. Your key developers should not only have top notch technical skills, they should have outstanding business and behavioral skills along with values that match those of your organization.

How to Staff for Growth

The following sections describe some of the more successful ways that top software development organizations recruit their best talent. Techniques discussed include internal referrals, campus recruiting, agencies, newspaper, and other print media ads, job fairs, Internet ads, and perhaps one of the least considered, acquisitions. No matter if you use one of these techniques or all of them, what you should do is establish metrics. If you were to invest $10,000 in any of these techniques, how many successful new hires could you expect to gain from each one? Good metrics will not only help you spend your recruitment dollars wisely, but can also help you justify the recruitment expense in the first place.

Internal Referrals

Successful software development organizations usually find a large number of their new hires from internal referrals. Good developers typically know other developers and are perhaps the best judge of how suitable a candidate is to join their team. Furthermore, few developers would want to work with a poor performer, even if he or she were a close friend. Many software development organizations further encourage internal referrals through some sort of employee referral program. Among high-tech companies it is not uncommon to find referral bonuses of $1,000 to $5,000 or more for referring new software developers. As such programs have become quite commonplace, leading companies try to provide further incentives such as entering each employee whose referral is hired into a drawing for further cash or other incentive prizes ranging from stock options to weekend getaways and exotic vacations. The total cash outlay is still less than what would be charged by most technical recruitment agencies.

Campus Recruiting

Campus recruitment is another place many development organizations look to find new talent. While the top universities may offer the best chance of finding great developers, the competition there will also be most fierce. There are several ways to increase your chance at college recruiting. First, you should select what schools you are going try and recruit from. When targeting a school for recruitment, try to find out as much as you can about the school to determine if you want to expend your resources recruiting there. Some schools have great technical reputations that are based on their electrical engineering or physics departments and may not concentrate at all on software development. The school's web page is always a good place to start if you are not familiar with a particular school. If there are alumni of the school in your organization, they are another good source of information. Finally, don't forget to contact the school's career center and discuss what skills you are looking for. The more information you have the better.

Besides a school's reputation, there are other items to consider when choosing a school to recruit from. You should consider not only the school's reputation for producing software development talent, but also consider the school's location. If the school is not local to your work location, relocation of the new hire will be another consideration. Of course many students are willing to relocate for a great job but it is likely to be an issue with at least some candidates. Finally, try to get current employees who are alumni of the school involved in your recruiting efforts. There is no one better than alumni to return to campus and help recruit new graduates. If alumni are not available for the actual recruiting trip, you might at least try to get them to speak via telephone with any finalists that are selected.

As with recruiting in general, don't consider campus recruiting a one-shot a year opportunity. While a majority of students graduate in the spring, good candidates are likely to be graduating at the end of each quarter or semester. There is likely to be less competition for these candidates as many companies will only interview on campus once a year. You should also look for ways to keep alumni and other interested employees involved with targeted campuses. Many schools have some sort of professional organization or affiliation program your company might get involved in. These provide extra opportunities for you to get your name in front of students and prospective employees. Also, you may want to consider internship or co-op programs. There is no better way to find great employees than to have them work part time for you while they are still in school.

An excellent example of a school-affiliated program is the UCLA Anderson School of Management's IS Associates program. For over twenty years, the IS Associates have brought together CIOs and other IS executives with students from the school's MBA program. Besides the obvious recruitment opportunities, the IS Associates events provide much-needed occasions for CIOs to network with their peers. In return, the IS executives and their companies provide financial support for the Anderson School, occasionally do duty as guest lecturers, and participate in quarterly events and seminars. The IS Associates also co-sponsor UCLA's week-long *Managing the Information Resource* (MIR) program. Many top CIOs and their direct reports from Los Angeles and across the world have attended this course, the second longest running such program in the country.

Agencies

The reputation of technical recruitment agencies is often placed just above or below used car salesmen. Used correctly, however, a good technical recruiter can be an excellent source of software development talent for your organization. Like any group, there are good and bad recruitment agencies. The organizations that use agencies most successfully typically establish a relationship with a small number of technical recruiters who they learn to trust. You should take the time to meet with the agency and describe the types of individuals you are looking for. Having a personal relationship with the recruiter will greatly increase your chances of getting qualified leads. Be sure to take the time to provide feedback to the recruiters when you do get resumes, as this will also help them understand the type of person you are looking for.

Newspapers and Other Media

Open the Sunday paper in any major metropolitan area and you are likely to find hundreds of advertisements for software developers, ranging from tiny two-line ads to multi-page spreads. While an expensive newspaper ad may provide you with a large number of references, you had better be prepared to screen them closely. Most software development organizations find that newspaper ads tend to generate the highest percentage of unqualified responses. What this means is you must be willing to invest the resources necessary to properly screen the resumes that you get back from newspaper ads.

One of the problems with newspaper ads is your best software developers are likely to be content in their current job and probably aren't spending their time reading the classified ads of the Sunday paper. You should consider more targeted advertisement such as in IEEE or ACM publications and journals. A one-page add in *IEEE Software* is at least pretty much guaranteed to be read by a software development professional, although not necessarily one looking for a job.

Job Fairs

Job fairs can be a lot like newspaper ads in that there is no way to pre-screen the people who attend. If you are going to use job fairs for recruitment, be sure you are targeting the correct one. A general engineering job fair will have lots of attendees who have never written a line of code in their life. For the best results, try to target a job fair that is very specific to software development.

Internet

Like newspaper ads, there is no way to pre-screen who will be reading your Internet job ads. With a little extra work, however, there is a way to generally monitor who is reading your Internet ad. You should use this to your best advantage. One networking company noticed a large number of "hits" on their web site from a competitor. They modified their job listing page to automatically recognize when someone from that competitor was accessing an on-line job listing and provided them with a special banner greeting. Another company recognized that their Internet job listings were being accessed most often during working hours, when someone's boss was likely to walk around the corner. They thus added a "quick escape" button at the bottom of each job listing page that jumps you to a product catalog page. Much better, they figured, to be researching a competitor's product catalog than to be researching their job listings.

There is no end to what features you might add to an Internet job listing. The most important, however, is how easily the candidate can apply for the job if it is of interest to them. The best job listings will identify multiple ways to respond, including traditional mail, fax, e-mail resume submission, and on-line forms to request more information.

Acquisitions

There are many reasons companies are acquired. Recruitment of software development personnel doesn't always make the top ten, but should be considered as a source of new development talent.

What to Look for and How to Look for It

The interview process, be it a couple hours or a couple of days, is an important first step in establishing a relationship with a prospective employee. Software developers are in high demand and so the interview is as much your chance to sell the candidates on your organization as it is their chance to show you their skills. During the interview process, three types of skills are examined: the candidates' technical skills, their business skills, and their behavioral skills. Besides one-on-one interviews, having a candidate interview with a group of your current developers can be very insightful. Since most development involves group interaction, there is no better way to start evaluating this than during the interview process.

Technical Skills

The technical skills segment of an interview is where you start to categorize a candidate's technical skills. Many candidates will put a broad range of technologies on their resume. You need to ascertain which of these the candidate is really an expert at as opposed to something they read an article on two years ago.

Values

Last but certainly not least important, the interview is a good chance to start evaluating a candidate's values and seeing if they align with those of your organization. Below is a list of what many development organizations categorize as winning and losing values along with sample questions you might ask a candidate.

Winning Values

A good software developer needs to be able to take initiative. No organization can afford to simply have software "factory workers" to whom you hand detailed requirements and later are returned perfect code. Will the candidate run that test one more time just to be 100% sure the program is operating correctly? Will they look for ways to improve the design they are working one? There are countless ways developers' initiative will lead you to more successful software.

A good developer needs to be dedicated to his or her work. There are likely to be times when your project will require extra dedication from each developer to meet an upcoming schedule milestone, solve a difficult bug, or meet some other constraint.

Other values to look for in developers include:

- flexibility
- openness
- respect
- honesty
- trust

Losing Values

Just as there are winning values to seek out in software developers, there are definitely also losing values you should avoid. These include:

- individual contribution at the expense of the team
- developing alone in the closet and not talking to anyone or asking for guidance or input.
- proprietary knowledge and ownership
- strict organization structure and hierarchy
- risk adversity
- purists
- superiority

8

Retaining the Best Talent

As discussed in Chapter 7, recruitment and retention in a successful software development organization are closely linked. The best practices presented in Chapter 7 for recruitment will undoubtedly carry over and help with retention. As discussed in the last chapter, if you hire software developers with backgrounds closely matched to your organization's job requirements and culture, you will be setting the stage for high retention and low turnover. This chapter presents additional best practices used by a variety of software development organizations to retain their best talent.

Successful software development organizations recognize the importance of retaining their best talent and continuously look for creative ways to do so. Long gone are the days when you could hire a COBOL programmer and expect them to stay on board until they retired. Before you are able to retain your key employees, however, you need to be able to identify who they are. Retaining key employees is important in any technical field. Not only do you have lost productivity while you look for a replacement candidate, there are the intangible costs. How long does it take for a new employee to come up to speed on a project? The bigger the project the longer it takes. Competitive compensation is certainly one part of the retention picture, although it is only a starting point. Software developers are valuable for their technical knowledge, which becomes quickly out-of-date. Developers thus tend to value positions that provide ample opportunities for training, both formal classroom training and on-the-job training. Besides such items as compensation and training, however, corporations in today's job market are going to extremes to retain their best employees. Of course the best way to improve retention is to improve recruitment and hiring, topics discussed in the previous chapter. If you hire the right individual for your organization, he or she is more likely to stay around and turn into a valuable long-term employee.

Compensation Philosophy

Since compensation is an important retention criteria, it's good to start by defining and understanding the compensation philosophy you want to pursue. Most development organizations feel they need to pay in the top 25% of what similar companies pay to attract and retain the top talent. This is probably a good starting point, although there are certainly counter examples. The IT department of a large upstart movie studio targets pay at the bottom 50% of industry rates. It is still able to attract and retain good candidates because of the glamour associated with working for the upstart company and because many employees believe the experience will qualify them for much higher paying positions later in their career. A large software company is known for offering employees low base pay that employees accept because of historic gains from the company's stock plan. Government agencies such as NASA who continually push the edge of technical possibilities attract developers for lower than industry salaries simply for the chance to work on exciting projects.

Total Compensation Strategy

Today, most large companies emphasize their total compensation strategy. Base pay and traditional medical or dental benefits are just part of what many companies provide. Helping employees realize and identify the value of 401k plans, employee stock purchase plans, or even such things as discounted childcare are important retention factors. This assures an employee will consider all these factors should they ever look at opportunities elsewhere.

Base Pay

An employee's base pay typically represents the largest part of his or her total compensation. For developers, typical base pay is 90% to 80% of total target compensation with the remainder being performance-based. As a senior developer or architect starts to have a larger impact on project success, some pay plans put more base pay at risk (i.e., base pay drops to 70% of total) in return for higher target incomes.

Traditional Benefits

Most organizations today will provide medical and dental benefits, life insurance, and disability insurance. An organization will typically not be able to provide more additional retention factors in this area as long as they meet what is typical in the field. The real area to differentiate an organization is through creative benefits.

Creative Benefits

Creative benefits are anything that do not fall into the traditional benefits category. This is an area where companies may provide significant retention incentives, often at a lower cost than more traditional benefits. Six digit salaries and lucrative stock options are not the only things software development team members look for. Some examples that have been used by different companies with large software development organizations follow.

- A large aerospace company built an on-site child care facility for its employees. Rather than directly subsidize child care rates, the company simply provided the land and buildings for the facility and outsourced its operation. Child care rates were fixed at local averages, but because the child care provider did not pay any facility costs, they could provide a much higher adult to child ratio and thus provide better care for the children. This was perceived as a major value to employees and undoubtedly helped keep many from considering other companies.

- A Hollywood computer game development company allows staffers to bring their dogs to work with them. Not stopping at that, the com-

pany even supplies unlimited Milk-Bones^{TM} dog biscuits in their
offices for all canine co-workers.

- Onsite or nearby subsidized health clubs is a common benefit at many
  Silicon Valley software development companies. Besides simply a
  retention aid, the side effects of better employee health, lower stress,
  and reduced medical costs commonly associated with individuals
  who exercise regularly greatly benefit the company.

- A midwest life insurance company worried about losing Y2K specialists is offering bonuses totaling up to twenty percent of annual
  base pay to software developers who stay on board until January,
  2000. Rather than offer the bonus in cash, choices include home computers, trips to Disney World, or a year's supply of pizza.

Short-Term Incentives

Short-term incentives are typically bonuses tied to meeting project or group-
specific milestones. short-term incentives help motivate employees to do the
best thing for the project they are working on.

Long-Term Incentives

The most common long-term incentive in most software development organizations is stock options that vest over multiple years. Here is an example
of how stock options work. Rather than give an employee a cash bonus, a
grant of stock options might be given instead. There are many types of stock
options programs but consider the simple example where the stock options
vest at twenty percent a year for five years. Using this example, an employee
granted 1,000 options in January 2000 could exercise 200 options in January
2001, and 200 options each subsequent year until January 2005. Typically
all unexercised options would carry over until the end of the option period.
The grant price of the stock is typically the selling price of the stock when it
was issued, or some discount thereof. Here is how an employee would benefit from stock options given this simplified scenario.

In January 2000, the stock price, which in this case was used as the grant
price, was $100. Here is how the employee exercised her options.

Table 8–1   long-term Option Example

Year	Options Exercised	Selling Price	Profit
2001	200	$120	$4000
2002	200	$140	$8000
2003	0		
2004	400	$150	20,000
2005	200	$200	$20,000
Total	**1000**		**$52,000**

The total gain to the employee was thus $52,000, given this scenario. Until the options are fully vested, they have a potential value to the employee that will most likely be weighted before any decision to leave is made. Of course, this value is based on the stock's appreciation. If the stock price were to drop below the initial grant price of $100/share, the options would be worthless to the employee until the stock once again rose above the grant price.

Besides the potential for stock prices to drop, there are other possible retention implications behind stock options in certain scenarios. Consider the case of the network switch startup that gave all employees who joined the company during its first year a large number of stock options that vested over five years as in the above example. Rather than vest on a yearly basis, however, after the first year the stock options vested on a monthly basis. The company was very successful and its stock appreciated several times its original value. What the company did not anticipate, however, was the effect this would have when the company turned five years old. Many of the original employees felt their base salaries had not kept pace with outside competitors; however, the hefty monthly stock option cashouts more than made up for the difference. Once the stock options stopped at the five year mark, the company all of a sudden found itself at risk of losing many of their key, most experienced software developers. The moral of the story is that long-term stock options are only a retention aid until they are fully vested.

Job Rotations

Many companies have found that job rotations significantly improve retention within their software development organizations. The most successful type of job rotation seems to be one that is approximately eight weeks in length. Software engineers typically rotate out to a non-development organization, such as sales, marketing, IT operations, or finance. Rotations out to another development organization are possible but typically are only useful if there is a prototyping or other short-term development opportunity available. Transferring into the middle of a large project, however, may take a software engineer the bulk of eight weeks just to come up to speed on the project.

The downside to job rotations is that there is always a short-term cost to the hiring manager who must do without the rotating engineer. When implemented correctly, however, the retention, cross-training, and other benefits of a job rotation program far outweigh these short-term costs. In order to make job rotation programs more successful, many corporations have structured programs built around some basic guidelines. Here is how a sample job rotation program might work.

For starters, since job rotation programs are by nature cross-organizational, the support of the president or other executives whom all the organizations report to is needed to ensure success of the program. This executive should be responsible for assuring that each organization's VP or director also support the goals of the program. If it is not possible to obtain this support, it may be possible to start a smaller, more grass roots job rotation program by coordinating between different line managers, but the long-term success of such a program is not likely to be as great.

One manager is placed in charge of the job rotation program. That manager is responsible for administering the program, collecting requests for job rotations from across the corporation, and soliciting line managers for volunteers. Typically, this manager resides with the software development organization.

On a regular basis, the job rotation program manager solicits requests for job rotations and publicizes the program to all the target organizations. Some ways that this has been successfully done is by documenting previously successful job rotations and publishing this information on an internal "job rotation" web page.

Managers in the target organizations who believe they have a job rotation opportunity document their request and present it to the rotation program manager. The request typically includes: types of skills required, length of rotation, location of the rotation opportunity, and a description of tasks to be completed.

Job rotations seem to work best when the work is done at the target organization's work location. If work is done at the employee's home work location, it is often too easy to be distracted by daily tasks. However, on the flip side, some employees might make excellent rotation candidates but personal constraints may prevent them from working in a different geographic location for the time required. If a home location rotation is to be done, the rotation manager and the regular manager must make an extra effort to make sure the employee will not be interrupted in their rotation by regular job duties.

The job rotation program manager reviews all job rotation requests and determines which are appropriate to pursue. When properly implemented, most companies find that very few inappropriate rotation requests are presented. In most cases, the job rotation program manager can work with the requesting manager to modify the rotation request to best assure finding the right rotation candidate.

Approved job rotation opportunities are forwarded to all line managers. The line managers then forward requests they feel are appropriate and timely to appropriate members of their staff. Once line managers are properly educated on the benefits of job rotations, they become some of the biggest supporters of the program. Still, most companies find that allowing the line manager final choice as to how and when to publicize opportunities is appropriate. If a project is in its final month of development before a major deadline, a manager may not wish to have any of his staff off on a job rotation. Given that the job rotation program as a whole is well publicized, it will become rapidly apparent if a line manager never forwards any job rotation opportunities.

Software engineers wishing to apply for a job rotation must first discuss the opportunity with their manager. If the manager approves, the engineer responds to the job rotation program manager and the target manager expressing their interest and qualifications for the rotation opportunity.

The target manager selects the candidate most appropriate for the rotation and then works out details with the hiring manager as to timing of the rotation.

Some companies fund the payroll and travel expenses of the rotating engineer from a separate job rotation program budget. This has two advantages. First, it removes possible budget objections from the employee's line manager. Secondly, it encourages target organizations to submit meaningful and relevant rotation requests, since accepted requests, in effect, are extra budget for the project.

While a job rotation program may seem like a lot of work to implement, the rewards, especially in terms of retention, can be great. Here are some of the many benefits companies have attributed to job rotation programs:

Avoiding "the grass is always greener on the other side of the pasture" syndrome. Many software engineers may have interests in other opportunities in sales, marketing, IT operations, or some other part of the company. Job rotations give those engineers a low risk way to investigate these types of jobs. If the interest is still real after an eight week rotation, then perhaps it really is better for the company for that individual to consider a job transfer. In more cases than that, what the software engineer figures out is that every job has its pluses and minuses and that he or she really does want to remain in a software development organization. In either case, it certainly is better than having the engineer leave the company just to pursue another job change opportunity.

Reduced "job burnout." Like all high tech jobs, software development organizations tend to be high stress places to work. A job rotation gives an employee needed time off from the day-to-day job while continuing to provide value to the company.

Cross-training leads to better software designs. A few weeks in the field in a sales or marketing rotation can give software engineers more hands-on customer feedback about their products than they would normally receive in several years. A rotation in IT operations can give software engineers a realistic look at what is necessary to support their software projects after they are fielded. Much positive feedback can also be received when software engineers see end users actually using their products to run their company. All these types of experiences tend to be channeled back into better design choices by the software engineers on future projects after they have completed the rotation.

Finally, after completing a rotation, many employees have a new-found respect for their line manager. They realize that it was a hardship for their manager to sponsor the rotation and feel that their manager must really value their importance to the organization for supporting the program.

Mentoring

Mentoring programs are a useful retention aid for many reasons. Here are some of the ways that mentoring is used by different software development organizations.

As mentioned previously, one of the best retention tools is good hiring. Some software development organizations now assign a mentor to all job applicants who are being seriously considered for a position. Job applicants are matched up with an employee performing similar job skills and if possible within the same development organization. This gives the applicant a chance to talk to a peer and get honest feedback on what it's really like to work for the company. Most applicants are more likely to trust the opinion of an individual contributor on this type of topic than they are a manager.

The next important time to have a mentor assigned is in the first several months after a new hire joins a company. Every company has its own culture, and software development organizations are no exception to this rule. During the first several months, the mentor is an invaluable aid for everything from helping the employee with paperwork issues (how do I get my payroll check direct deposited) to helping come up to speed on the software design. A software engineer could spend a month reading over design documentation and actual code and not learn as much as by spending a day sitting down with a mentor who knew the software design inside out. The new hire's mentor may or may not be the same as the employee who was the mentor during the hiring process. Many times it helps to make both of these positions separate, giving the new employee more than a single person to turn to for advice.

In the longer run, its a good practice to encourage every engineer to have one or two trusted mentors to help guide their career. This type of mentor need not necessarily be in the same organization. Also, this is the type of mentor that cannot be assigned to someone as an applicant or new hire. These types of relationships need to develop mutual trust. What the managers job should be is to explain the value of having a career mentor and encourage new employees to seek out such individuals as they believe would make good mentors. In the end, it's each engineer's responsibility to select his or her own mentors.

HR Issues

When you have an employee who is not meeting the minimum requirements of the job, it is certainly time to get HR involved. However, if you wait until then, it may be too late to do anything to reverse the performance of the employee. The most successful HR policies start out with a general belief that every employee is valuable to the organization. At the same time, progressive HR managers recognize that an employee's performance may at times start to move on a downward track. When this starts to happen, the HR policies should be structured to do everything possible to get the employee's performance back on track and moving in the upward direction. Given today's job market for software development skills, improving a poor performer who has the necessary skills can be much easier than hiring to replace that individual.

9

Successfully Transitioning Developers

Every year, successful software development organizations are faced with new development tools, new languages, and entire new computing paradigms from which to choose. As IT managers try to evaluate the impact of new technology in meeting the company's business goals, they must weigh not only the merits of the technology but their ability to successfully transition their developers to these new methodologies. If developers can't be transitioned, then other choices must be made, include hiring different developers or choosing not to implement the new technology. This chapter examines many of the issues surrounding the successful transition of developers to new methodologies and makes recommendations as to how best to do so.

Why Transition Developers

If your software development organization is planning a major shift in development methodologies, many of your developer's technical skills will become instantly outdated. We are often asked by managers anticipating an organizational transition whether they should retrain their developers or simply hire new ones. A hint to our answer can be found in the ordering of the parts of this book, *People, Processes, and Technology.* While technical skills are very important to developer performance, mature processes and developer's business skills and personal skills can play a bigger role. New technical skills, given an individual's sound computer science background, can be easily taught. Business skills, including knowledge of corporate culture, the company's business processes, and domain knowledge can take years to develop. Personal skills, such as dedication, flexibility, and leadership are usually established early in one's career and are not at all likely to be taught. Our answer, therefore, is a resounding yes. Software development technology is constantly changing and healthy organizations should be continually looking for opportunities to transition developers to newer development technologies and methodologies.

Established IT organizations do not typically make a wholesale change in their technology overnight. This makes it easier to transition development organizations on a piecemeal basis. Before switching to a new technology, organizations typically pilot the technology on a prototype or small project. After gaining some experience with the technology, a strategic decision may be made to start employing that technology on new projects. It typically does not make sense to make major changes to a development methodology or underlying technology midstream in a project. Even after all ongoing projects have been completed and all new development is being done with a new technology, legacy software must still be maintained. Here is how we map the technology life cycle of an IT organization to the mix of developers in the group.

In any software development organization, there is likely to be some developers who are "early adopters" of technology. These are the individuals we target to become part of new pilot projects whenever a technology transition is being considered. We are often asked how to spot these early adopters. Generally, it is fairly simple. Every mainframe development group probably had one or more developers who experimented with web browsers during the early days of the web in 1994 and 1995. Maybe they did this on their home PC, or maybe they took a class at the local college. We look for these or other signs of interest in a new technology when selecting developers to pilot a new technology on the job. As these developers gain experience in the technology, they can then move on to become the design leads and mentors for other developers as new projects with the technology are started.

Having formal training processes in place to allow developers to be trained on new technologies is also a key factor to successfully transitioning developers. Many times, new technologies such as Java are adopted with such speed that traditional training organizations within a company cannot keep pace with the changes. This is where creative approaches can be useful:

- Consider using local university extension programs to supplement your in-house training.
- Partner with hardware and software vendors, or integrators, to obtain training resources.
- Use job rotations to place developers within other organizations that are already using the technology you wish to adopt.
- Create virtual teams of experts within the organization to share best practices on a new technology and train their peers.

An example of the latter approach is the Java ACES (Action-oriented Community of Expertise in Sales) group with Sun's field system engineering (SE) organization. As Sun prepared to publicly announce the Java platform in early 1995, Gary Oing, manager of the SE programs office recognized that the normal field training infrastructure could not possible train the entire SE organization in time to support the initial Java technology rollout. It was then that the Java ACES program was founded. The Java ACES were a small group of about 50 SEs who received special training in Java technology and then actively spread this knowledge about the entire field SE organization. Specifically, software development in Java was one of the key focus areas of the Java ACES. The program was so successful that it has continued as the Java platform evolves and has launched similar programs in other fast-moving technology areas such as High Performance Computing (HPC) and data storage systems.

In a large software development organization, you will undoubtedly find some developers who are resistant to developing new skills in order to transition to a new technology. You shouldn't expect or force every developer to transition. Sometimes a developer's knowledge of legacy (or soon to be legacy) systems is so valuable to the business that management would never think of letting that person go. Its important to remember that not all developers need transition to a new technology when it starts being introduced into an organization.

During a transition period, you may also want to consider using consultants to augment your internal staff. At the start of a project, consultants can help train your developers and help out in critical areas where you have not developed a critical mass of trained staff. One of the transition mistakes you should be careful to avoid when using consultants is having them take the lead role in the implementation of a new technology without involving and training your own staff. What we have seen happen many times is a development organization that decides to implement a new applications architecture or technology: they don't have the training staff to do this internally, so they go off and hire consultants to do the first project. The consultants complete the first project while the internal staff continues working on their existing projects. At the end of this cycle, your organization is no closer to having transitioned the development team than they were at the start. To address this issue, we recommend having at least a one-to-one ratio between your internal staff and consultants on any transition project. In addition, be sure to budget for at least a twenty percent overhead for consultants to complete on-the-job training.

At the tail end of an organizational transition, you might want to consider outsourcing any remaining development or maintenance of legacy applications. Outsourcing maintenance is perhaps a riskier proposition if the majority of the application knowledge base stays with your organization and transitions onto new projects. The remainder of this chapter examines some of the issues that arise when transitioning developers to new application architectures, programming languages, or development methodologies.

Mainframe to Client-Server

During the 1990s, many development organizations successfully made the transition from mainframe development to client-server development. Here are some of the lessons learned from these organizations:

- Mainframe developers generally have acquired much better data center operations disciplines than their client-server brethren. Make sure these disciplines are not lost when transitioning to a client-server environment. Just because a portion of an application runs on a distributed end user desktop rather than in a glass house data center, the same application testing, version and baseline control, error checking and recovery, and security needs to be built in to enterprise-wide applications, regardless of where they ultimately execute. Developers who grew up in the client-server world developing engineering or personal productivity applications where a software error affected only one or a few users, versus hundreds or thousands, tend to lack some of the mainframe development disciplines mentioned above.
- Client-server developers often are accustomed to operating with greater flexibility, allowing them to respond to new customer requirements in a more timely fashion. Part of this is because they don't always carry out all the mainframe disciplines listed in the first point

above. Part is just because client-server development tools and environments often affords better productivity. The challenge in a mainframe to client-server transition is to combine the best of both environments.

- When transitioning developer organizations, make sure to get everyone involved. This means not only the developers but also the system administrators, database administrators, even the office administrators and the receptionist. Even those not directly involved in a transition of skills should be aware of the transition and clearly understand the business reasons that are driving the change to the new technology.

- Most organizations transitioning to a new client-server development environment do not get rid of their mainframes, at least not on day one. This means that mainframe developer experience will remain an important skill in order to continue maintenance of legacy applications. In addition, most of those new client-server applications will probably require one or more interfaces to legacy mainframe. There is no better way to develop a client-server to mainframe interface than to have the developer who wrote the original mainframe application on your client-server team.

Mainframe to Web-Centric

Since web-centric software development is newer than client-server, there have been fewer examples of this type of transition to study. In general, all the points discussed for mainframe to client-server transitions above hold true. Here is an additional point to consider for this type of transition:

- Many software experts have commented that web-centric software applications really herald back to the mainframe days as now both data and applications are being re-centralized into larger servers. The water is further muddied as IBM and others release Java Virtual Machines, web server software, and other web-centric applications for allowing one to actually implement a web-centric design on a mainframe. Independent of hardware platform, however, the software architectures used on traditional mainframe applications and web-centric applications remain entirely different. Don't think your mainframe development staff can become instant web-centric experts simply by purchasing a web server for your mainframe.

Client-Server to Web-Centric

A client-server to web-centric application development transition is much easier than either of the two previous mainframe transitions. As in mainframe to web-centric, many of the client-server to web-centric transitions in large IT organizations are still underway and it is too early to draw many specific conclusions regarding this type of transition but some interesting observations are included below.

- Web-centric applications tend to start small with stand-alone prototypes or simple pilots. Many web-centric applications make software packages, operating systems, or hardware choices early on that are inherently unscalable. As the web-centric software marketplace is still immature, it is easy to write off lack of scalability with, "it will get better in the next release." Unfortunately, by their very nature, web-centric applications are often deployed in environments where user load is the hardest to judge and scalability is more important than ever. In a mainframe or client-server architecture, the application developer typically has a fairly good idea of what types of loads will be placed against the system. On the Internet, a web-centric application can go from one hundred to one million users virtually overnight. Scalability, at the software, hardware, and operating system level should be of utmost importance in any web-centric application.

Procedural to Object-Oriented

Transitioning a developer from a procedural to an object-oriented environment is both difficult and time consuming. This doesn't mean it can't or shouldn't be done, it just means you will need a lot of patience. Managers often underestimate the time required to make this transition because learning the syntax of an object-oriented language, in itself, can be a simple task. Truly understanding object-oriented technologies and becoming a skilled object-oriented designer are much harder tasks to complete. Here are some of the observations we have seen when developers are simply taught an object-oriented language without taking the time to learn object-oriented technologies.

- Without a strong foundation in object-oriented design technologies, developers often may not see the real advantages of object-oriented programming and will revert back to their level of comfort. You can, for instance, write a C++ program that uses absolutely no C++ unique language feature and in fact compiles correctly with a standard C compiler. We have seen many FORTRAN programmers, who after a short course in C++ can program in the language. All too often, however, their C++ coding structures looks surprisingly like FORTRAN, complete with liberal use of "goto" statements and a lack of classes.

- The developers learn object-oriented design but the senior software architects continue to design in a procedural model. What results is you may have low level design details that are implemented in an object-oriented fashion, but overall the application behaves very much like a procedural program.

Language-Specific Transition Issues

While it is more common in scientific programming groups than in commercial IT organizations, a large number of developers have transitioned from FORTRAN programming to C programming. Without a doubt, the hardest concept for a FORTRAN programmer just starting out in C to master is pointers. C provides a tremendous amount of programmer flexibility in its ability to use pointers. As in the case of procedural to object-oriented transitions, some FORTRAN programmers learn C and are very happy to program away without ever utilizing C's pointer facilities.

Perhaps more common in commercial IT organizations is to find developers who have transitioned from COBOL programming to C programming. Like the FORTRAN to C transition, this is a major change. On average, there are many more possible ways to write a code fragment in C than there are to write the code implementing the same functionality in COBOL. While a C programmer may describe this as flexibility, the COBOL programmer may define it as "more ways to make an error."

One of the simplest language transitions to make is from C++ programming to Java programming. The Java language reduces the complexity of C++ while remaining instantly familiar. While Java syntax is similar to C++, the Java language does not use the concept of pointers. Instead, all objects are referenced by true object handles. In addition, some of the more complicated object-oriented features of C++, like implementation inheritance and templates, have been removed from the Java language. In addition, Java's rich set of application programming interfaces (APIs) provides programmers with a wide range of pre-defined extensions to the language.

The transition from C to Java programming is only slightly harder than from C++. As there are no stand-alone functions in the Java language, all application functionality must be implemented as methods within a class. This at least forces a programmer to start thinking about object-oriented design. By contrast, as previously mentioned, a C programmer could start writing code verbatim in C++ without ever using classes, methods, or any other object-oriented structure.

Does Transitioning Work?

When you start out with a healthy organization and attempt to assimilate a new technology, our experience certainly indicates that transitioning developers works. In three sample mid-sized projects that we surveyed, over ninety percent of developers successfully transitioned to their new roles. The remaining ten percent were not necessarily bad developers, they just continued to be more comfortable and more productive working in their original environment. The surveys follow.

Project 1:

Application Domain: Signal processing.

Project Description: To implement a new set of signal processing algorithms

Total Developers: 12

Length of project: 11 months

Number of developers with at least average C skills at start of project: 5

Number of developers with at least average C skills after 2 months: 7

Number of developers with at least average C skills after 4 months: 10

Number of developers with at least average C skills after 11 months: 11

Project 2:

Application Domain: Custom text search and decision support.

Project Description: To re-architect a decision support application from a client-server to a web-centric architecture while modifying/adding approximately 75% of the original functionality.

Length of project: 9 months

Total Developers: 20

Number of developers with web-centric experience at start of project: 0

Number of developers with at least average web-centric skills after 2 months: 5

Number of developers with at least average web-centric skills after 4 months: 15

Number of developers with at least average web-centric skills after 9 months: 18

Project 3:

Application Domain: Manufacturing.

Project Description: To re-architect an electronics manufacturer's mainframe scheduling and production planning application to a client-server architecture using a commercial ERP package, including new interfaces to other legacy systems.

Length of project: 15 months

Total Developers: 40

Number of developers with client-server experience at start of project: 7

Number of developers with at least average client-server skills after 2 months: 12

Number of developers with at least average client-server skills after 4 months: 32

Number of developers with at least average client-server skills after 15 months: 37

Part 3

Processes

The Software Life Cycle

Many people view the software development life cycle as that time between when a programmer sits down to write the first line of code for a program to when the completed program successfully compiles and executes. Successful software development organizations have much more complete definitions of a software life cycle. These life cycle definitions start with early requirements gathering and analysis stages and proceed through ongoing operations and maintenance. The maturity of a software development organization, in fact, is closely related to its understanding of the software life cycle and the underlying processes and procedures required to successfully develop software. The Software Engineering Institute has captured this in a model, called the Capability Maturity Model for Software. This is a model for judging the maturity of the software processes of an organization and for identifying the key practices required to increase the maturity of these processes. This chapter introduces the Capability Maturity Model and then discusses how it applies during the software life cycle, from initial requirements definition to production acceptance.

The Capability Maturity Model for Software

The United States Government, as one of the largest developers and users of software in the world, has always been very concerned with improving software processes. As a result, the Software Engineering Institute (SEI) was created. The Institute is a federally funded research and development center which has been run under contract by Carnegie Mellon University since 1984. The SEI is staffed by software professionals from government, industry, and academia. The SEI's web site, at http://www.sei.cmu.edu, contains information about all the activities of the institute. One of the most important contributions to software development to come out of the SEI is its series of capability maturity models, which describe how to measure the maturity of software development organizations. The SEI has defined six capability maturity models:

1. SW-CMM: A capability maturity model for measuring software development organizations.
2. P-CMM: The people capability maturity model, for measuring an organization's maturity in managing its people.
3. SE-CMM: A capability maturity model for measuring system engineering organizations.
4. SA-CMM: A capability maturity model for how an organization acquires software.
5. IPD-CMM: A capability maturity model for measuring an organization's ability to perform integrated product development.
6. CMMI: The capability maturity model integration.

The CMMI is the most recent focus of the SEI's activities and currently exists in draft form. This project's objective is to develop a capability maturity model integrated product suite that provides industry and government with a set of integrated products to support process and product improvement. This project will serve to preserve government and industry investment in process improvement and enhance the use of multiple models. The project's output will consist of integrated models, assessment methods, and training materials.

The first capability maturity model developed by the SEI was the capability maturity model for software, also known as the SW-CMM. It was first developed in 1987 by Watts Humphrey and William Sweet. The SW-CMM defines five levels of maturity commonly found in software development organizations and describes processes required to increase maturity at each level. While concepts such as network computing and the Internet were unknown then, the SW-CMM remains a benchmark by which software development organizations are judged. The Software Engineering Institute has updated the model since then, with the latest version being the SW-CMM version 2 draft C, released in October of 1997. The basics of the model, however, have not changed. Now more than ever, as development organizations are forced to work to schedules on "Internet time," process maturity remains critical to software development organizations.

The capability maturity model for software categorizes software development organizations into one of five levels according to the maturity of their processes. A brief description of each of the five maturity levels is given below along with key process areas for each level. Within each process area, a few representative traits of organizations performing at this level are listed. The complete SW-CMM, of course, includes many more details than are possible to cover in this chapter.

Level One: Initial

At this level, software development is ad hoc and no well-defined processes are followed. As such, organization focus is typically placed on those key developers, or "heroes," who happen to fix the software bug of the day. Organizations at this level of maturity are not likely to be successful at delivering anything but the most simple software projects. An organization operating at this level might expect to take six to nine months to move to level two, assuming a proper management team was in place with a focused effort to improve the organization.

Level Two: Repeatable

At this level, there is a focus on project management to bring repeatability to the software development processes. The key process areas expected to be mastered by organizations at this level are listed below.

- Requirements Management: software requirements are developed prior to application design or coding; at each step in the software design process, requirements are mapped to software functions to assure all requirements are being met; software testing includes requirements traceability matrices.

- Software Project Planning: software projects are scheduled and budgeted accurately; software engineers of the right skill mix and experience are assigned to each project.

- Software Project Control: software projects are tracked against their plan; proper management oversight is used to identify project risks instead of waiting until delivery dates are missed.

- Software Acquisition Management: any third party software acquired for use on the project is properly evaluated for training, performance, usability or other limitations it may impose on the project.

- Software Quality Assurance: each developer is held accountable for software quality; quality metrics have been established and quality is tracked against these metrics.

- Configuration Management: a software revision control system is used by all developers for all project code; software baselines are properly established and tracked.

Having these processes and their management in place will typically result in organizations who can deliver small to mid-sized projects in a repeatable fashion. Organizations at this level who do not move toward level three often fail when they undertake larger projects or fail to meet cost, quality, and schedule constraints that become imposed on them. Level two software groups are fairly common to find among the IT organizations of large corporations where software development management has been made a priority. Moving to the next level, however, requires a concentrated effort in software process development and might take anywhere from 12 to 24 months for a typical level three organization.

Level Three: Defined

Organizations at level three have moved on from simple project management of software development to focus on the underlying engineering processes. The key process areas expected to be mastered by organizations at this level are listed below.

- Organization Process Focus: a process focus is ingrained into the culture of the development organization.

- Organization Process Definition: the organization translates its process focus into the clear definition of processes for all aspects of the software development process from initial requirements definition to production acceptance.

- Organization Training Program: the organization not only trains all software engineers on the software technologies being used, but also on all processes.
- Integrated Software Management: organizations have implemented the categorization, indexing, search, and retrieval of software components to foster reuse of software as much as possible
- Software Product Engineering: individual software products are not simply developed in isolation, but are part of an overall software product engineering process that defines a business-wide applications architecture.
- Project Interface Coordination: individual software projects are not defined in isolation.
- Peer Reviews: peer reviews of software are accomplished at various places during the software life cycle, after design is complete, during coding, and prior to start of unit test.

Achieving level three of the capability maturity model is the goal of most large software development organizations. Levels four and five go on to define additional criteria that very few organizations are able to meet.

Level Four: Managed

At this level, the entire software development process is not only defined but is managed in a proactive fashion. The key process areas expected to be mastered by organizations at this level are listed below.

- Organization Software Asset Commonality: besides enabling reuse through software management, reuse is built into the design process by following common design standards, interfaces, programming guidelines, and other standards.
- Organization Process Performance: the organization has established metrics for evaluating the performance of its software processes.
- Statistical Process Management: statistical methods are used and managed in the development, implementation, and tracking of process use and effectiveness.

Organizations at level four thus not only manage the quality of their software products, but can manage the quality of their software processes and understand the second order affect of process quality on product quality.

Level Five: Optimized

This is the "Holy Grail" of software development. In fact, very few large organizations have ever achieved a level five score in SEI evaluations. To do so requires a demonstration of continuous process improvement in software development. The key process areas expected to be mastered by organizations at this level are listed below.

- Defect Prevention: the organization not only focuses on quality assurance, that is, finding and correcting defects, but on defect prevention.
- Organization Process and Technology Innovation: the organization continually innovates both in new processes that are developed and in new technology that is applied to the software development process.
- Organization Improvement Deployment: continuous process improvement in software development is not just a buzzword but is planned, executed on, and tracked against the plan with ongoing feedback loops.

Certainly many organizations have achieved some of these criteria on some projects, however achievement of level five requires universal adherence by all software development groups and on every project.

The software processes of the SW-CMM can be applied across the entire software life cycle, from requirements gathering through final testing. The rest of this chapter provides a brief description of different stages of the software development process.

Requirements Analysis and Definition

This is where every software project starts. Requirements serve many purposes for a software development project. For starters, requirements define what the software is supposed to do. The software requirements serve as the basis for all the future design, coding, and testing that will be done on the project. Typically, requirements start out as high-level general statements about the software's functionality as perceived by the users of the software. Requirements are further defined through performance, look and feel, and other criteria. Each top level requirement is assigned to one or more subsystems within an application. Subsystem level requirements are further refined and allocated to individual modules. As this process points out, requirements definition is not just a process that takes place at the start of a development project, but is an ongoing process. This is especially true when a spiral development model is used. The ability to manage the definition and tracking of requirements is a key process area required of level two organizations by the SW-CMM.

System Architecture and Design

The system design stage is where the software architect plays a crucial role. The architect takes the output from the requirements stage, which states what the software is supposed to do, and defines how it should do it. This is a crucial stage for any software project because even the best programmers will have trouble implementing a poor design.

Test Plan Design

Designing your software test plan is really part of system design, but we have decided to break this out into a separate stage because it is so often overlooked. Many great software designs end in unsuccessful projects because no one thought about how the system would be tested.

Implementation

During the implementation, or coding stage of a software development project, software engineers complete detailed level designs and write code. One of the key processes level three organizations complete during the implementation stage is peer reviews. During a peer review, a group of developers will meet to review a software module, including the code under development, the detailed design, and the requirements of the module. To someone who is not a software developer, getting a half dozen people in a room to review, line by line, hundreds of lines of code in a software module may seem like a large waste of time. In reality, however, code reviews are one of the common processes followed by successful software development organizations of all kinds. Here is the outline for a sample code review:

Attendees

We typically try to have between four to eight code reviewers (peers of the developer) from the same or related application development teams. The developer's manager attends if possible. We typically try to involve a system architect or senior developer as a facilitator for the code review.

Ground Rules

We have found that these ground rules are essential to making a code review productive. We always review the ground rules at the start of each code review.

- No grading. The purpose of the code review is not to grade or otherwise measure the performance of a developer, but to identify and resolve any issues while the code is still under development. Unless this is perfectly understood and practiced, we often find a developer's peers are unwilling to raise issues with code in front of a manager or more senior developer for fear of having a negative impact on the developer. This dilutes the entire value of the code review.

- No incomplete phrases. During the review, incomplete phrases are typically well understood by all given their context. However, two weeks later, a developer will typically not be able to understand the meaning of an incomplete phrase noted in the meeting minutes. When everyone speaks and writes in complete sentences, it makes follow-up on the review much simpler.

- Majority rules. Everyone must agree up front that when issues are raised, they will be discussed until everyone is in agreement. This is a peer review by developers working on the same or closely related applications. If there is any question as to the validity of the design or of a code segment, this is the time to resolve it. If there is not 100 percent agreement, then those in the minority must ultimately, if they cannot sway others to their case, side with the majority view.

- Stay intellectually committed. It takes a lot of effort to follow, line by line, the code of another developer. However, everyone in the code review is making a major investment in the review for the benefit of the entire team. Everyone needs to be 100 percent committed to the review process and not duck what they perceive are issues.

Requirements Review

The developer presents the requirements that have been allocated to the module.

Design Review

The developer presents the detailed design of the module. Visual aids used include flow charts, UML diagrams, call graph trees, class hierarchies, and user interface components.

Code Review

At this point, the facilitator takes over and walks everyone through the code. This frees the developer to concentrate on listening to and documenting comments made by the reviewers.

Summary

The findings of the code review are summarized by the facilitator. If necessary, specific design modifications are agreed to. If major design changes are required, a follow-up code review will always be conducted. If only minor code changes are identified, no follow-up review will typically be required.

Validation and Testing

Many people do not understand why software is so prone to errors and in fact simply accept software bugs as a fact of life. The same people who accept their PC rebooting twice a day would, however, be intolerant of picking up the phone and not receiving dialtone because of a software bug in the telephone company phone switch. One can easily think of other examples of mission critical software, such as control software for nuclear power plant operations or the software in your car's anti-lock brake computer. Even state-of-the art development techniques cannot eliminate 100 percent of software bugs but proper software validation and testing can go a long way toward detecting most bugs before software is released to end users. This section discusses some of the common types of testing performed during the software development life cycle.

Unit Testing

Unit testing is the testing of a single software module, usually developed by a single developer. In most organizations, unit testing is the responsibility of the software developer.

Subsystem and System Testing

An application typically is made up of one or more software modules. System testing will test all software modules in an application. On larger applications, this may be preceded by subsystem testing. One of the focuses of subsystem and system level testing is to test all the interactions between modules.

Black-Box and White-Box Testing

Two different approaches to developing software tests are black-box and white-box test design methods. Black-box test design treats the software system as a "black-box," and doesn't explicitly use knowledge of the internal software structure. Black-box test design is usually described as focusing on testing functional requirements. Synonyms for black-box include: behavioral, functional, opaque-box, and closed-box. White-box test design allows one to peek inside the "box," or software component, and focus specifically on using internal knowledge of the software to guide the selection of test data. Synonyms for white-box include: structural, glass-box, and clear-box.

While black-box and white-box are terms that are still in popular use, many people prefer the terms "behavioral" and "structural." Behavioral test design is slightly different from black-box test design because the use of internal knowledge isn't strictly forbidden, but rather simply discouraged. In practice, it hasn't proven useful to use a single test design method. Many organizations use a mixture of different methods so that they aren't hindered by the limitations of a particular approach.

It is important to understand that these methods are used during the test design phase. The influence of the test design method used is hard to see once the tests are implemented. Note that any level of testing (unit testing, system testing, etc.) can use any test design methods. Unit testing is usually associated with structural test design, simply because the developer designing a unit test is typically the same person who wrote the code. Subsystem and system level tests are more likely to use behavioral test design methods.

Alpha and Beta Testing

Alpha testing refers to internal company testing of an application prior to its external release. Beta testing is typically done by external users prior to official release of the software. In both cases, users exercise the application software for its intended purpose and report back any bugs they may encounter. Many companies have found both alpha and beta testing extremely useful because it allows much more extensive testing than could have ever been accomplished solely by the in-house development and quality assurance teams.

Several years ago, Sun Microsystems began an extensive alpha test program of its Solaris operating system. Literally hundreds of engineers throughout the company who were unrelated to the actual operating system development installed early builds of Solaris, often six months or more before customer release. This testing was so successful that the Solaris group went the next step and began installing weekly alpha release updates on their main file server machine, providing production service to over 400 engineers. It certainly doesn't take long to get bugs fixed in that environment. The Solaris alpha test program was so successful that many other software product groups within Sun are now alpha testing their software on internal engineering desktops and servers.

Beta testing may also have the advantage of providing users early access to new features and thus building or maintaining a customer base in rapidly changing markets such as the Internet. Netscape has certainly been one of the most widespread sponsors of beta test programs. Some of Netscape's web browser products have undergone half a dozen or more beta releases with millions of users. Before widespread use of the Internet such feedback was impossible simply because of distribution issues. Netscape can beta test six releases, one per week, of its software with a million or more Internet downloads for each release. Just to produce and distribute a million CDROMs would take six weeks for most software vendors.

Stress Testing

The purpose of stress testing is to ascertain that application software will meet its design requirements even under full performance loads and under all possible input conditions. Because software performance is so closely tied to system hardware, stress testing most often is accomplished on the actual production hardware, or a replica thereof.

Production Acceptance

After all other testing has been completed, the final step is for software to undergo production acceptance. This is where operations personnel will integrate the software into a production baseline and perform final regression testing. The main purpose of these tests is to document the correct operation of the software in its production environment and address all issues related to its production rollout. A production acceptance process tailored to client-server systems is presented in the book titled *Managing The New Enterprise*. Chapter 13 presents our own version of production acceptance, the Web-Centric Production Acceptance process, which is specifically tailored to today's web-centric applications.

Rapid Application Development

For the last ten years, many software projects have incorporated the use of "Rapid Application Development" methodologies in an effort to decrease development times. RAD, as it is generally referred to, incorporates an umbrella of methodologies based on spiral, iterative development technologies. RAD techniques range from the simple use of GUI development tools to quickly build prototypes, to processes incorporating complete, cross-functional business analysis. Since January 1997, Cambridge Technology Partners, one of the early practitioners of RAD, adapted their methodology to address the special needs of electronic commerce. Dubbed CoRAD, for customer oriented RAD, Cambridge's methodology brings together a unique combination of technical, business, creative, and cognitive disciplines to implement high impact, successful electronic commerce solutions. If you are even considering building an electronic commerce application, you should read this chapter closely to avoid the pitfalls many early electronic commerce sites faced because they concentrated too narrowly on either the technical or creative side of electronic commerce. Furthermore, you need to realize that e-commerce isn't just about building a web site – it's about building a whole new business channel.

CoRAD projects consist of five distinct phases: strategic planning, product definition, product design, product development and product delivery. CoRAD treats your electronic commerce project as a product because that is how customers will view it. Successful web sites have to be launched, marketed to customers, and provide incentives for customers to try them out, just like traditional consumer products. They will compare your web site against your competitors', judging its usefulness. If the site crashes or takes too long to download, customers will go elsewhere. The role of technical, business, creative, and cognitive specialists in each phase is described below. Before discussing each phase of the CoRAD methodology, however, let's spend some time describing why it is needed in the first place.

Why Another Methodology?

Cambridge first started developing its RAD methodology for developing client-server solutions in 1991. Over the years, as client-server technologies matured, Cambridge continued to evolve its RAD model. Internet applications, however, including electronic commerce, extranets, on-line communities, interactive marketing, and interactive web services place new demands on software over and above traditional client-server development. The CoRAD methodology brings together four key disciplines for the rapid development of an Internet application:

- Technical
- Business
- Creative
- Cognitive

Internet applications and online business have placed new technical demands on software architecture. Often, it is impossible to accurately predict how many people will use an Internet site. For example, when Netscape sized its first web site, it considered the NCSA site from which the original Mosaic web browser was distributed. At the time, NCSA was receiving 1.5 million "hits" per day. Netscape wanted to be able to handle at least three times that load and designed its site for 5 million hits a day. That number was surpassed in Netscape's first week of operation and the site routinely handles 150 million or more hits per day, or 100 times the original NCSA reference. While your site may not see this amount of growth, experts say an Internet architecture should be capable of scaling to handle ten times the expected load without reaching an architectural bottleneck. On an Internet site, you will have to consider the scalability of your application software; networking and security software must also scale commensurately with application usage.

Electronic commerce applications also have a major business impact. They affect how you market your products, how you sell, and how you service your customers. How will you transition your people to work in this new environment, or will you need new people? What new business processes will be needed? Will you need new channels or partners?

Finally, the creative and cognitive skills needed for successful Internet applications are substantially different than traditional internal client-server applications. No matter how good the technology employed, the business goals of your electronic commerce application cannot be successfully achieved unless the targeted customers use the solution you provide. Experience on the Internet has proven this is not always the case. Today's electronic commerce customers typically have a choice. They may choose to use your interactive solution or choose not to. They may choose a competitor's web site or they may use another traditional channel offered by your own company. Traditional client-server application users have used the application because they had no choice. The Internet changes the relationship between application and content. To successfully design for the web you need to be able to influence your customers to choose your content from your site. Your electronic commerce application is merely the means for them to do so, rather than an application that is forcing them to do so. CoRAD's creative and cognitive disciplines come into play in creating an application with content that customers will choose to view. This is done using a five step process as shown in Figure 11-1.

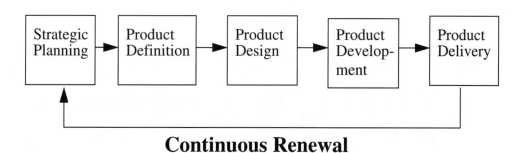

Continuous Renewal

Figure 11–1   The CoRAD Approach

Strategic Planning

The CoRAD methodology starts with a three to six week strategic planning workshop where Cambridge helps its clients identify and prioritize the electronic commerce initiatives that will give them the highest return on investment. Cambridge examines the internal factors that could contribute to or impede the success of an e-commerce endeavor – i.e., existing Internet initiatives, technical infrastructure, operational processes, organizations, and staffing. It also conducts an external assessment in which it focuses on competitors in the industry and e-commerce best practices from other industries. A strategy and a work plan are developed that include recommendations for the next phase.

Product Definition

The next phase of an engagement is a three to six week product definition workshop. This step, much like a traditional software requirements analysis, is the key to avoiding surprises halfway through the project. The product definition stage begins by defining the scope of the project including identification of the target customers, their needs, and the functions the site must perform. Sample customers are identified and, if possible, interacted with, to understand the design context. This is where cognitive disciplines become an absolutely crucial element of successful web implementations. This helps derive a more complete understanding of your customers, including their environment, habits, goals, and conceptual models. In turn, this helps you define an electronic commerce product that is truly intuitive for your specific customers to use. Use of these cognitive experts continues through the product design and development stages.

In parallel with gathering information about the customer's requirements, the product definition phase examines several technology choices. These choices include everything from development environments to hardware platforms to integration with existing systems. Existing network and security infrastructures are also examined to evaluate if they are e-commerce ready. This typically involves IT executives as they are the ones who ultimately will have responsibility for operating the site. This results in the selection of a technology framework for the project.

Another parallel task in product definition is an analysis of your business environment. The goal of this analysis is to identify any needed process, such as marketing plans, or organizational changes. Business goals are clarified and critical success factors are established. These may range from specific dollar sales to more subjective qualities such as customer loyalty indexes. A cross-functional consensus on the product is established when possible, along with executive buy-off.

Most importantly, the first prototype of the product is developed. Even at this early stage, you should avoid building user-interface-only prototypes. Prototypes, although they may lack some of the final functionality, should incorporate all the key business logic of the product. Both user interfaces and back-end databases are easier to derive once the business logic has been defined than visa-versa.

Product Design

The third phase in Cambridge's CoRAD methodology is the product design stage. The emphasis during this six to twelve week phase is on architecture. The technologists architect an infrastructure for your product that is secure, scalable, and reliable. The creative and cognitive designers build on the work begun in the prototype to architect a powerful and effective user interface for the customer. A good rule of thumb for web applications is they should be so simple to use that no help screens are required. While this may seem limiting, it is indeed true. PeopleSoft, for example, a popular vendor of enterprise resource planning applications, has designed all its web-deployed interfaces without help screens. Also during this phase, the business consultants architect new processes and organizations to align the functionality in the application with the delivery capabilities of the organization. Customer testing of the prototype also continues during this phase, allowing additional feedback to be gathered and incorporated into the evolving design.

Product Development

During the six to twenty week product development, the focus turns to implementation. The software is written and the content is refined. At the same time, the organization is prepared to assimilate the changes the product will impact prior to its launch. Larger scale customer pilots are undertaken and more feedback gathered. This helps ascertain that the product meets the requirements for the release and that it's fast, reliable, and intuitive. Depending on the application, internal tests may also be useful for stressing the application and finding bugs before public release.

Product Delivery

The final phase in the CoRAD methodology is product delivery. This phase has two parts: preparation and execution. During rollout preparation, a conversion strategy is developed if any conversion from an existing system is being done. This is followed by conversion program design and the development of the conversion programs. Rollout execution involves the complete installation of the application in the production environment for the extended user community.

Cambridge's CoRAD methodology is just one example of a rapid application development methodology. Like many methodologies, CoRAD is designed to be tailored to the individual projects where it is applied. No matter whether you use CoRAD, or your own version of a rapid application development methodology, your software project is more likely to be successful if some sort of RAD approach is followed.

12

Software Productivity, Metrics, and Quality

Software development organizations are today constantly looking for ways to increase both developer productivity and code quality. The first step toward improving either is to establish productivity and quality metrics and benchmarks for your organization. Without a benchmark, you have no way to determine when you have improved or how to measure yourself against other organizations. After you have established a benchmark and determined your weak areas, one of the next steps is to train your staff where you perceive weaknesses or room for improvement. Next, look at your total development environment and be sure to address all possible areas for improvement. For instance, studies have shown that the design of developers' workspace can have a large effect on their productivity. Quality must address not only software bug reports, but quality at every step of the software life cycle, from initial requirements to areas like documentation. This chapter addresses these and other important areas to consider when attempting to put in place any software productivity or quality programs.

Code Metrics

Today, a number of different tools exist to measure code metrics. Metrics are available to measure many aspects of code, from code size, to code complexity, to errors, and other code performance metrics. One of the first developers of coding metrics was Thomas McCabe, who in 1976 developed a mathematical technique, the cyclomatic complexity metric, which measures the control structure of software. This metric characterizes software in terms of numerical measures of complexity. Using such metrics, it is possible to identify software modules that would be difficult to test or maintain.

Since McCabe developed the first software metrics, a number of other types of software metrics have been developed, including:

- Halstead metrics
- Line count metrics
- Object-oriented metrics
- Boolean metrics

No matter what metrics you decide to use, here are some common traps to avoid when implementing a software metrics system:

- *Lack of management commitment:* Management commitment is critical to the success of any metrics program. If the reasons behind the metrics program are not explained to the developers in a clear fashion, they are not likely to support the program. The management team should not only verbally support any metrics program, they should make it clear that metrics will be a requirement of job performance. Of course before managers can express to developers why a good metrics program is being required, they must first be educated themselves as to the value of software measurement. A good resource is the book *Practical Software Metrics for Project Management and Process Improvement.*

- *Lack of communication and training:* Communication as to why a metrics program is being used is crucial to the acceptance of such a program by developers. Developers need to view the metrics program as a step toward improving the quality of the software project, not as a personal measurement of productivity. Once the reasons for the metrics program are clearly communicated, individual developers will need to be trained on the metrics tools being used in order to make sure the right data is collected at the right time.

- *Measuring the wrong thing at the wrong time:* Some metrics programs go overboard and start collecting hundreds of metrics on day one. When too many metrics are collected too early in a program, the large amount of data that results can often be meaningless to management. On the other hand, if you start out collecting only one or two metrics, the results may be similarly ambiguous. The right solution is to decide what aspects of the development team's work is most important to understand in order to meet the business goals of the organization and then start by collecting a sample of related metrics. As you gain experience with these metrics, you can then add or remove individual measurements depending on the usefulness they are providing.

- *Using metrics data as part of developer performance reviews*: The most sure-fire way to ruin any metrics program is to tie specific metrics to an individual's performance review. If developers think the metrics program is simply a "big brother" attempt by management to rank developers, they will either stop reporting metrics completely or simply report metrics that make them look more favorable. The solution is to make it clear to developers that the metrics program is being instituted to better understand the development process, not to rank individual developers. Furthermore, you should control the scope of visibility of different types of metrics. For instance, certain metrics should be kept private to the individual and their manager, while other metrics should be shared with the entire development team.

McCabe Metrics

The following is a sampling of some of the McCabe metrics that can be collected by a number of automated metrics tools.

Cyclomatic Complexity

Cyclomatic complexity is a measure of the complexity of a module's decision structure. It is calculated based on the number of linearly independent paths that also equates to the minimum number of paths that should be tested. Low quality and error-prone software often display a high cyclomatic complexity.

Essential Complexity

Essential complexity is a measure of the number of unstructured constructs contained in a module. Unstructured constructs tend to decrease code quality and make it more difficult to modularize code. With unstructured constructs, making changes in one part of the code often causes errors to appear in other parts which may depend on the changed code.

Module Design Complexity

Module design complexity measures a module's decision structure as it relates to other modules. This quantifies how much effort will be required to integrate and test the module with subordinate modules. A high module design complexity leads to a high degree of control coupling between modules, making it difficult to isolate, maintain, and reuse individual software components.

Design Complexity

Design complexity measures the interaction between modules in a program. This metric provides a summary of the module design complexity and thus a good estimate of the overall integration testing effort that will be required by the program. A high design complexity implies complex interactions between modules, which leads to a difficult-to-maintain program.

Number of Lines

The number of lines in a program is one of the most basic of all coding metrics. As such, this metric by itself does not offer much value if taken in isolation. This metric is also one of the most overused and misused metrics. We have seen many organizations measure number of lines on a single project and then use this figure as a "magic number" to which future project sizing and developer performance will be measured. Of course this is the wrong approach to take. It is very easy for a developer to produce huge volumes of code that are of poor quality and otherwise score very poorly against any other metric. However, we have seen this happen in more than one case when management insisted on simply measuring the number of lines produced. Nevertheless, the number of lines, when used in conjunction with other metrics, does contribute to an understanding of a program. Generally speaking, smaller modules (with fewer lines) will be easier to understand and maintain.

Normalized Complexity

Normalized complexity is simply a module's cyclomatic complexity divided by the number of lines of code in the module. This division factors the size factor out of the cyclomatic measure and identifies modules with unusually dense decision logic. A module with dense decision logic will require more effort to maintain than modules with less dense logic.

Global Data Complexity

Global data complexity measures the complexity of the global and parameter data with a module. Global data is data that can be accessed by multiple modules in the program. The use of global data introduces external data coupling to the module that can lead to potential maintenance problems.

Pathological Complexity

Pathological complexity measures the degree to which a module contains extremely unstructured objects. This reveals questionable coding practices such as jumping into the middle of loops. Control structures such as these represent the greatest level of risk and should generally be redesigned.

The Impact of Workspace on Productivity

It today's highly competitive environment, many companies try to cut costs by eliminating private offices, moving employees to cubicles, and shrinking the size of cubicles. While this can certainly cut real estate costs, it is important to look at the impact of workspace on productivity to see if there are associated cost increases due to lost productivity. An internal software productivity study done at a large aerospace company compared two groups of programmers. In the first group, programmers were given private offices with ergonomically designed workstations where they could work in undisturbed concentration. The second group was placed in open cubicles with standard office furniture. The skill sets of both groups were matched as closely as possible. The programming assignments given to each group were also matched in difficulty and size. After an eighteen month study, two of the most interesting results were:

- The programmers with private offices developed 22% more lines of code than the second group.
- The programmers with private offices had 27% fewer software problem reports filed during subsystem test and system integration testing.

While this study is over fifteen years old, its results are still reflected in the current practices of leading software development companies. Here are some of the best practices top software development companies use today in designing workspaces:

- Programmers should have private offices with closing doors so they can work undisturbed.
- Workstations (desk, chair, etc.) should be ergonomically designed and adjustable to accommodate different sized employees.
- In windowed offices, office layout should allow the programmer to work without having to stare out at busy intersections, sidewalks, or other public areas that would distract his or her attention.
- Office spaces and meeting rooms should have adequate whiteboard space on walls that will not be obstructed by office furniture. Large whiteboard spaces are crucial to program design.
- There should be plenty of meeting areas and public spaces to foster both informal gatherings that improve team communications. Software development facilities at Xerox PARC still include the famous "beanbag room" where developers gather for informal conversations. Much of the cost justification for more public gathering spaces is achieved through smaller offices, something most programmers find a worthwhile trade-off.

Make versus Buy

Software development organizations routinely consider make versus buy decisions to determine if a software library, utility, tool, or application should be purchased from a third party or developed in-house. Many times these decisions are tainted because software developers sometimes like to develop their own versions of code rather than re-use existing code. This is a cultural issue that needs to be addressed rather than ignored. No development organization today can afford to build every last library and utility from scratch. Whether you are considering a math library for fast fourier transforms (FFTs), a configuration management utility, or an entire application, make versus buy decisions should be based on more than simply the cost of developing the application in-house versus the purchase price of the application.

Here are some other things to consider if you plan on buying software:

- What training costs will be incurred before your staff can successfully utilize the software?
- What quality and performance criteria does the software meet and are these up to the minimum standards of your organization?
- How easily will the software integrate with your current environment and how much time and effort will be invested in writing conversion and translation tools?
- How will maintenance of the purchased software be incorporated into your overall software maintenance plan?

On the flip side, here are additional criteria to consider if you plan on developing the software in-house:

- Do you have adequate staff to complete the software without sacrificing ongoing development projects?
- Is the software strategic to your business? If so, there are more likely to be intangible benefits such as developer experience that are gained by writing the code in-house. For instance, an organization developing scientific software may want to write their own FFT routine – an organization specializing in business software may not.
- Can you use this software on more than one project? Leveraging the development cost over several projects, versus paying multiple license fees, may impact a financial decision.
- Do you have a separate budget for staff versus purchases? In many organizations, staff payrolls are part of preallocated budgets and software purchases are funded from different funds. As short-sighted as it seems, some organizations develop their own software package instead of purchasing one simply because they already have a budget assigned for development staff and financial controls prohibit them from spending that money on purchasing software.

The Value of Domain Knowledge

As software processes and the programming skills of developers improve, domain knowledge becomes more and more a differentiator to successful software development organizations. In days past, the Unix wizard, who enlightened new programmers with lore and knowledge of the C language, was often regarded as the most valuable development team member. If your development organization already has skilled programmers in place and has implemented a complete set of software development processes, the most valuable programmer is likely to be the one with the greatest domain knowledge on the application being developed. Consider how domain knowledge is used throughout the software life cycle:

- During requirements definition, the software engineer with domain knowledge will already understand the problem you are trying to solve and thus will be more likely to capture requirements correctly on the first attempt.
- When interacting with users, the software engineer with domain knowledge will already understand the terms and domain-specific vocabulary used. This will make it easier to translate user needs into correct requirements.
- During software design, the software architect with domain knowledge will be better able to decompose software requirements into specific application modules, objects, and operations. This is especially true if an object-oriented design methodology is used. In object-oriented design, software architects often try to map real world objects onto their software equivalents. This is often very difficult to do if you do not properly understand the problem domain.
- During software testing, a software engineer with domain knowledge will have a better idea how the application will be really used and thus can often devise better test cases that more closely match real life use.

Of course if you believe that domain knowledge truly is beneficial to a software development team, the next question to answer is how can developers have much domain knowledge when they have been off writing code for years? Here are some ideas:

- Some developers that have been working in a specific application area for many years actually have as much domain knowledge as most of the end users. The software development manager should recognize this and use domain knowledge as a criteria when assigning developers to projects.

- Consider using job rotations as a way for software developers to gain domain knowledge. For instance, if your group develops financial software, have a developer go off and work on a project for your corporate controller for six weeks to gain experience.

- If you don't have domain knowledge within your development team, look for ways to get end users involved in your development team, perhaps on a job rotation basis. Even without any software development experience, I have seen end users make excellent suggestions during design reviews, simply based on their domain knowledge.

The most successful software organizations have institutionalized acquiring domain knowledge into their development processes. They do this as part of their everyday recruiting, training, and retention efforts. Whenever possible, get end users involved in the software development processes. Recognize the value of domain knowledge in your development organization and you to will be on your way to more successful software development.

The Importance of Standards

Software standards play an important role in the development of successful software projects. A typical software project will be subject to many standards, from enterprise-wide architecture standards to project-specific coding style guidelines. Developers who have worked in smaller organizations with fewer standards are often surprised at the large number of software standards some groups have. Standards, if imposed too early during the development of a new technology, can stifle innovation. Organizations producing large, complex software projects, however, cannot successfully do so in the long run without careful selection of the appropriate standards. This section discusses some of the various types of standards that are typically found in successful software organizations.

Enterprise-Wide Architecture Standards

You should only have a few enterprise-wide architecture standards and they should be simple ones. Some examples of these standards would be:

- All information should be delivered to users in a web browser format.
- Interfaces between systems should use a publish and subscribe methodology for information exchange.

Note that these standards are both hardware platform and software technology independent. For instance, in the first standard, there is no statement that says the web browser should be on a Unix workstation, a PC, a Mac, a TV boxtop browser, or for that matter a cell phone display. Each department can choose its platform based on its specific needs. This is not to say that the IT group might not choose to implement a standard corporate desktop, it is just that this decision would be independent of the software architecture standard. Similarly, in Standard 2 above, publish and subscribe is a generic technology. You might implement it with a CORBA-based system, a relational DBMS, or even a FORTRAN program.

Coding Standards

Code conventions are important to programmers for a number of reasons:

- 80% of the lifetime cost for a piece of software goes to maintenance.
- Hardly any software is maintained for its whole life by the original author.
- Code conventions improve the readability of the software, allowing engineers to understand new code more quickly and thoroughly.
- If you ship your source code as a product, you need to make sure it is as well-packaged and clean as any other product you create.

For the conventions to work, every person writing software must conform to the code conventions. Everyone. There are many sample coding standards for various languages available on the Internet. In Appendix B, we have included a sample Java coding standard.

Help Standards

There is nothing more frustrating than getting a non-descriptive help message from an application that confuses you more than it helps you. In the early days of software development, "Help" information was contained in long rows of three-ring binders stacked along the wall of the terminal room. As window-based interfaces became popular, user interface coding stan-

Chapter **12** ∣ Software Productivity, Metrics, and Quality

dards allocated standard positions for the "Help" button. For instance, the Macintosh has perhaps the most standard Help button location that is always on the top right of the menu bar. Today, of course, help standards specify much more than the location of the Help button. Four of the more popular help standards include Microsoft's WinHelp, Oracle Help, Netscape's NetHelp, and JavaHelp. Each provides a set of utilities for authoring, storing, delivering, and displaying help within applications.

From implementing a standard "Help" screen to making sure developers have adequate whiteboard space, these are some of the many factors that will effect the productivity of your programmers and the quality of the code they will develop.

Web-Centric Production Acceptance

You've recruited, hired, trained, and retained the best software engineers, architects, and managers in the industry. You've established a world class software development organization for these engineers to work in. You've bought the best software development tools money can buy and each developer has a top-of-the-line workstation and a private office. Your glass-house computer room is filled with high-powered file servers, DBMS servers, and the latest networking gear. Your software development team has worked for months to prototype, design, implement, and test a web-centric application, assuring every user requirement is met. You've worked with the IT operations staff to put in place a Service Level Agreement. Your long overdue vacation plans are looming on the horizon and it seems like your project is nearly complete. Surprise! There is still one more task to do before you can claim a successful web-centric software development project – a very big task. We call it the Web-Centric Production Acceptance (WCPA) process.

The WCPA is our most important process. Implementing a WCPA process often makes the difference between the success or failure of a web-centric software development project. We have worked with many Fortune 500 companies who have attempted to deploy web-based applications, some successfully and others ending in project failure. Many of the failures were due to the absence of a process to deploy, manage, and support distributed, web-centric applications and their supporting infrastructure across the enterprise.

The WCPA started life as the Client/Server Production Acceptance (CSPA) process, described in Managing the New Enterprise. We have modified the CSPA process to specifically address the requirements of developers working on web-centric applications. Like the CSPA, the WCPA is our way of transitioning applications from development to production, i.e., deployment. It's also our way of making sure customers get the same reliability and security for their globally deployed Intranet, Extranet, and Internet applications as they did with their mainframe or client/server applications. The WCPA is our way of improving and maintaining IT and customer dialogue for systems support and development. Just as web-centric is a revolutionary computing paradigm, the WCPA is our contribution to a new age of IT customer relations enabled by personalized, web-based communications.

The WCPA Chronicle

In *Managing the New Enterprise,* the development of the CSPA process at Sun from 1989 to 1993 is described. During that time, Sun transitioned from a mainframe-based IT organization to a Unix client-server one. Starting in 1993, Sun once again started a transition, this time to a web-centric IT infrastructure. It is from these experiences, and those of our many customers, suppliers, and partners, that the WCPA evolved. While Sun does not have an official process named the WCPA, we have coined this term for the entire collection of production acceptance processes used for web-centric applications. Before describing the process in detail, it is interesting to describe how it evolved internally at Sun.

In 1993, software developers in Sun's IT organization were as unfamiliar as anyone with the web. Inside SunLabs, Java was still known as the Green Project, known only to James Gosling and a small circle of other researchers. Other Sun developers, however, had crossed paths with Marc Andreesen, who at the time was developing the Mosaic web browser at the National Center for Supercomputing Applications at the University of Illinois. More than a few beta copies of the Mosaic web browser had been downloaded at Sun and were being used to access a few experimental web servers on Sun's Intranet. By March of 1993, enough engineers had downloaded copies of Mosaic that demand was rising to allow HTTP traffic through Sun's firewall. Sun's IT organization thus became involved with the web when Sun's first HTTP proxy server was set up inside Sun. All web traffic for Sun passed through this single proxy machine and over Sun's T1 line to the Internet.

By late 1993, Sun's marketing organization had become aware of the web and was looking for ways to publicize Sun's presence on the Internet. The January 1994 Winter Olympics in Norway were around the corner, being sponsored as usual by IBM. While it was too late for Sun to sponsor the Olympics, they were able to arrange for an electronic feed of all Olympic results. Sun set up a web server in Norway to bring these results, for the first time ever, to the web in near-realtime. In addition, during January 1994, the www.sun.com site went live. Since Internet bandwidth across the Atlantic was still limited, Sun set up a series of Unix scripts to mirror the Olympic results from the Norway server to www.sun.com, a server physically located at Sun's Northern California headquarters. The lessons learned during this event would become the start for the WCPA process.

During early 1994, more and more Sun engineers began experimenting with Mosaic and other early web browsers and servers. At the time, these were still unsupported by Sun's IT organization. The power of this technology and growing external interest in the web did not go unnoticed by Sun's marketing department. Sun had sometime earlier signed up as the official computer sponsor of the 1994 Soccer World Cup event and this seemed like the perfect venue for demonstrating Sun's ability to run large web sites. On the June 17th opening day and throughout the following thirty days, the main World Cup web server, a Sun SPARCCenter 2000 with four CPUs and two T1 links to the Internet, handled over six million accesses – a world record.

Using experience gathered during the World Cup, Sun continued to expand its external and internal use of the web. In July of 1994, Sun's Intranet, called SunWeb, started life as the first internal web server fully sanctioned and supported by Sun's IT department. During the remainder of 1994, Sun continued to expand the content available on its web site, including:

- August 1994 - Sun's online catalyst catalog (3rd party software) was launched, complete with WWW links to vendor's sites.
- October 1994 - Sun's telemarketing group, SunExpress, published the first Sun online catalog (online ordering was not yet available).
- December 1994 - Sun's Reseller Resource web site went live.
- December 1994 - Sun's WABI product became the first downloadable software to be available on the site.

Sun's webmaster at the time performed the job on a part-time basis, stealing away an hour here and there from his day job to manage the site. As a production machine, www.sun.com was subject to Sun's own CSPA processes. This meant, for instance, twenty-four hour monitoring of system status, CPU load, and other critical factors. Of course the CSPA process did not address any web-server specific performance factors and thus the WCPA continued to evolve. At the time, this meant the addition of some simple scripts that monitored web server "hits," which of course was a number that soon became of interest to marketing.

Throughout the second half of 1994 and the first half of 1995, traffic to www.sun.com more than doubled every month, as measured by the WCPA scripts. In late May of 1995, two significant events were expected to drive web traffic to www.sun.com even higher. First, during the SunWorld event, the Java platform was officially introduced to the public. In addition, after having grown haphazardly over the last eighteen months, the site was ready for a redesign. A new format was introduced with monthly cover pages and feature stories. However, site analysis for June 1995 showed that www.sun.com traffic had grown by only ten percent over the previous month. Sun's IT department, following their CSPA processes, declared there was no problem with the server which in fact was running at less than 25% utilization, even during peak times. Marketing, of course, became concerned and started monitoring site traffic on a weekly basis. To make matters worse, site traffic during the first two weeks of July 1995 showed absolutely no growth in accesses.

After some analysis, it was finally determined that it was Sun's single T1 link to the Internet that had become the bottleneck. In mid-July, a second T1 link was added as an emergency measure. Immediately, traffic returned to its previous growth rates. It was at this point that the CSPA and WCPA processes started to merge, as it became apparent that the two could not be separated. Within a few months, the second T1 link was starting to become fully loaded, only this time everyone knew about it beforehand. Before any bottlenecks in network performance were hit, Sun upgraded its Internet link to a T3 line.

The WCPA process continued to evolve as Sun's internal and external use of the web grew. In September of 1995, Sun's IT organization introduced support for Netscape Navigator and started transitioning users off Mosaic. By late 1995, the SunWeb Intranet consisted of over 300 web servers with nearly a million pages of content. In addition, Sun's IT organization started to roll out its first Java-based applications. During 1996, the content and applications available on SunWeb continued to grow. To conserve both internal and external bandwidth, Sun deployed a series of caching proxy servers.

With the launch of Sun's JavaStation network computer in the fall of 1996, Sun made the next big move in evolving its Intranet and the WCPA. This was called the JavaStation 3000 project. The goal of the JavaStation 3000 project was to replace the Sun workstations on 3000 employees' desks with JavaStations. Not only did this accelerate the application development schedule for Sun's IT organization, but it also proved to be a valuable proving ground for Sun's own technology. Eventually, over 5000 JavaStations were deployed to employees' desktops, providing a complete office computing environment built entirely around 100% pure Java applications. By the end of 1998, nearly all of Sun's internal applications will have been ported, rewritten, or replaced by Java applications.

As Sun re-architected its internal applications and processes around the web, employees became more and more confident doing their daily work in a browser environment. This also changed the way Sun's IT organization needed to think about remote access, at the time provided only via secure dialup lines. Sun's goal was to provide employees with secure access to internal web-based resources through the public Internet from any Java-enabled, SSL (Secure Socket Layer) supported web browser. As a result, Sun.Net was born. Today, Sun.Net enables employees to browse millions of internal web pages and run applications ranging from e-mail to network management from any web browser worldwide.

The WCPA Questionnaire

The WCPA process starts with a questionnaire that helps the software development team, the IT operations team, and the end user customer access the readiness of the complete environment surrounding the deployment of a new application. When used effectively, this questionnaire is filled out during the entire development process, rather than waiting until immediately prior to deployment. The first section of the WCPA covers the operational environment the application will be deployed in:

- Hardware (CPU, memory, disk, network)
- Operating system
- Disk layout (RAID level, connectivity, etc.)
- Filesystem table
- Database requirements
- Job/batch schedules
- Error messages and handling

The second part of the WCPA questionnaire describes support requirements of the application, including:

- Interdependencies of the application on other jobs and systems
- Capacity planning
- Systems availability (online availability, backup windows, etc.)
- Testing plan (alpha, beta, preproduction, stress testing, and so on)
- Training of users and IT support staff
- Documentation for users, help desk staff, operations staff, etc.
- Administration processes
- Support procedures (hardware, OS, network, application, 3rd party vendors, etc.)

The third part of the WCPA questionnaire deals with exception procedures or any specialized requirements of the application including:

- Security
- System moves/changes
- Critical system messages
- Filesystem backup and archives
- Disaster recovery

Personalized Communications

The WCPA places a special emphasis on communications between the three stakeholders in a successful software development project: the developers, the IT operations staff, and the end users. From the very beginning of the process, the WCPA opens the lines of communication between all three groups. The database administrators, system programmers, production control personnel, and computer operations work closely with application developers and end users to understand the requirements necessary to implement and support a distributed web-centric application.

The WCPA's approach of personalized communications contrasts starkly with earlier models of software development, such as waterfall software lifecycles. The WCPA is proactive, not reactive. In the past, the only time MIS would get involved with users was when a problem occurred. Someone would call the Help Desk. The Help Desk would call data center operations.

Operations would come to resolve the problem. That was and still is the paradigm in many data centers. This paradigm, however, does not work for today's web-centric applications environments. You need to work closely with your users to solve the business issues of new applications or they will never be successful, no matter how skilled your developers become.

The WCPA is responsible for setting everyone's expectations, for communicating roles and responsibilities, and for establishing how groups and individuals – customers and the data center – work together. It is a service-level agreement between different organizations.

The WCPA is also the communications vehicle to ameliorate the cultural differences among Unix, PC, and mainframe personnel, applications development, IT support, users, and the data center as they come together to support web-centric projects. Personalized communications is not just a buzzword. It is a new way of doing business and working together for the benefit of the whole enterprise.

Internal Support Agreements (ISAs)

Service-level agreements have long been the mainstay of mainframe production systems and larger Unix client-server systems. On the web, however, service-level agreements become much harder to define and monitor. No longer are all the components of the application residing in a glass-house data center, or even distributed within a company. web-based applications may span multiple companies in an Extranet or, in the case of the Internet, may span across the world. The WCPA questionnaire, when filled out, helps span the many environments of the web and becomes a template for an internal support agreement between users and IT.

The internal support agreement is aimed at three groups: business managers receiving IT services, who need to ensure that the services delivered are in line with their business requirements at a cost they are prepared to pay; the system administration staff, who deliver these services and need to fully understand the commitments that customers require in order to provide quality service; and the new enterprise network services staff, who coordinate the delivery of these services across the web to their respective business units or external customers to ensure maximum contribution to business effectiveness.

With an internal support agreement, both internal and external customers can understand the kinds of service they should expect from their computer resources and how those resources are expended. On the other side, an internal support agreement makes sure system administration personnel understand their jobs well – what services they provide as well as those they don't provide.

The differences between applications development and operational support are well publicized and have been going on for decades. Even when development and operations were centralized under one MIS organization, finger pointing was common behavior and everyone had no choice except conform to the same rules and guidelines. Networked computing has changed all that. Most of the issues centered around implementation and support of mission critical applications. Development would blame operations for messing up a restart or operations would blame development for lack of QA or support on their part. There were many issues of this nature.

In many companies today applications development is located within the business unit or division for business reasons – this is good for quickly responding to business issues and requirements, but puts additional friction between the groups. After decentralization, companies must also deal with the cultural differences that occur. Many of the younger development staff come from a Unix, NT, or client/server background. So now you often have Unix mentalities versus legacy culture mixed within the same development organization.

In the early days of client/server computing, development organizations would attempt to support their own servers. Today, most development organizations want centralized IT to support their servers for system administration functions such as tape backups and restores. This is not much different than the old way of doing business when operations would support the development environment on the mainframe. One of the cultural changes that must be addressed when IT takes control of development servers is ownership of "root" authority (security privileges). Development organizations without IT support often enjoy the freedom of being on their own and having root authority.

One of the hottest topics when IT support first meets with development groups is the discussion of who will own "root" functionality. This generally starts out as a pleasant discussion with mutual respect among the participants. Development requests IT perform system administration functions while they keep root authority. IT responds that the only way to effectively perform system administration functions and to maintain integrity is for the data center to own "root". This is the only way IT can maintain high reliability, availability, and serviceability (RAS) with their limited resources. Development then typically responds that they cannot effectively complete their jobs if they don't have root authority. Many companies solve this dilemma by having joint root authority – the data center owns it and several of the senior developers are also provided with root access. An internal support agreement is an excellent place to document such a root access policy. This model has proven to work well for many development organizations. A sample internal support agreement is included in Appendix C.

Roles and Responsibilities

The following sections detail the various roles and responsibilities of IT personnel and support services typically included in the WCPA guide.

Internet Engineering

Internet Engineering is the group responsible for operating the company's Internet access. In a large company, it is typical to have multiple, geographically separate routes from internal networks to the Internet, both for load sharing and reliability. Internet Engineering is responsible for the principal external servers in the "demilitarized zone" or DMZ. The DMZ is that portion of the network that sits behind the first firewall but outside of the main internal networks, as shown in Figure 13-1.

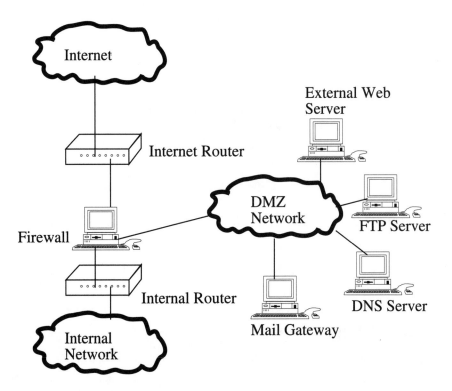

Figure 13–1   Sample Internet Firewall and DMZ Network

Typical responsibilities of Internet Engineering include:

- Determining requirements for Internet connectivity
- Contracting for ISP (Internet Service Provider) services
- Installing and maintaining external web, ftp, and e-mail servers
- Installing and maintaining external DNS and other directory servers
- Monitoring ISP performance and service level agreements

Security Engineering

Security is a specialized enough topic that it is called out separately in the WCPA. Typical responsibilities of Security Engineering include:

- Designing and maintaining firewall complex, possibly in conjunction with Internet Engineering
- Working with Internet Engineering to assure security of all external servers
- Working with Network Engineering to assure security of all internal networks
- Working with WebTone engineering to provide secure access through the firewall
- Designing and implementing methods for remote user authentication and data encryption

Network Engineering

Typical responsibilities of Network Engineering include:

- Determining internal networking requirements, both for WANs and LANs
- Contracting with Telcos for WAN services
- Installing and maintaining all WAN and LAN routers, switches, and hubs
- Determining impact of new applications on the network

WebTone Engineering

Typical responsibilities of WebTone Engineering include:

- Working with Internet engineering to hand off incoming and outgoing web, ftp, and e-mail traffic
- Installing and maintaining internal DNS and other directory services
- Providing internal web server hosting
- Designing and maintaining a network of internal proxy cache servers at strategic points on the corporate Intranet

Technical Support

Typical responsibilities of Technical Support include:

- Determining physical location of all server equipment
- Installing network connections and power
- Installing hardware, including third party equipment
- Conducting preventive maintenance diagnostics on all equipment
- Partitioning the disks during OS installation
- Configuring operating system specific parameters
- Applying any operating system patches required
- Assisting database administration with DBMS installations
- Installing any unbundled software products, such as tape management, disk mirroring, etc.
- Installing all required data center utilities
- Configuring and maintaining system security
- Monitoring system performance and capacity (CPU, memory, disk, network)
- Managing backup tape integrity and storage
- Providing on-call support, 7x24, or as specified
- Performing disaster recovery drills
- Establishing end-of-life plans to deactivate servers and applications
- Providing online availability statistics
- Providing system tuning for peak performance
- Performing capacity planning
- Establishing network connections to LAN and WAN, including ISP (Internet Service Provider) connections
- Providing and maintaining network databases such as DNS, LDAP, NIS, NFS, Primary Domain Controller (NT), Backup Domain Controller (NT)
- Performing security audits; monitoring security access
- Establishing user accounts and system (root) accounts
- Monitoring all daily processing
- Starting/restarting production jobs and applications
- Scheduling all online and batch processing
- Evaluating, developing, and implementing utilities and tools to support servers and applications in the production environment

Hardware Support

Typical responsibilities of Hardware Support include:

- Supporting and resolving all hardware problems
- Handling all preventive maintenance within the data center for mission-critical servers

Applications Support

Typical responsibilities of Applications Support include:

- Providing second-level application support as required
- Working with technical support and database administration to resolve complex application problems

The WCPA Process

The WCPA process is synergistic, much in keeping with the web philosophy of shared resources. The various business units dictate what technologies and applications they want and need and entrust the data center to provide the technology and to reliably and securely support those applications.

It takes from one week to more than three months for an application to wind its way through the WCPA process, depending on its size and process for deployment. Working in Internet time, this is about half as long the CSPA process for an equivalent client-server application. In shortening the production acceptance cycle, we have not cut corners, but rather found ways to use web technology to speed up the process. We begin the WCPA process by assigning a data center WCPA committee to work closely with the developers and users of a new application, preferably starting with its design stage. A WCPA web page is established for each project, serving as a focal point for communication during the entire process. Table 13-1 provides a summary of typical WCPA implementation schedules.

If you are a user or a developer of an application requiring data center staff

Table 13–1 Sample WCPA Implementation Schedule

Phase	Activity	Duration	% of WCPA Process
1	Information Gathering	1 week	10%
2	Resource Planning	2 weeks	20%
3	Implementation	6 weeks	50%
4	Production Cutover	2+ weeks	20%

support, your first contact is Production Control. We assign a data center operations analyst to oversee the WCPA process and manage the WCPA committee.

This committee consists of Technical Support, Database Administration, Security Engineering, WebTone Engineering, Internet Engineering, Production Control, and Computer Operations personnel from the data center, along with the application's project leader.

The team collaborates to foster the application all the way through the alpha, beta, and preproduction stages. Once an application is finally ready for production use, the data center infrastructure takes charge of its implementation and security. Root access to the application is controlled by Technical Support, regardless of where the application's server is located, and all changes must follow the change control process.

Preparing an application for production happens in four phases.

Phase I is the information gathering phase. Phase I takes about a week to initially complete, and then continues as needed throughout the WCPA. During the initial phase, the user will contact Production Control and fill out the online WCPA questionnaire available on the Production Control web page. This questionnaire contains general information about the project, including its name, the names of its development group, owner and leader, a description of the application, whether it needs a database, what type of hardware it will use, whether it requires continuous (7x24) support, where users are located, and expected target dates for server installation, alpha and beta tests, production freeze, software distribution, WCPA questionnaire sign-off, and a production implementation date.

Phase II is resource planning time. The Production Control Operations Analyst assigned to the project reviews the questionnaire and, based on the application's needs, formulates an appropriate WCPA committee and works with Technical Support to define data center space, equipment, personnel allocations, and costs to support the project. The Operations Analyst also works on the WCPA questionnaire with the application's project leader. The project leader orders needed equipment with the recommendation from Technical Support. This is where the Production Guide, which includes the services provided by the Data Center, the Personalized Communications, and the Internal Support Agreement come into place. Here it's important to communicate the services provided, set expectations, and, more importantly, communicate the services not provided.

Phase III is the implementation period. It usually takes one month to complete, depending on the size and complexity of the application. Technical Support personnel install the necessary hardware, software, and all supporting utilities on the server. The tape librarian is instructed to create tapes with labels for the backup process. The data center's Database Administration people work with the application developers to prepare the supporting database (if needed), then relay disk partition information and database creation scripts for installation and execution by Technical Support. Applications Development installs the application and performs testing.

Finally, in Phase IV, the application and all data center support services are brought online and tested for as long as it takes to ensure the application can run reliably in a production environment. Also, during this final phase, the Operations Analyst adds the application to automated systems that track server and application availability worldwide.

Once fully completed, an application's WCPA questionnaire, hardware, and software are maintained by the data center. Database Administration maintains and upgrades the database and software, making any needed system changes such as adding dump devices, increasing database sizes, and analyzing and reconciling maintenance errors. Production Control manages job scheduling, restarts applications, and makes network support file (DNS, etc.) changes, as necessary. Technical Support maintains the operating system software and hardware, formats and repartitions disks, installs unbundled software, and maintains and configures system security and network services. Once the application is ready for production, the committee approves the WCPA for sign-off. It now becomes a working service-level agreement for supporting the application in production. Any deviations must go through the Change Control process.

What IT Should/Should Not Support

In deploying web-centric applications, it is often more important for IT to know what services you don't provide, particularly in those gray areas where previous practices might lead to differences of opinion unless support policies are clear. For instance, in a traditional client-server environment, IT controlled not only all servers, but all desktops where client software was installed. In a web-centric approach, no client software other than a Java-capable web browser needs to be pre-installed. All application software can be downloaded at run time. In such a scenario, especially if the application is deployed over the Internet, IT may have no control of client desktops, other than to specify a minimal browser revision level. If a business unit uses some special, non-IT supported browser and the application runs into difficulty, IT might do an initial diagnosis but normally should pass along the problem to the business unit, who chose the unsupported browser in the first place.

Besides caveats, there are a variety of responsibilities IT and business unit customers accept as part of the Internal Support Agreement. Customers are responsible for providing the list of services they need to support their operations. The levels of service should be held to as few categories as necessary. Customers are expected to work closely with IT to ensure all users carefully select, control, and regularly change user passwords, according to corporate security policy. Final configurations are the responsibility of IT, implemented and supported as defined by the WCPA questionnaire. In cooperation with the local facilities organization, any distributed web and proxy servers are managed to ensure an adequate environment for systems. The Internal Support Agreement also spells out what some consider the ultimate responsibility: funding. The business units, not IT, should be responsible for obtaining funding and approval for all their appropriate capital assets to ensure sufficient computing resources. They are responsible for future adds, moves, and changes, as well as funding for those future systems. If management doesn't allocate money and resources to meet those customer needs, IT and the customer must and will negotiate a reduced level of support.

Finally, anything included in the service-level agreement and budgeted for IT services, will be provide by IT. Anything not included is either done without or later negotiated.

The WCPA is not foolproof. In fact, there are many ways to defeat its purpose:

- Put an application into production without thorough testing and documentation.

- Treat every application as an exception and take shortcuts.
- Reassign application developers to new projects before completing deployment of the current application.
- Be too busy to thoroughly document.
- Let the WCPA gather dust, versus making it an ongoing process.

Barring such willful ignorance or neglect, the WCPA doesn't just happen on its own. Here are some things you can do to make sure the WCPA succeeds in your organization:

- Start early; don't wait until an application is nearly ready for production.
- Intimately involve developers and users; build their sense of ownership.
- Always adhere, without exception, to the WCPA for new applications and releases.
- Clearly spell out and document responsibilities and duties in the WCPA questionnaire.

Part 4

Technology

14

Programming Language Features

Ever since 1949, when John Mauchly developed Short Order Code, the first high-level programming language, software developers have debated which programming language was best. Most experienced software developers, however, will agree that every programming language has its pros and cons, depending on the application. There is no single language that is best for all software projects. Apart from language features, many external factors such as programmer familiarity, hardware platform, development tool support, and legacy code interface issues impact a project's language choice. In addition, different types of applications will be better suited to one language or another. This chapter provides a brief overview of the features available in some of the more common programming languages. The main benefits of each language are discussed, along with disadvantages that the language may present to your software project.

C

The C language was originally developed in 1972 by Brian Kerninghan and Dennis Ritchie of AT&T. C is a general-purpose programming language that features economy of expression, modern control flow and data structures, and a rich set of operators. Because it is not a very high-level language, C is good for low-level systems-oriented programming such as writing operating systems or compilers. It is also used as the output of front-ends of compilers for more high-level languages. On the other hand, C's lack of restrictions and its generality can make it more convenient and effective for tasks than supposedly more powerful languages. This is of course a double-edged sword. While C's flexibility provides convenience for experienced programmers, it also provides very fertile ground for the introduction of errors and bugs by programmers less familiar with the language. Mastering the use of pointers in C, for instance, is one of the most difficult tasks to accomplish for programmers experienced only in non-pointer based languages like FORTRAN. C's flexibility, therefore, increases the importance of having well-defined style guides and programming standards in place.

The first version of C was developed for the Unix operating system running on the DEC PDP-11 computer. Today, C compilers are available for nearly all operating systems and hardware platforms, ranging from PCs to Unix systems to mainframes. For many years after its introduction, the most formal definition of the language was contained in the reference manual, *The C Programming Language*. The formal definition of the C language is now contained in the ANSI C standard, first published in 1988.

The predecessors of C, BCPL and B, were typeless languages. By contrast, C provides a variety of data types including characters, integers, floating point numbers, pointers, arrays, structures, and unions. C clearly shows its history, however, in that it is not strongly typed like languages such as Java or Ada. C provides the basic control-flow statements required to implement structured programming, including "if" statements, switch statements, while, for, and do loops, and early loop exits (break statements). The ANSI C standard also added the definition of a standard C library. This library specifies functions for file input and output, memory allocation, string manipulation, and other common functions. Many of these functions, while formalized in the standard, existed in earlier implementations.

C++

The C++ language, as the name implies, is based on extensions to C. Designed by Bjarne Stroustrup of AT&T in the mid-eighties, C++ added a number of object-oriented features to C. While one can certainly write object-oriented code in C, there are no facilities in the language to support it. C++ added common object-oriented language features such as classes and methods to C. Most early C++ compilers, in fact, were nothing more than front-ends that translated C++ code into C and then invoked the C compiler.

Because it is a superset of C, C++ has always been a much more complicated language to learn. For many years, different vendors added their own specific extensions to C++, trying to provide more and more functionality. As a result, the C++ standardization process took many years to complete. Finally, in September of 1998, the C++ standard was finally published by the ISO. Compilers that are ISO C++ compliant are still very rare. In addition, the standard C++ library is relatively new, and millions of lines of existing C++ code that use proprietary libraries are still in use.

FORTRAN

The first compiler for FORTRAN, which stands for FORmula TRANslator, was developed by John Backus and his colleagues at IBM in 1957. As one might guess from its name, FORTRAN is often used for programming scientific applications involving heavy use of mathematical formulas. Early FORTRAN programmers, lacking much of the programming theory that is well-known by any first year computer science student today, made heavy use of "goto" statements to control execution flow in their code. Of course old habits are hard to break. Even after Edsger Diijkstra wrote about the harmful effects of the "goto" statement in 1968, starting the structured programming trend, many FORTRAN programmers continued to write their code with "goto" statements.

Despite its simplicity and lack of modern syntax, FORTRAN continues to make up a large percentage of the code in production today. Outside of scientific programming applications, little code is developed today in FORTRAN but its huge installed base continues to make it an often-encountered language in legacy applications. Because of its structure, FORTRAN is well suited for the development of scientific programs and the optimization thereof. FORTRAN does not contain pointers and thus many compile-time optimizations are simplified. Furthermore, many FORTRAN scientific function libraries have been highly optimized over many years of progressive tuning.

FORTRAN has, of course, been modernized over the years. The last two FORTRAN language standards, FORTRAN 90 and FORTRAN 95, have modernized the language with the inclusion of several new features. To date, however, the FORTRAN 77 standard remains the most widely used dialect of the language.

Ada

In the early 1980s, the United States Department of Defense recognized the need to address the language requirements of large scale mission critical programming projects. In order to do so, they sponsored a contest to see who could develop the best new programming language. The winning team was made up of several companies led by Honeywell-Bull with Jean Ichbiah as the chief architect. The resulting language, named Ada, is a very complete high-level language and incorporates almost every programming construct known at the time of its design. Unfortunately, compiler technology in 1983 was not well suited to the completeness of Ada's design which, in part, led to Ada's reputation as a complex language. While Ada is more complex than Java, it is actually far less complex than C++. Today, compiler technology has caught up with Ada's design and there are many excellent compilers available. In 1995, Ada became the first object-oriented language to become an international standard. While Ada has seen widespread use on military software projects, its use in commercial applications has been more limited. Surprisingly, given its Department of Defense heritage, Ada has seen perhaps more commercial use in Europe and elsewhere overseas.

BASIC

As the name implies, BASIC (Beginner's All-purpose Symbolic Instruction Code) is a very simple language developed with beginning programmers in mind. BASIC was developed in 1964 by John Kemeny and Thomas Kurtz at Dartmouth. Since then, many variations of the language have been developed, the most popular of which is certainly Microsoft's Visual Basic language. To this day, however, BASIC remains a language for beginning programmers and not many large, complicated applications are developed for it. The market for ActiveX components however, many of which are written in Visual Basic, remains very strong.

Java

Most computer bookstores today carry more Java programming books than any other language. Even so, many software developers are still unfamiliar with Java as a programming language much less the overall Java environment and all it encompasses. Java's popularity has been fueled by its adoption as a *de facto* standard for programming Internet and intranet applications at a time when both of these areas are seeing exponential growth. There are a number of different Java environment subsets and APIs; however the Java language is common to all of these. This section starts by discussing the Java language and then provides an overview of the four primary Java environment subsets: Java Card, Embedded Java, Personal Java, and the complete Java environment. While the Java language is very stable in its current state, many of the Java APIs continue to evolve. Our discussion of Java APIs is thus limited to some of the more popular APIs that were defined as of late 1998 when this book was written.

Java was developed in the early 1990s at Sun Microsystems Labs by a team led by James Gosling. At the time, Gosling was part of a team developing a prototype hand-held controller for consumer electronics projects. The team wanted a simple, object-oriented, and familiar language for their project. They started with C++ but after several weeks decided its complexity was excessive, given the goals of their project, internally referred to as the "Green" project. A number of other languages were considered and rejected as alternatives. In the end, Gosling and his team decided to develop a new language which they called "Oak." A working prototype of their first device, the "Star 9," was developed to test the language but never saw its way into production. In late 1993, however, as the world wide web was just starting to become popular, Gosling reconsidered Oak as a language that could be used for Internet applications. By early 1995, Sun had developed a web browser, called WebRunner, capable of executing small Java programs, called applets, that were downloaded when referenced on a web page. In May of 1995, the language and browser were renamed and introduced to the public as the Java language and HotJava browser.

Many early uses of Java were to create "applets," small applications that ran within a web browser (Java also supports the creation of complete stand-alone applications.) More recently, Java has become popular for server side programming leading to the creation of "servlets." A servlet is akin to a Java applet except it executes within a web server, versus an applet which executes within a web browser. Java's component technology, JavaBeans, has also been extended for server-side usage, now called Enterprise JavaBeans.

From its roots as a language for programming the "Star 9," simplicity has always been one of the overriding design goals of the Java language. Java was designed such that it could be programmed without extensive programmer training while staying roughly attuned to current software practices. The fundamental concepts of the Java language can be grasped quickly and programmers can be productive from the start.

The Java language was also designed to be object-oriented from the ground up. After 30 years of research use, object-oriented technology has finally found its way into the programming mainstream. The needs of distributed client-server based systems coincide with the packaged, message-passing paradigms of object-based software. To function within increasingly complex heterogeneous, network-based environments, programming systems must adopt object-oriented concepts. The Java language provides a clean and efficient object-based development environment.

While Java's design makes it perhaps the simplest object-oriented language to use, the combination of "simplicity" with "object-oriented" must be taken carefully. To make the most of an object-oriented language, a developer must start with an object-oriented architecture. One of the reasons object-oriented technology has been so slow to catch on is that creating a good object-oriented architecture for a software project remains a relatively difficult task. Not all software architects have the necessary experience with object-oriented technology to do so. While the Java language simplifies the implementation of object-oriented architectures, it does not necessarily simplify the design of such architectures. We have seen very large Java projects, some over 50,000 lines of code, whose architecture is not at all object-oriented. Without proper training in and understanding of object-oriented design, many C and FORTRAN programmers have developed Java code whose structure bears a strikingly familiar resemblance to programs they may have written in C or FORTRAN.

The simplicity of the Java language owes much to its similarity with C and C++. Even though C++ was rejected as an implementation choice for Gosling's "Star 9", Java's syntax was kept as close as possible to that of C++. At the same time, many of what Gosling and his team felt were the unnecessary complexities of C++ were removed from Java. Making the Java language a minimal "subset" of C++ while simultaneously retaining its "look and feel" means programmers can migrate easily to programming in Java. The Java learning curve can be as low as a couple of days for an experienced C++ programmer.

Java is most often used as an interpreted language. When you "compile" Java source code into a.class file, you are not converting it to a machine specific executable. Instead, compiled Java code is represented in the.class file as architecture neutral "bytecode." The bytecode is simply a compact representation of the original Java syntax that has been checked for static (compile time) errors. To execute the bytecode, it must first be interpreted by a Java Virtual Machine (JVM), which translates the bytecode into the underlying hardware architecture instructions. This process is outlined in Figure 14-1. As an interpreted language, Java's development cycle is much faster than traditional compiled languages. The old edit-compile-link-debug cycle is reduced to just compile and run. When you are satisfied with the application, you can obtain maximum performance by using a built in, just-in-time compiler to compile the Java intermediate code into machine code.

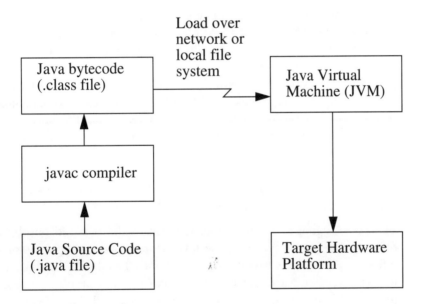

Figure 14–1   Java Code Execution in the Java Virtual Machine

The popularity of Java and the almost universal availability of JVMs for every operating system have led to bytecode cross compilers for other languages. For instance, there are now compilers available that can generate Java.class files from Ada code.

Java applications are portable across multiple platforms. While basic portability is a result of the Java bytecode and Java Virtual Machine design, portability considerations extend down to the language level. For instance, the primitive data types are all well defined. Integer primitives include an 8-bit `byte`, a 16-bit `short`, a 32-bit `int`, and a 64-bit `long`. There is no ambiguity in the length of integer types as is present in different implementations of C and C++. Real numeric types and their arithmetic operations are defined by the IEEE 754 specification. The `char` data type is based on sixteen bit Unicode characters. Boolean is also a primitive data type as it is in modern C++, where it is called `bool`. The preciseness of these primitive data type definitions help to keep Java applications portable across a wide range of platforms.

For most programmers, the Java language presents two major and very obvious departures from C and C++. First, in Java, all pointer manipulation is implicit and programmers do not directly deal with pointers or pointer arithmetic. Secondly, Java's robust run-time system manages memory for the programmer. These two features of Java remove some of the most common C and C++ bugs, memory leaks, and invalid pointers. The Java language completely removes the memory management load from the programmer. C-style pointers, pointer arithmetic, and C memory management functions such as malloc and free do not exist. Automatic garbage collection is an integral part of the Java language. Once you have allocated an object, the Java run-time system keeps track of the object's status and automatically reclaims memory when objects are no longer in use, freeing memory for future use.

The Java language's memory management model is based on objects and references to objects. Because the Java language has no implicit pointers, all references to objects are through symbolic "handles." The Java memory manager keeps track of references to objects. When an object has no more references, the object is a candidate for garbage collection. While the Java language has a "new" operator to allocate space for objects, there is no explicit "free" operator.

One of the common criticisms of previous garbage collection schemes is that they tend to run at inappropriate times, creating poor interactive response or interrupting time-critical server code. In Java, this problem is largely solved by running the garbage collector in a low priority thread. In the 1.1 release of

Java, the garbage collection scheme was expanded to include a distributed garbage collector for Java objects created through the Java RMI (remote method invocation) API. Much additional work on garbage collection performance is now being completed and will be incorporated into the 1.2 release of the Java Development Kit (JDK).

Java's built-in garbage collection is just one example of the use of language level multithreading in Java. Chapter 19 of this book describes multithreading in more detail. While multithreading in general is not new, Java is one of the first languages (besides Ada) to support multithreading at the language level. Java's multithreading features make it easy for programmers to directly implement multiple concurrent threads of activity into their program. With Java, there is no longer any reason for a user interface to display an hourglass cursor while it waits for a database query to execute, or for any other asynchronous action, for that matter.

Java is dynamically adaptable and can load new code modules as needed from multiple sources, even across a network. Java's widespread use in networked applications has often raised questions about its security. Java's security beckons from its original design as a language for programming networked applications. Security is built in at the language level. For instance, while pointers are the cause of many common C bugs, they are also the starting point of many viruses and other network security breaches. The lack of arbitrary pointers in the Java language eliminates a whole class of potential security holes. Such language level features form Java's first defense against malicious use. The second security barrier stems from Java's interpreted nature.

Before Java bytecode is interpreted and executed by the Java Virtual Machine, it must first pass through a bytecode verifier. Because the bytecode preserves the structure and syntax of the original code, the bytecode verifier can check for illegal type manipulations, parameters, and other potential security breaches. Thus even a malicious compiler cannot create insecure Java bytecode because this would be caught at run time by the bytecode verifier. The Java run time environment can also implement additional security constraints by limiting which hosts a Java applet downloaded over the network can communicate with.

The original Java release contained a basic set of class libraries, called packages, used by most Java programs. The java.lang package contained the basic language foundation classes. These classes implement wrappers for the primitive types, threads, exceptions, string, and a variety of other fundamental classes. The I/O package implemented basic input and output classes.

The AWT class library (Abstract Windowing Toolkit) implemented basic functionality found in graphical user interfaces such as buttons, scrollbars, fonts, color, and events. A utility package provided a variety of encoder and decoder techniques, date and time, hash table, vector, and stack classes. The network interface class library extended the functionality of the I/O class library with network communication classes such as sockets.

These class libraries, plus others defined since, have become know as the "core" Java APIs. Any full Java implementation must implement the complete set of core Java APIs. Besides the core APIs, a number of extended Java APIs have also been defined, such as the Java3D API. Java implementations have the option of supporting the extended APIs. Over time, some extended APIs have moved into the core set and programmers should check the documentation on the http://java.sun.com/products/ web page for the latest status of any API.

Besides being extended with new APIs, several "subsets" of the Java core APIs have been defined for specific application environments. These include JavaCard for smart cards, Embedded Java for embedded devices, and Personal Java for devices such as PDAs. Each of these Java environments supports the full Java language with the difference being simply in the set of class libraries that are guaranteed to exist in the implementation.

COBOL

COBOL was developed in 1959 by the Committee on Data Systems Languages (Codasyl). The Codasyl committee named the language they created COBOL, for Common Business Oriented Language. As the name implies, it was specifically targeted at the needs of business computing applications. Today, COBOL is perhaps best known for being the greatest source of potential Year 2000 (Y2K) problems. Much of this reputation is due to the fact that many COBOL programs still in operation were originally developed many years ago and were never expected to last until the turn of the century. COBOL is still the primary development environment for many mainframe applications, however it has never seen much use in the Unix or PC world.

LISP

The other major language besides COBOL to be developed in 1959 was LISP. LISP, which stands for LISt Processing, was developed by John McCarthy for artificial intelligence applications. For the most part, LISP has not seen widespread use outside of the academic community. One exception to this was during the mid 1980s, as "expert system" technology, often written in LISP, saw a flurry of commercial use. Several computer vendors, including Symbolics (now defunct), Xerox, and Texas Instruments, even developed special purpose workstations during this time that were specifically designed to execute LISP code. While Simula, developed in 1967, is generally credited with being the first object-oriented language, LISP certainly contributed greatly to the experience base of object-oriented programmers. Symbolics developed their own object-oriented extensions to LISP called Flavors, that later became the basis for the Common LISP Object System which is now a part of the standard Common LISP language. Xerox, in part out of its experiences with LISP, developed Smalltalk, an object-oriented language that is still used today.

Scripting Languages (Perl, awk, Tcl, ksh)

Modern scripting languages were first popularized by simple Unix scripting languages such as "sh." The sh language, short for shell, was one of the first Unix scripting languages. Unlike compiled languages that are transformed into machine code executables, script files are executed directly by a script interpreter. A file containing a sh language script, for instance, can be directly executed with the sh command. There are a number of Unix scripting languages based loosely on sh. The "csh" scripting language, for instance, adds features to more closely resemble the C programming language syntax. The "ksh" and "tcsh" scripts are yet more advanced scripting languages based on sh.

Along with general purpose scripting languages, early Unix programmers developed a number of other special purpose scripting languages that are still in widespread use today. For instance, the "awk" language was designed specifically for string handling and manipulation functions.

Over the years, scripting languages continued to grow in complexity and competed in functionality with traditional programming languages. Tcl, for example, is a modern scripting language that is often used for visual programming. Perl, another scripting language, is used extensively in web programming.

The main benefit of scripting languages is the flexibility and rapid development they afford to programmers. It can often be simpler and quicker to program a small task in a scripting language than in a compiled programming language. Most scripting languages are intended for implementing functionality that resides in a single file. This limits their practical use to programs of several hundred statements or less. Another disadvantage of scripts is their often cryptic syntax. The same syntax that makes it easy to accomplish so much in a few dozen lines of code makes for difficult reading. Finally, because most scripts are executed in an interpretative fashion, there are few opportunities for run time optimization. Compute intensive code almost always executes faster as a compiled program than as the equivalent script.

Software Development Tools

A wide range of development tools have been available for many years to help developers write code more efficiently. These tools range from specialized single function tools to complete tool suites addressing all stages of the software development life cycle. Given the maturity of the tool market, it is still quite surprising to find so many programmers utilizing no more than a simple text editor and basic compiler for their development. Part of the problem, no doubt, can be lack of proper processes in development organizations, as described in Part 3 of this book. The other part of the problem is that most tools, despite their fancy user interfaces, are no panacea for software development. An unskilled developer with great tools will still be less successful in developing software than a good developer with no tools.

Today, many vendors package development tools together in a so-called integrated development environment (IDE). Some IDEs started out as single-function tools and evolved as vendors added more functionality or merged their product with others to provide customers a more complete single-stop solution. It is common for IDEs to address software development from either the user interface point of view or the database point of view. Not surprisingly, IDEs that started out as simple GUI development tools often take the former approach while IDEs that started out as database access tools often take the latter approach. Both of these approaches can be sub-optimal for modern multi-tier software architectures. If you design your code by starting with the user interface, you often end up designing the database to match the user interface. If you start designing your code with the database, you can end up developing your user interface to match the database design. In either case, business logic often gets mixed in with both the user interface code and the database code instead of being isolated in a stand-alone module. The best tools let you start by defining your business logic and then help you derive both user interface and back-end database design based on the requirements of your business logic.

Despite the limitations of many tools, a good IDE or other development tool, used properly, will contribute much to the success of your project. This chapter discusses some of the various classes of tools available including IDEs, GUI development tools, database tools, and testing tools. Examples are given of some of the more popular tools in each category. Where possible, tools supporting the Java language have been given as examples because of the popularity of the Java platform. As there are literally hundreds of development tools, the ones presented in this chapter are not meant to be an all-inclusive list. This chapter further describes some of the components that might be found in an IDE, such as code editors, compilers, profilers, and debuggers.

Interactive Development Environments

A good interactive development environment (IDE) will contain a full range of code editing, analysis, debugging, and test tools for use throughout the development life cycle. A good IDE will also provide tight integration of its component modules to facilitate a programmer moving through the edit-compile-debug cycle. Such integration requires more than a common tool launcher and common look and feel. It should also include a robust inter-tool communications backend. For instance, from a debugger window you should be able to launch a text editor to open up at the line being edited, or even better, allow editing directly in the debugger window. Without switching context, the tool should also allow the compiler to be invoked against the file that was just edited. Some of our favorite tools along with a brief description of their features are included below and summarized in Table 15-1.

Table 15–1 Interactive Development Environments

Tool Name/Vendor	Languages Supported	Platforms	Comments
Bean Machine IBM	Java	Windows, OS2, Unix	Visual applet and JavaBean generation
Builder Xcessory Pro Integrated Computer Solutions	Java, C, C++	Unix, Windows (target only)	Excellent GUI builder with strong cross-platform target support
CodeWarrior Professional Metrowerks	Java, C, C++, Pascal	Unix, Windows, Mac	One of the best tools if you need to support Unix, Windows, and Mac platforms
Java Workshop Sun Microsystems	Java	Solaris, Windows	Written 100% in Java; tools based on a web browser metaphor
JBuilder Imprise	Java	Windows, AS400	Great database support
SuperCede for Java Supercede	Java	Windows	Good ActiveX/JavaBean interoperability
UIM/X VisualEdge Software	Java, C, C++	Unix, Windows, Mac	Great support for C/C++ and Motif to Java migration
Visual Cafe for Java Symantec	Java	Windows	Good multithreaded debugger
VisualAge IBM	Java	Unix, Windows	Includes incremental compiler and automatic version control
Visual J++ Microsoft	Java	Windows	All the bells and whistles you can use in Windows

BeanMachine

BeanMachine is a visual applet authoring tool with wizards. It supports text, audio, and animation. JDBC capabilities provide open data access from text files, spreadsheets and relational data. A publish tool puts the finished applet, compiled Java, HTML, and all the media needed by the applet into a single directory. BeanMachine supports Windows, OS2, Solaris, HP/UX, and AIX.

For more information on BeanMachine, see the IBM web page at http://www.ibm.com.

Builder Xcessory Pro

Builder Xcessory Pro is a GUI builder for developing Java, C, and C++ front-ends. It provides strong cross-platform support for all the top Unix environments including Solaris, HP/UX, AIX, and Irix. While the development environment runs only on Unix, applications can be deployed on Unix, Windows, or Java platforms. The tool includes drag & drop, WYSIWYG, and instant play/build capabilities. Builder Xcessory Pro can generate Java-only code and includes a class browser for Java classes generated by the product.

For more information on Builder Xcessory Pro, see the Integrated Computer Solutions web page at http://www.ics.com.

CodeWarrior Professional

Supports Windows, MacOS, and Solaris. CodeWarrior Professional is an integrated set of tools that allows you to edit, compile, and debug C, C++, Java, and Pascal programs. The Java compiler supports the generation of both .zip and .jar files. This is one of the best tools if you need to support both Java and C code across all three platforms.

For more information on CodeWarrior, see the Metrowerks web page at http://www.metrowerks.com. Note that while the official company name is "Metrowerks," they have smartly allocated both the "metrowerks.com" and "metroworks.com" domain names.

Java Workshop

Supports Solaris and Windows. Java WorkShop 2.0 is unique among development tools in that it is written entirely in Java. It is a complete visual development environment for JavaBeans, Internet and intranet Java applets, and applications. JavaWorkshop features include a visual GUI builder, a project and portfolio manager, source editor, class browser, build manager, profiler, Java compiler, project tester, graphical debugger, remote debugging, support for team development, online help and tutorials. All user interface functions of the tool are presented using a browser-like interface that helps developers quickly familiarize themselves with the tool.

For more information on Java Workshop, see the Sun Microsystems web page at http://sun.com.

JBuilder

Supports Windows and AS400. Despite a corporate name change, the former Borland corporation continues to put out one of the more popular PC-based development tools. Anyone who has ever used Imprise's Builder product will be instantly comfortable with JBuilder. It features JavaBeans component creation, a scalable database architecture, visual "Two-Way" development tools, and the ability to produce "100% Pure Java" platform-independent applications, applets, servlets, and JavaBeans. The product's open environment supports JDK 1.1.x, JDK 1.2, JFC/Swing components, JavaBeans, Enterprise JavaBeans, CORBA, RMI, JDBC, and all major corporate database servers. JBuilder is perhaps one of the best general purpose IDEs for developers whose applications will involve a large amount of database connectivity and this is where the tool shines above its competitors. In addition, JBuilder is one of the few IDEs to support the AS400 platform.

For more information on JBuilder, see the Imprise web page at http://www.imprise.com.

SuperCede for Java

Supports Windows. Supercede is one of Microsoft co-founder Paul Allen's many start up companies. Nevertheless, their product, Supercede for Java, competes directly with other IDEs from Microsoft. Supercede is a very interesting IDE with database development capabilities, integrated C++ compiler, ActiveX/JavaBean interoperability, support for generation of Intel executables and DLL's, support for JDK 1.1 and JavaBeans, and Super-Cede's Flash Compiler technology.

For more information on SuperCede for Java, see the SuperCede web page at http://www.supercede.com.

UIM/X

UIM/X supports Windows, MacOS, Solaris, HP/UX, AIX, Irix, and Linux. It started out many years ago as a Unix based X-Windows development tool for C and then C++. It is therefore no surprise that this tool includes a Migration Assistant, which converts Motif interfaces into 100% Pure Java. The Java development mode provides interpretive design, a graphical connection editor, a graphical constraint editor, a declaration editor, and a method editor. The tool also includes a handy run mode for quickly switching between designing and testing of user interfaces. If you have a large amount of cross-platform Unix/Motif code you want to convert to Java and reuse, this is one of the best tools available.

For more information on UIM/X, see the VisualEdge Software web page at http://www.visualedge.com.

Visual Cafe for Java

Supports Windows. Building on the success of its C/C++ based Visual Cafe IDE, Symantec Visual Cafe for Java is one of the best overall tools for Windows developers. Symantec's Just-In-Time compiler consistently offers some of the best Java performance on Windows. Visual Cafe provides extensive debugging support, including multithreaded application debugging. The Database Development add-on provides extensive database connectivity support for all the major database platforms.

For more information on Visual Cafe for Java, see the Symantec web page at http://www.symantec.com.

VisualAge

Supports Windows, Solaris, AIX, Irix, and Linux. VisualAge supports a wide range of features including code editing, incremental compilation, debugging, and automatic version control. It also includes a Visual Builder to assemble Java applets, Java applications, and JavaBeans from pre-selected parts on the visual builder palette.

For more information on VisualAge, see the IBM web page at http://www.ibm.com.

Visual J++

Supports Windows. In the Microsoft tradition, Visual J++ provides more features than perhaps any other IDE on the market. Unfortunately, many of the advanced features of Visual J++ are only available if you are willing to sacrifice Java's portability outside of the Windows environment. Productivity features such as a fast Java compiler, debugger, GIF/JPG editor, macro scripting, and a post-build process for packaging and deployment are all included. It also supports ActiveX so developers can integrate Java with existing DCOM applications. Visual J++ also features a GUI designer to visually create forms or import resources from existing Visual C++ or Visual Basic applications.

For more information on Visual J++, see the Microsoft web page at http://www.microsoft.com.

GUI Development Tools and Libraries

Today, just about any software program that requires user interaction will have a graphical user interface. While the graphical user interface is the most visible part of a program, it typically is not the largest part. Nevertheless, a good GUI development tool can provide a large productivity increase for a programmer compared to hand developing the same code. Traditionally, GUI development tools were targeted at a specific windowing environment, such as Microsoft Windows, X, or Macintosh. Some GUI tools were cross-platform and generated code for more than one target platform. The problem with many cross-platform GUI tools is they are targeted to the least common denominator feature set of their target environments. This tends to produce user interfaces that are a compromise of what is possible with a single environment tool. Of course this has all changed with Java technology.

In its original 1.0 release, Java supported a set of user interface components called the Abstract Windowing Toolkit (AWT). In the 1.2 release, Java's GUI functionality was dramatically improved with the user interface components of the Java Foundation Classes (JFC). These components (nicknamed "Swing components") are written in Java, without window-system-specific code. This permits a customizable look and feel without relying on the native windowing system and simplifies the deployment of applications. This feature gives users the ability to switch the look and feel of an application without restarting it and without the developer having to subclass the entire component set. The same Java application could, for instance, switch dynamically at run time into a Windows look and feel, an X look and feel, or the developer's own custom look and feel.

The JFC contains all the common components normally found in a user interface, including

- Windows
- containers
- menus
- labels
- buttons
- checkboxes
- choice lists
- text fields
- scrollbars
- sliders

Often, a GUI development tool will be packaged as part of a larger IDE suite. When selecting an IDE for Java development, you should be sure to select one that supports at least the Java Foundation Classes and the full JDK 1.1 or later release. In addition, you may wish to purchase additional user interface components, typically packaged as class libraries. The widespread use of Java has greatly increased the number of prepackaged GUI components available. There are hundreds of packages available from small shareware packages purchased off the net to sophisticated component collections from established software vendors. Here is just a small sampling of the GUI packages available on the market.

Table 15–2   GUI Development Libraries

Tool Name/Vendor	Languages Supported	Platforms	Comments
Chart.J Rogue Wave Software	Java	Any Java platform	Prebuilt and custom chart types
ILOG Jviews ILOG	Java	Any Java platform	Creates 2 D structured graphics displays like maps and network topologies

Table 15–2   GUI Development Libraries

Tool Name/Vendor	Languages Supported	Platforms	Comments
JWave Visual Numerics	Java	Any Java platform	2 D and 3 D graphics

Chart.J

Supports Windows and Solaris. Rogue Wave was one of the first companies to start packaging and selling C++ class libraries and continues to expand its product offerings with a wide range of Java-based components. Chart.J includes JavaBeans components for use with a JavaBeans-aware graphical tools along with a programmatic interface that can be used to incorporate customizable, dynamic charts into Java applets or applications. Chart.J provides prebuilt chart types, or developers may use the charting primitives to create composite chart types by mixing and matching any combination of overlays. Chart.J's data model provides for dynamic updates of charted data, and built-in callback mechanisms provide drill-down capability for various portions of a chart.

For more information on Chart.J, see the Rogue Wave Software web page at http://www.roguewave.com.

Jviews

Supports Windows, Solaris, and HP/UX. ILOG's JViews is a 100% Java class library for developing 2 D structured graphics diagrams. It complements existing GUI components (AWT, Beans, etc.) to create interfaces such as network topologies, maps, process control screens, or customized editors.

For more information on Jviews, see the ILOG web page at http://www.ilog.com.

JWave

Supports Windows and Solaris. JWave is a set of Java classes for creating basic presentation graphics and performing Visual Data Analysis (VDA) within an applet or application. Components use PV-WAVE as a graphic server to create the graphics. The PV-WAVE server can either run on a remote machine on your inter/intranet, or as a local process on your machine. Components produce static 2 D and 3 D graphics, animations, and 3 D VRML worlds. If you are already using PV-WAVE, you will find this package to be a must-have.

For more information on JWave, see the Visual Numerics web page at http://www.vni.com.

Database Tools

Almost every software development tool vendor has some sort of tool that can be loosely categorized as a database tool. These fall into three general categories. First there are the major database vendor's products. The vendors each have their own development tools such as Oracle's Developer 2000 or Sybase's Powerbuilder. The database vendor's tools tend to start with the database design and derive user interfaces based on the database structure. Such tools are a great fit if you are primarily developing a database-centric application with a single DBMS. One of the disadvantages of this approach, however, is that database schema changes can wreck havoc on your application. Each of these tools does provide multi-DBMS support; however, it is no surprise that each vendor's tool typically works best with its own database.

The second category of database tools come from the traditional Interactive Development Environment vendors such as Symantec or Imprise. These tools tend to start with the user interface design and then add features for mapping user interface elements (forms, text fields, etc.) to database tables. Such tools tend to provide better cross-DBMS support while they may lack some of the fancier features or capabilities of the DBMS vendor's tools. Imprise has a reputation for being the vendor who provides the best database integration in their development tools; however, all vendors tend to leapfrog each other with new capabilities with each new release.

The third category of database tools can be categorized as middleware tools. Such tools specialize in providing connectivity between multiple databases and multiple development environments. In Java-based applications, database interaction has been simplified by Java's JDBC (Java Database Connectivity) API. The JDBC API defines a vendor and in fact database architecture neutral interface for accessing data. An application written to the JDBC API could switch at run time between storing data in a relational DBMS, an object-oriented DBMS, or even a flat file. The promise of this approach is that, when combined with other building blocks, it will let developers concentrate on coding the business logic of their application and then derive both the database structure and the user interface as dictated by the business logic. Once again, here is a small sampling of some of the tools available.

Table 15–3 Database Tools

Tool Name/Vendor	Languages Supported	Platforms	Comments
Blend.J Rogue Wave Software	Java	Any Java platform	Great add-on to other Rogue Wave tools
CocoBase Thought Inc.	Java	Any Java platform	Glues together JDBC, CORBA, and RMI
Developer/2000 Oracle	Java, C, C++, others	Windows, Unix	Oracle's flagship development tool
GemStone/J Gemstone Systems	Java	Any Java platform	Three-tier transactions support
Jaguar CTS Sybase	Java, C, C++	Windows, Unix	ActiveX and JavaBeans support in a high performance transaction server
NetDynamics Sun Microsystems	Java, C, C++	Windows, Unix	Load balancing for high-end scalability

Blend.J

Blend.J integrates Rogue Wave's JWidgets and Stingray's Objective Blend into a collection of 45-plus controls. It provides both JFC and AWT support, with controls that offer the same interface but different implementations, allowing developers to swap implementations rather than rewriting code. If you are using any of Rogue Wave's other tools and need to access information from a database, you should consider this tool.

CocoBase

CocoBase is centrally managed middleware for making databases Internet-accessible. It sits on top of the JDBC drivers and uses CORBA or RMI to access and manipulate databases and data stores as first class application objects without putting SQL in the client or server. CocoBase glues together the GUI, ORB (or RMI), and JDBC driver of the developer's choice. There are three versions of this tool available. The free version is a persistent object storage facility with embedded XDB's Jet Store BTree Engine. CocoBase Lite is a dynamic object to relational mapping tool. The enterprise version includes tools for mapping objects and converting tables to objects.

For more information on CocoBase, see the Thought Inc. web page at http://www.thoughtinc.com.

Developer/2000

Developer/2000 is Oracle's flagship enterprise application development environment. It includes a form builder and an integrated reporting and charting tool for relational database application development.

For more information on Developer/2000, see the Oracle web page at http://www.oracle.com.

GemStone/J

GemStone/J is a three-tier, integrated transactional server for Java and CORBA, based on distributed JavaBeans and other enterprise services. GemStone/J utilizes key standards such as CORBA/IIOP and JDBC to ensure interoperability and integration with all data sources. It provides an open application development environment for distributed Java applications. In conjunction with the GemStone/J tools and services, APIs, Java, and JavaBeans applications can be flexibly partitioned between client and server.

For more information on GemStone/J, see the Gemstone Systems web page at http://www.gemstone.com.

Jaguar CTS

Jaguar is a component transaction server designed for delivering scalable, transaction-based applications for the Internet. It supports multiple component models including JavaBeans and ActiveX. It provides connection management, session management, monitoring, multi-database connectivity, and point-and-click administration.

For more information on Jaguar CTS, see the Sybase web page at http://www.sybase.com.

NetDynamics

NetDynamics is a visual development environment for generating server-side Java database applications. Scalability and performance result from a combination of request brokering, load balancing, multiple database connection management, and distribution over multiple CPUs.

For more information on NetDynamics, see the Sun Microsystems home page at http://sun.com.

Testing Tools

As with other specialized tools, many IDEs contain some sort of testing tool. Bundled test tools typically are focused at testing single applications only. Before deploying any sort of enterprise-wide application, however, you probably will want to perform some type of end-to-end network level application testing. Here are a few of our favorite testing tools.

Table 15–4 Testing Tools

Tool Name	Languages Supported	Platforms	Comments
JavaScope Sun Microsystems	Java	Any Java platform	Code coverage and metrics, written entirely in Java

Table 15–4 Testing Tools

Tool Name	Languages Supported	Platforms	Comments
Pegasus Ganymede Software	Java, C, C++	Unix, Windows, Mac	End-to-end network testing
WebLoad Radview Software	Java, C, C++	Unix, Windows	Web server loading; includes most security protocols

JavaScope

JavaScope measures how thoroughly Java applications and applets have been tested. The tool provides a range of code coverage metrics, including method coverage, branch coverage, logical coverage, and relational coverage. The tool is written entirely in Java, generates editable Java scripts, and runs on all platforms with a conforming version 1.1 JDK. There are two companion products to this tool: JavaSpec for automating testing of non user-interface components, and JavaStar for testing of user interface components. JavaStar includes a complete record, playback, and compare facility and recorded scripts can be easily edited.

For more information on JavaScope, see the Sun Microsystems web page at http://sun.com.

Pegasus

Ganymede's testing tools provide the capability to perform end-to-end performance testing of networks at the application level. Given the increasing complexity of today's network-centric applications, the use of a tool such as this is almost a necessity for any enterprise-wide application. Pegasus provides trend analysis, reporting, and troubleshooting modules to help manage application operating and service level agreements. Its forte is in throughput and response time testing of complete application environments.

For more information on Pegasus, see the Ganymede Software web page at http://www.ganymedesoftware.com.

WebLoad

During the 1994 World Cup, in the early days of the Web, Sun Microsystems set a world record for web site traffic by recording five million "hits" to the World Cup web site during a six week period. Today, a number of busy web sites get over five million hits an hour. Furthermore, today's sites aren't just serving up static text and graphics. Many sites include complicated back-ends with database connections, CGI applications, and Java servlets. Web-Load does exactly what its name implies. WebLoad lets you simulate hundreds to millions of visits to your web site while monitoring throughput and response time. For ecommerce web sites, WebLoad supports all the common browser encryption schemes. WebLoad also lets you simulate new HTTP features such as running sessions with the HTTP keepalive option set (which allows the TCP connection to remain opened for the entire session, improving performance for most types of page loads).

For more information on WebLoad, see the Radview Software web page at http://www.radview.com.com.

Web Authoring Tools

Web or HTML authoring tools aren't exactly software development tools per se; however, since most software developers will have to develop at least a few web pages in their career, a few words on the topic are appropriate. Web authoring tools used to be their own special class of tools. Today, nearly every popular word processor provides some capability to at least export data as HTML. Even Microsoft, king of proprietary formats, has announced plans to switch to HTML as the default file format in its upcoming Office 2000 release. For simple web authoring, however, we tend to stick with one of two tools. Netscape includes an excellent web authoring tool, dubbed "Composer", with the "gold" or "professional" versions of its web browser. When working on Macintosh platforms, however, we often start up Adobe's Page Mill tool (also available on Windows). Page Mill offers better support for authoring media-rich web pages, including drag and drop capability for images, audio and video clips, animations, and other (especially other Adobe) tools. PageMill also includes a whole suite of web site management tools for checking links and otherwise keeping your web site up to date. If you must use a Microsoft product, their FrontPage web authoring tool is also an excellent product.

Table 15–5 Web Authoring Tools

Tool Name	Languages Supported	Platforms	Comments
Netscape Composer	HTML, JavaScript	Unix, Windows, Mac	Best cross-platform support
Adobe Page Mill	HTML, Javascript	Mac, Windows	Great Mac support and integration with other graphical tools
Microsoft FrontPage	HTML, Javascript	Windows, Mac	Great Windows support

Code Editors

Every software developer tends to have a favorite text editor, from old Unix favorites such as "vi" and "emacs" to modern window-based editors. A good IDE will not only provide a full featured editor, it will allow the developer to transparently substitute his or her favorite text editor as the default.

Besides normal text editing features, a good software development text editor will be context sensitive for one or more particular programming languages. A context sensitive editor understands the basic syntax of the language and can add such useful features as:

- automatic indentation of nested code blocks
- automatic identification (via flashing or some other highlighting) of matching parenthesis or other code block delimiters
- bolding or other highlighting of language keywords, global variables, etc.

Compilers

Besides the obvious requirement of correct code compilation, compilers can be measured on a number of other features including:

- speed of compilation
- speed of the code produced
- compactness of code produced
- the degree of customization provided to the developer

The speed of a compiler is important during development as code is continually being edited, compiled, and debugged. A good compiler will include options for at least three levels of compilation. Most compilers have a basic mode that does not produce any debug information or perform advanced optimizations. When compiling a large program during development, this option may be used for most of the code as it is usually the fastest. For any code segments being actively debugged, the developer will want the compiler to produce additional debug information as output for use in debugging. Typical programs take longer to compile in this mode as the compiler does extra work to produce the debug information. The slowest compilation speeds will usually result when additional optimization levels are turned on. While optimization levels will vary by compiler, in most cases you should look for a compiler that offers optimizations that:

- add several additional general purpose optimization levels
- optimize for specific CPU instruction sets
- optimize for specific CPU architectures

As additional optimization levels may lead to varying behavior in certain types of code, you should always be sure to test software that has been compiled at the optimization level you plan to use when distributing the software. For instance, most Windows 95 software is only compiled at optimization levels supported by a 386 CPU. This is because a 386 is the minimum CPU requirement for Windows 95. Someone writing high performance code who knew it would only be executed on the latest Pentium CPU would want to be sure to compile the code with all Pentium specific optimizations turned on to make sure the code executed as fast as possible.

Most compilers work in a two step fashion. First, the compiler translates the source code into object code, which is a machine representation of the actual CPU instructions to be executed. The second step of compiling is referred to as linking. In linking, the compiler (or linker) takes all the object code files produced in step one, links any needed libraries (or at least links stubs to these libraries if dynamic linking is supported), and produces the final executable file. If a function is statically linked, the code for that function is included in the executable file. If a function is dynamically linked, only a code stub and not the actual function code is included in the executable file. Dynamically linked code is referenced at execution time and only then is the referenced code loaded. Dynamic linking is typically used for operating system and system library functions that are always assumed to be present on the target platform. Static linking is typically used for user-developed code since that would not be otherwise present in the base platform.

In large programs consisting of thousands of functions and hundreds of files, program link time may be much longer than the compile time of any single file. To speed up the edit-compile-debug cycle on large programs, some advanced compilers support a feature typically referred to as "fix and continue" or incremental linking. This allows a developer to recompile individual files and, via dynamic linking, "patch" the executable with the changes without relinking the entire executable. On a large program this can turn a five minute re-link into a simple 10-20 second recompile.

Debuggers

After a code editor, the debugger is probably the tool used most often by a developer. Most IDEs will include a source code debugger. The debugger allows you to view the source code of a program as it is being executed by the compiler. Common operations of a source code debugger include:

- single stepping through code, executing a single line of code at a time
- the ability to single step into a function call, or simply to single step over all statements in a function without following function calls
- the ability to set breakpoints at any line or function in the source code
- the ability to set a breakpoint based on an arbitrary code expression
- the ability to set and display variables in the program, including complex structures
- the ability to view the call stack
- a disassembler

Code Analysis

To help support the development of large programs, a good IDE will have several kinds of code analysis tools. One of the most basic is a call graph browser. A call graph, as the name implies, simply provides a graphical representation of function calls in the program. A call graph allows you to start at any function in your program and trace up or down the call tree to view program flow. Additionally, a call graph browser will also give you the option to view function parameters.

For object-oriented languages, IDEs will also provide a class browser. A class browser allows you to graphically view the relationships between classes, including superclasses and subclasses.

Another useful code analysis tool is a context sensitive search tool. This may be a stand-alone tool or may be integrated into the editor or other code analysis tools. For a simple program, simply searching for a variable or function name based on a text search may be sufficient. In a large program, searching for a common text string may produce hundreds of irrelevant matches. A good search tool understands the syntax of your program and allows you to limit your search in one of two manners, by syntax or by scope. A syntax limited search would look for a text string matching only the designated syntax. For instance, you could search for global variables while excluding functions and local variables of the same name. A scope limited search would look for a text string only within a function, library, or other type of code block. You should make sure the search tool allows you to specify both syntax and scope limiters at the same time. Other common search features include the ability to do case sensitive searches and complete word versus partial word searches.

Performance Analysis Tools

No matter how fast CPUs get, it always seems we are trying to squeeze more performance out of our software. A good performance analysis tool will provide you with statistics to help you do so. A performance analysis tool works by gathering data during one or more sample executions of your code. Thus the more real to life your test set is, the more useful the output of your performance analysis tool will be.

One of the simplest yet most useful performance analysis tools is a run time histogram. Such a tool shows you graphically what functions are using up the most time in your program and how often that function was called. In many cases such a tool will allow you to concentrate your performance tuning on the areas that have the greatest potential payback. After all, achieving a 50% speedup in a segment of your code that is only using up 1% of the execution time does little to speed up the entire program. It would be ten times more effective to concentrate on getting a 10% speedup in a segment of the code that was using 50% of the execution time.

Another useful performance analysis tool is a loadmap generator. A loadmap generator examines a running program to look for ways in which code could be rearranged to improve locality of reference. It is not uncommon today to have program sizes that exceed the capacity of the four to eight megabyte caches found on modern CPUs. Often, a compiler can do little to determine run time locality of reference. A loadmap generator examines locality of reference at run time and provides hints to the linker for more efficiently arranging code so as to optimize cache misses. Just like run time histograms, however, a loadmap generator is only as good as the code sample that was used to generate it.

Component Tools

Component Tools let you develop applications by combining, modifying, and customizing existing components such as ActiveX controls or Java-Beans. Often, such tools are either embedded or bundled with a general development tool suite. If you are developing ActiveX controls, which currently implies that you are targeting a Microsoft Windows only environment, then Microsoft's own tools such as Microsoft J++ are hard to beat. The only caution is that while tools such as Microsoft J++ can be used to develop pure, cross-platform Java code, doing so disables many of their advanced features. Use the tool's advanced features, which is what differentiates the tool in the first place, and you once again become locked into a Microsoft Windows environment. A good cross-platform alternative is Sun's JavaStudio tool for creating applications from JavaBeans. Besides producing 100% pure Java code, JavaStudio itself is written in Java. That means the tool can run on any platform supporting the correct Java virtual machine. Some of the Interactive Development Environment tools previously discussed that support JavaBeans development include Symantec Cafe, Sun's Java Workshop, and Imprise's JBuilder.

CASE Tools

Computer Aided Software Engineering tools address the front-end of the software development life cycle starting with requirements analysis, definition, and tracking. Most CASE tools provide one or more methods of program modeling, typically based on either an object-oriented or structured programming paradigm. One of the best CASE tools for the Unified Modeling Language (UML) is Rational Rose, developed by Rational Software, which just happens to be the creator of UML. Rational Software has captured a large share of the UML tool market, and according to IDC's May 1998 report has more market share than the next three vendors (Select, Cayenne, and Platinum) combined.

Rational Rose includes support for C++, Java, Visual Basic, and Ada languages. Some of its other popular features include:

- support for UML modeling
- component-based development
- visual Differencing tool
- Corba/IDL generation
- Database Schema Generation (DDL code)
- MS repository integration
- Multiple diagram types including Use Case, Sequence, Collaboration, Class, State, and Component diagrams

Version and Baseline Control

Even the smallest development projects should utilize some sort of version and baseline control tool. Two mainstays of the Unix world are the Source Code Control System (SCCS) and the Revision Control System (RCS). Both tools provide the basic functionality needed to establish a baseline, let multiple developers in a workgroup check in and check out files, and track multiple code trees. Both tools also provide a wide range of advanced capabilities sufficient for almost any sized project. Unfortunately, the standard versions of these tools rely on simple command line interfaces. Many vendors wrap graphical user interfaces around these tools to create their own version control tools.

As with many types of tools, the widespread adoption of the Internet and Java have led to interesting new products with features never imagined several years ago. Sun's JavaSafe product, for instance, is one such tool. It provides all the features of traditional version control tools, but since it is written entirely in Java it runs in any web browser. In effect, it uses a web server/web browser paradigm to check in and check out code. Such a tool can greatly simplify remote workgroups working over an Intranet or even over the Internet.

The ClearCase product family offers software configuration management (SCM) products for software teams in Windows and Unix development environments. ClearCase provides comprehensive configuration management, including version control, workspace management, build management, and process control.

16

Selecting Your Hardware Environment

Most software development books don't spend much time discussing hardware environments. Software, of course, ultimately executes on a hardware platform and the two are thus closely linked. This has been so since the early days of software. In fact, John Mauchly, who in 1949 developed one of the first high-level programming languages, called Short Order Code, had three years earlier been the co-designer of the ENIAC, one of the first large-scale digital computers. Today, however, software developers have a much broader choice of hardware platforms (and software languages) to select from for their projects. Selecting the proper hardware platform for your production and development environment can have a major impact on the success of your project. The most important thing to remember about this chapter, however, is this one big rule about hardware: Given today's economics, it is acceptable to waste money on hardware overcapacity. The reason is very simple. The tight labor market for software developers means skilled software engineers can demand premium salaries. Entry level software developers can easily make $50,000 a year and developers experienced in specialized skills such as object-oriented development can demand six figure salaries in some markets. At the same time, Moore's Law continues to apply as hardware becomes faster (and correspondingly cheaper) every year. This is illustrated in Figure 16-1.

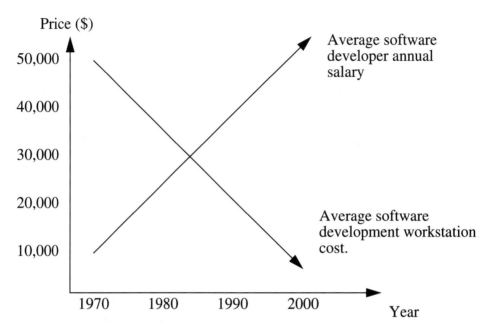

Figure 16–1   Trends In Hardware Costs versus Labor Costs

In spite of the realities of relative hardware versus labor costs, many organizations are still not taking this into account. One reason is that hardware costs may still be analyzed in isolation. For instance, does a $10,000 workstation make a developer twice as productive as a $5,000 workstation? Probably not, but this is not the right question. To justify the $10,000 workstation's acquisition costs, it need only make a $50,000/year developer ten percent more productive to pay for itself in one year! Furthermore, hardware costs amount to only a small fraction of the life cycle cost of a workstation – the bulk of this cost is incurred for system administration. A more expensive workstation does not cost any more, and may actually cost less to administer, than a lower priced system.

Your software project will most likely require a lot more hardware than development workstations. Depending on the project, you will require one or more different servers. You will also want to separate out your development environment from your production environment, with possibly a third set of hardware for quality assurance and testing. Some applications, such as the popular enterprise resource planning package SAP, in fact, utilize methodologies that specifically require separate sets of development, quality assur-

ance, and production hardware. This chapter takes a look at some of the different types of workstation and server hardware that will be needed by most development projects while examining some development infrastructure components, namely networking and storage, that are changing even faster than the host platforms they are connected to.

One place to start when evaluating hardware platforms is with audited benchmarks. The two primary benchmark auditing and publishing organizations are SPEC, which covers CPU, NFS, and Web benchmarks and the Transaction Processing Council (TPC) which specializes in database benchmarks. This chapter suggests some of the SPEC and TPC benchmarks that might be appropriate to consider for different types of servers. However, using a benchmark without considering the details can lead to many incorrect assumptions. To help you better understand these benchmarks, this chapter reviews several benchmark reports, exposing the details and providing references for further study.

Developer Desktops

Whether you are using Unix workstations or PCs for development, you should invest in a high-end desktop for each developer. Marginal differences in acquisition costs are well worth the investment given the additional productivity you will gain. While Moore's law quickly makes any desktop configuration guide obsolete as of late 1998, a suggested minimum developer configuration is shown in Table 16-1

Table 16–1 Recommended Developer Desktop Configuration

Component	Minimum Capacity/Speed
CPU	350 MHz
CPU Cache	1 MB
Memory	128 MB
Local Disk	4GB, 7200 RPM
Monitor	21 inch high resolution color
Network Adapter	100 Mbit/second

Let's examine each component and its role in development.

CPU speeds continue to increase with no end in sight. For instance, Sun's UltraSPARC processor roadmap, shown in Figure 16-2, show CPU speed increasing from 143 MHz in 1995 to 1.5 Ghz in 2002, roughly doubling every year as predicted by Moore's Law. The faster the CPU, the more productive the developer will be. Even if you use central compile servers for large compile jobs, most developers will make use of their local CPU for small compile jobs. In addition, developers tend to run many tools in parallel. It is not uncommon for a developer to have a dozen or more development tool windows open at any one time and be quickly switching back and forth between them.

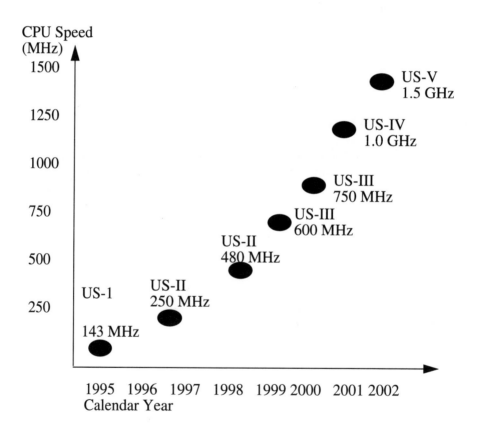

Figure 16–2   UltraSPARC CPU Roadmap

Chapter **16** I Selecting Your Hardware Environment

Aside from CPU speed, cache size is one of the most important performance indicators of a desktop system. Today's CPUs operate several times faster than main memory and special cache memory is used as a buffer to decrease overall memory access times and increase total memory system performance. You should select the largest cache size available on your CPU, typically 1 MB or more.

Software development, especially with modern interactive development environments, is especially memory intensive. You should start out with a minimum of 128 Mbytes of memory for each desktop. If you don't have enough memory, processes will get swapped out to disk and switching between development windows will slow down dramatically. You should evaluate your memory needs by exercising the proposed desktop with the full suite of development tools the average programmer will be using. This will help you get a much better idea of memory sizing for your choice of tools. Adding more memory to a developer's workstation is often one of the easiest and cheapest ways to increase productivity.

One of the often overlooked components of a workstation is the disk subsystem. Just about any computer advertisement will include two similar models, where the higher priced system includes a larger capacity disk drive. However, drive performance criteria, starting with RPMs, are the most important performance criteria versus capacity. Most low-end PCs still use 4500 or 5400 RPM drives. Higher priced models, especially those using SCSI drives, typically run at a minimum of 7200 RPM, and 10,000 RPM drives are rapidly being introduced into the marketplace.

Development Servers

Many studies have shown that the five year total cost of ownership of a desktop system can easily range over $10,000 per year in 1998 dollars. That's an average of over ten times the acquisition costs assuming a $5,000 high-end desktop. A large part of the total cost of ownership is in system administration. Thus the easiest way to save on desktop costs is not to buy cheaper desktops, which would decrease productivity, but to have the right server infrastructure to allow you to centralize desktop management. There are at least three common functions that should be centralized to servers. These are file, compile, and database services.

File Server Benchmarks

A properly configured file server on a modern network (such as fast ethernet) can provide faster file services to a development desktop than a local disk drive. The file server can also provide much better reliability and availability than individual disk drives. Finally, centralizing file storage greatly simplifies backup and other administration tasks.

The industry standard benchmark for file server performance is the SPEC SFS97 (formally called LADDIS) benchmark, which can be found at http://www.specbench.org.

There are two primary performance figures quoted for this benchmark, throughput (in operations per second) and response time (in milliseconds). It is important to consider both numbers, as response time generally rises as throughput increases. Besides looking at the ramp-up in response time, there are other reasons you should look closely at the test details and consider the appropriateness of these numbers. Tables 16-2 through 16-6 describe some of the detailed results of the SPEC SFS97 benchmark using a Sun Enterprise 6002. These results are used to illustrate some of the detailed results of the benchmark and other items you should consider when reviewing a benchmark such as this.

One important item in the test details is the number of network interfaces used. In this benchmark, there were 9 network interfaces used, which works out to an average of approximately 3,000 operations per network interface. If your development network utilizes a single 100 Mbit fast ethernet network, you would be wasting about 88 percent of the Enterprise 6002 server if you utilized it only for file services. In real life development environments, it would be very uncommon to see loads of more than 2,000 operations/second on any 100 Mbit network segment. The moral is, before considering any benchmark number, make sure that your environment would be capable of making use of the benchmarked system.

Table 16–2   SPEC SFS97 Results for Sun Enterprise 6002

Throughput (ops/sec)	Response (msec)
5036	5.3
7563	5.9
10034	7.0

Table 16–2   SPEC SFS97 Results for Sun Enterprise 6002

Throughput (ops/sec)	Response (msec)
12634	10.0
15168	9.9
17689	12.7
20258	13.9
22788	15.3
25329	19.7
25465	19.1
25639	28.8

If you were to simply look at a summary listing of the SPEC SFS97 results, you would see this benchmark listed as 25639 operations/second with an overall response time of 9.94 msec. As with all benchmarks, you need to be very careful when looking only at summary numbers. The overall response time in the summary refers to the average response time while the operations/second refers to the maximum throughput. Careful examination of the detailed results will show that at the maximum throughput, response time is nearly three times the average response time. Different benchmark results will have different throughput/response curves and it is thus important to compare not just actual maximum throughputs but also throughput versus response.

Now lets take a closer look at the server configuration and availability data for this benchmark.

Table 16–3   Spec SFS97 Server Configuration and Availability

Attribute	Value
Vendor	Sun Microsystems Inc.
Hardware Availability	March 1998
Software Availability	May 1996
Date Tested	February 1998

Table 16–3 Spec SFS97 Server Configuration and Availability

Attribute	Value
Model Name	Sun Enterprise 6002
Processors	18 336 MHz UltraSPARC II
Main Memory	8 GB
Operating System	Solaris 2.5.1

Several important things to note on the server configuration include the number of processors, main memory, and hardware/software availability. Vendors may publish Spec benchmarks as long as the hardware and software used will be generally available within six months. You should not compare one vendor's currently shipped systems with those that another vendor will ship in six months. The next section of the Spec SFS97 report specifies the server tuning used. These parameters will be important if you are trying to re-create similar results to those published in the benchmark. You should note how many specific parameters need to be tuned. If you need to tune dozens of parameters to obtain the benchmark results, this may indicate that it will be very difficult to tune the server to your specific workload, which may vary greatly from the benchmark workload.

Table 16–4 Server Tuning Parameters

Parameter	Value
Buffer Cache Size	Dynamic
Number of NFS Processes	839
Fileset size	246 GB

The next section of the benchmark report describes the network subsystem used. To achieve the published Spec SFS97 results, vendors typically use very large network subsystems. If your network is not of the same or greater capacity, you will not be able to achieve the same result.

Large benchmarks also tend to stress the disk subsystem of the host computer. Here is the disk subsystem used in the test.

Table 16–5 Network Subsystem

Parameter	Value
Network Type	100 Mbit Fast Ethernet
Number of Networks	9
Number of Network Controllers	9
Protocol Type	UDP
Switch Type	9 SunSwitch

Table 16–6 Disk Subsystem

Parameter	Value
Number of Disk Controllers	13
Number of Disks	364
Disk Type	2 GB, 7200 RPM
Number of Filesystems	360
File System Configuration	Default

Compile Server Benchmarks

Software developers have a unique ability to ferret out the fastest, most underutilized system on their network and then use that system to run compile jobs. Your local policy or security may, of course, limit such activity. Nevertheless, providing some sort of compile server for your developer environment may make sense. Often, a file server may double as a compile server. A number of different factors will impact compile speed, including complexity of the application and compiler optimization or debug level. A simple compile with no debug or optimization level usually compiles fastest. Adding debug information typically slows down a compilation as does performing additional compile-time optimizations. Compiling often stresses the integer performance of a CPU. In fact, one of the components of the standard components of the SPEC integer benchmark is a compile benchmark called 126.gcc. Below is a summary of the SPECint_rate95 benchmark for a Sun Ultra Enterprise 6000 server.

Table 16–7   SPECint_rate95 Benchmark Summary

Parameter	Value
Model	Sun Enterprise 6000
CPU	Thirty 336 MHz UltraSPARC II
Memory	8 GB
Disk	4x4.2 GB
Hardware Availability	March 1998
Software Availability	August 1998
OS	Solaris 2.6
Compiler	Sun C 5.0

Here are the specific results for each of the subtests within the SPECint_rate95 benchmark

Table 16–8   SPECint_rate95 Subtests Results

Benchmark	Base Number Copies	Base Run Time	Base SPEC Ratio	Peak # Copies	Peak Run Time	Peak SPEC Ratio
099.go	30	398	3122	30	384	3236
124.m88ksim	30	193	2663	30	131	3910
126.gcc	30	227	2019	30	227	2022
129.compress	30	141	3454	30	120	4055
130.li	30	198	2596	30	132	3887
132.ijpec	30	207	3133	30	199	3264
134.perl	30	208	2469	30	120	4276

Table 16–8 SPECint_rate95 Subtests Results

Benchmark	Base Number Copies	Base Run Time	Base SPEC Ratio	Peak # Copies	Peak Run Time	Peak SPEC Ratio
147.vortex	30	244	2987	30	191	3818
SPECint_rate_base95			2771			
SPECint_rate95						3480

Database Server Benchmarks

One of the most common database server benchmarks is the TPC suite of benchmarks. As in any benchmark, your application performance may be vastly different from the benchmark. You should, therefore, only use benchmarks as a starting point in comparing hardware platforms. There are two major benchmarks included in the TPC suite. The first is the TPC-C benchmark that measures server performance on a set of transaction processing workloads. This workload is characterized by a large number of small transactions. The second benchmark is the TPC-D benchmark that measures server performance on a set of online application processing, or data warehouse, workloads.

Here is a sample report showing the TPC-C benchmark for a Sun E6000 server. All published TPC results are available on the TPC web page at http://www.tpc.org. While the total TPC-C throughput attained by many vendors is quite impressive, few applications require a $6 million database server capable of handling forty-four thousand users. As with all benchmarks, you should consider not only the absolute number published but also the details of the benchmark report to determine if this is a valuable benchmark or not for your application.

Table 16–9 E6000 TPC-C Benchmark Summary

Parameter	Value
Platform	Sun Enterprise 6000
TPC-C Throughput	51,871.62 tpmC

Table 16–9 E6000 TPC-C Benchmark Summary

Parameter	Value
Price/Performance	134.46 tpmC
Availability Date	February 23, 1998
Operating System	Solaris 2.6
Database	Oracle8 Enterprise Edition 8.0.3
Processors	Two nodes, each with 22 250 MHz CPUs
Number of Users	44,000
Total System Cost	$6,974,524
Main Memory	5.5 GB (node 1), 6 GB (node 2)
Disk Controllers	40 Fiber Channel
Disk Drives	1188 4.2 GB SCSI
Front-end Systems	26 UltraServer 1 Model 170

Web Server Benchmarks

One of the common web server benchmarks used today is the SPECweb96 benchmark. Like other benchmarks, it is important to consider the details of the benchmark result along with the summary figures. Let's start examining the SPECweb96 result by using one of the published results for Sun's Ultra Enterprise 450. The benchmark results are broken down further as detailed in the following tables.

From the summary table (Table 16-10), you should first notice the availability dates for the hardware and software. As in the other benchmarks, be sure you are comparing currently available software and hardware configurations as the SPEC benchmarks allow data to be released up to six months before scheduled availability of the platform.

Table 16–10 SpecWeb96 Summary

Parameter	Value
Platform	Sun Ultra Enterprise 450

Table 16–10 SpecWeb96 Summary

Parameter	Value
Software	Solaris 2.6/Sun WebServer 1.0
Hardware Availability	August 1997
OS Availability	August 1997
HTTP Software Availability	August 1997
Processors	Four 296 MHz UltraSPARC II
Memory	2048 MB
Disk Controllers	Internal
Disk Subsystem	Two 4.2 GB disks

Table 16–11 Response Time

Throughput (ops/sec)	Response (msec)
300	3.8
600	4.1
900	4.4
1201	4.9
1500	5.3
1800	5.8
2099	6.6
2401	7.8
2700	9.8
2905	21.8

The second table shows the response time at various throughput levels. Note that in this particular benchmark there was a steep rise in the response time to achieve the last few hundred operations/second. In web server performance, it is especially crucial to monitor both throughput and response time.

In most cases, your web server performance is likely to be bottlenecked by network throughput. Table 16-12 shows the network subsystem used to achieve the throughput on this particular test. Since most web sites do not currently have dual 622 Mb/sec ATM links to the Internet, these results may be meaningless if you are trying to determine the performance you will actually receive using a different speed network link.

Table 16–12   Network Subsystem

Parameter	Value
Number of Controllers	2
Number of Networks	2
Type of Network	622 Mb/sec ATM

Finally, lets take a look at the operating system tuning that was required to achieve these results. If the server requires extensive tuning, it may be very difficult to tune the system to your local site's requirements. If only a few tunable parameters are modified, it is much more likely you will be able to use the system in your environment with little modification.

Table 16–13   OS Tuning Parameters

Parameter	Value
tcp:tcp_conn_hash_size	262144
ba:atm_pfifos	0
tcp_close_wait_interval	60
web server: cache_small_file_cache_size	24
web server: cache_large_file_cache_size	1240

Network Infrastructure

For nearly twenty years, network infrastructure remained fairly static. In 1983, for instance, the first Sun-1 workstation shipped with 10 Mbit/second ethernet standard. In 1995, Sun's SPARCstation 20 workstation still shipped with a 10 Mbit/second ethernet interface. FDDI technology extended networking speeds to 100 Mbit/second, but this high speed technology was typically reserved for backbone networks connecting large servers. In November of 1995, Sun started shipping 100 Mbit/second fast ethernet as standard on its UltraSPARC-1 workstations. This trend was quickly endorsed by the volume PC marketplace and in 1997, more than 50% of the ethernet network interface cards shipped by all vendors were capable of running at 100 Mbit/second. In 1998, all the major network equipment vendors are shipping 1,000 Mbit/second gigabit ethernet switches. During the last three years, most network managers have started to change over from a shared hub-based infrastructure to switched networking devices supporting full channel speeds on each point-to-point link.

Disk Storage Architecture

Traditionally, disk storage was attached to a single host. Workstations, Unix servers, and mainframes each had their own directly attached storage. Three types of disk arrays are commonly found on servers:

- JBOD: (Just a Bunch of Disks). Independent disks sharing a common enclosure and host interface controller.

- RAID: (Redundant Array of Inexpensive Disks). Software is used to make otherwise independent disks appear as a single disk. The most popular form of RAID is RAID-5, where data is striped across multiple disks along with additional parity bits to enable the system to recover from any single disk failure. RAID-5 systems are further differentiated depending on whether the RAID software runs on the disk array controller, referred to as hardware RAID-5, or on the host operating system, referred to as software RAID-5.

- Mirrored: Data is written in parallel to two separate disk drives, often used in conjunction with disk striping and also referred to as RAID 0+1. This provides the highest reliability since a mirrored disk array can continue to operate at full performance even in the event of multiple disk failures.

If you wanted to share data between hosts, you typically copied the data to the remote hosts storage system. There was no easy way to share storage devices other than a few dual-ported disk subsystems that might support two hosts at most. This led to the creation of server-centric storage islands as illustrated in Figure 16-3

.

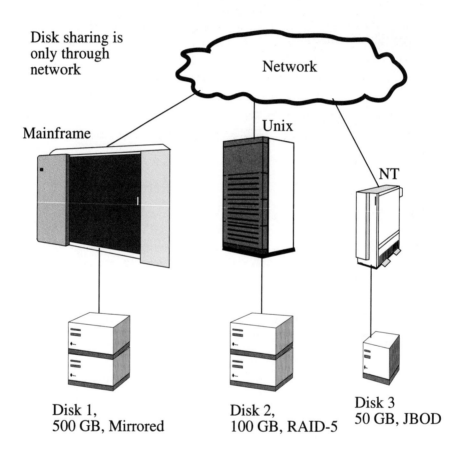

Figure 16–3   Host Attached Storage

The next major architectural change in storage was to build large storage systems, front-ended by intelligent controllers, that could attach to many (several dozen or more) servers. This approach offered the advantage of being able to more easily share your available storage, possibly between heterogeneous hosts. If today you need 500 GB on a mainframe and 100 GB on a Unix server, but next year your plans call for 100 GB on the mainframe and 500 GB on the Unix server, then this is a good approach. Entire companies, such as EMC, have based their building of large storage systems using this exact approach.

However, upon closer examination, such centralized storage approaches do have their drawbacks. The wide diversity of applications supported in a typical enterprise today have vastly different storage requirements. For instance, Online Transaction Processing (OLTP) systems typically perform a large number of small, random writes to a storage device. A disk subsystem optimized for OLTP typically would include a large nonvolatile cache to speed up database synchronous write operations. On the other hand, an Online Analytical Processing (OLAP) application, such as a data warehouse, typically performs large read operations and simply requires the highest disk read throughput available. A large disk system cache might do nothing but slow down the operation of such a system. It is difficult to satisfy both requirements with a single storage subsystem.

Furthermore, as an organization grows, even the largest centralized storage subsystem becomes too small and you have to add another. With large centralized systems there is a high marginal cost to add a new storage subsystem. Eventually, what happens is that you simply extend your original server-centric storage islands to become larger storage-centric islands as shown in Figure 16-4.

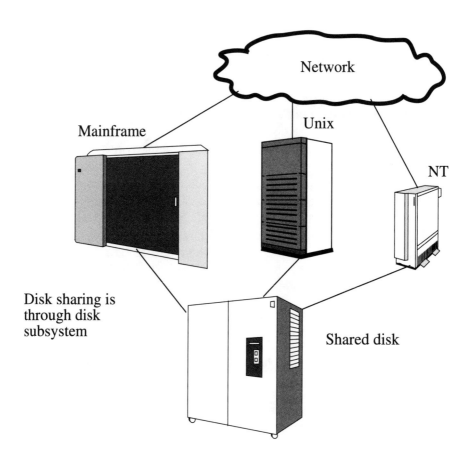

Figure 16–4   Centralized Storage

The best possible solution to the storage problem will likely come from network attached storage subsystems. Such systems are being enabled by the rapid adoption of Fiber Channel Arbitrated Loop (FC-AL) disk drives and associated hubs and switches. Such an architecture allows you to deploy storage networks using the FC-AL standard. This allows you to mix and match various FC-AL storage subsystems depending on the storage requirements of your particular application. Much like in Ethernet networks, the storage devices are shared between all hosts on the FC-AL network. When needed, intelligent controllers can be used to provide nonvolatile write caching, RAID, mirroring, or even orthogonal storage functions such as backup and recovery. The resulting architecture would look much like that shown in Figure 16-5.

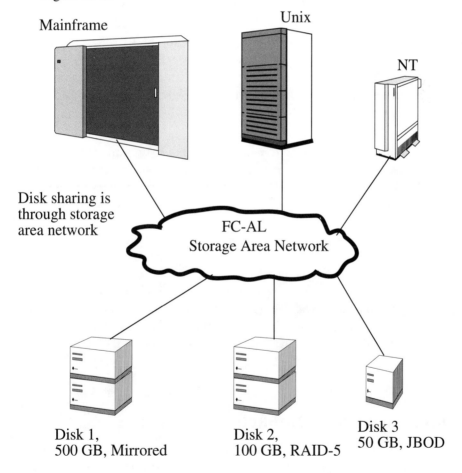

Figure 16–5   Network Attached Storage

Single Function versus General Purpose Servers

A general purpose Unix or NT server, whether in a development or production environment, is capable of performing many different functions at the same time. For instance, a development server might be both an NFS file server, a compile server, and a database server. This flexibility comes at the cost of some complexity. Some hardware vendors have taken the approach of producing single function servers that are optimized for performing a single operation, such as file serving. Examples of such servers are the dedicated file servers produced by both Network Appliance and Auspex. Such a single function server can potentially have easier administration and provide better performance per CPU cycle because it is optimized for a single, or small set of tasks. On the other hand, a general purpose server has the flexibility that it can be used to run multiple applications.

Especially when it comes to file servers, the bottleneck in most systems is the network, not necessarily the file server. Even modest sized general purpose servers provide much more file system capacity than can be utilized by most development networks. This was illustrated in the SPEC benchmarks reviewed earlier in this chapter.

A good compromise to the single function versus general purpose server argument is to use general purpose servers but limit the number of functions hosted on any single server. For instance, consider a development environment with requirements to support database, file, web, e-mail, calendar, and directory services. Rather than use six separate servers, you might want to combine these functions into two servers, one for database, file, and web serving and a second server for e-mail, calendar, and directory services. There are a number of advantages to this approach. First, by limiting the number of functions on any single server, you simplify administration of the server and reduce the potential of application conflict. Secondly, such an approach is more scalable. Finally, the inherent redundancy of multiple servers allows you to implement clustering solutions to provide high levels of continued application availability even when one of the servers has failed.

Architecture Issues Impacting Software Design

Each year, hardware vendors introduce larger and larger servers with ever increasing capacity. At the same time, software places ever increasing demands on systems as more users undertake more compute intensive tasks than ever before. For the last three decades, however, Moore's Law meant that even if a fast enough machine wasn't available when you began a large software development project, one probably would be by the time you finished. Today, while CPU speeds still continue to double annually, server designs are simply running into speed of light constraints as vendors try to place more and more CPUs into the same sized cabinet. At the same time, the growth of corporate Intranets and the Internet have meant that user populations, instead of doubling, often grow by a factor of ten times or more overnight. So how can more complicated software meet these growth requirements as individual CPU speeds only double annually and theoretical constraints limit potential server growth? The answer is various combinations of hardware architectures including SMP (symmetric multiprocessing), MPP (massively parallel processing), NUMA (non-uniform memory architecture), and clustering. Below we introduce the reader to the major server architectures being promoted by hardware vendors today and describe the impact of each on software design.

SMP Architectures

The SMP, or symmetric multiprocessor, hardware architecture is the most popular multiprocessor hardware architecture in use today. The "symmetric" in SMP refers to the symmetric relation between CPUs and memory. SMP designs use a shared memory architecture where all memory is shared equally among all CPUs. An SMP server typically has multiple CPU and memory banks and any CPU can access any memory bank in an equal amount of time, hence the "symmetric" nomenclature. A typical SMP design is shown in Figure 16-6. SMP servers range in size from two CPU Pentium PCs to Sun's 64 CPU Enterprise 10000 (Starfire) server. Because CPU to memory access speeds are constant, no special tuning or software changes are required for multithreaded applications to gain near-linear performance improvements as CPUs and memory are added. Typical multithreaded applications (see Chapter 19) will see over 90% performance improvement for each CPU added in an SMP system. Eventually, however, physical and electrical limitations will limit how many CPUs can be connected with an SMP architecture.

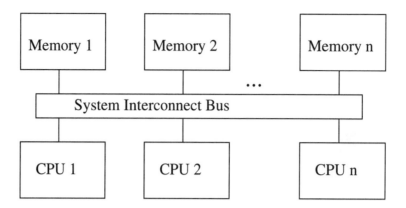

Figure 16–6 SMP Design

In any SMP design, the ultimate hardware limit is the performance of the system interconnect, or backplane. There are two primary measures of backplane performance, throughput and latency. Throughput is determined by the combination of a backplane's clock rate and its width. A 64 bit (8 byte) wide backplane running at 100 MHz has a theoretical bandwidth limitation of 800 Mbytes/second. This bandwidth must be divided between all the CPUs, memory banks, and I/O devices on the backplane. At 100 MHz, typical speed of light propagation delays in silicone limit backplane lengths to about 19 inches, or about the width of a standard computer equipment rack. This in turn limits the number of CPUs that can be mechanically connected to a backplane in a 19 inch rack to about 64, give or take a factor of 2. The second measure of backplane performance is its latency. Backplane latency is measured as the delay from when a backplane transaction is initiated (i.e., a CPU to memory transfer) to when it is completed. Once again, speed of light limitations in a 19 inch backplane lead to best case latencies of several hundred nanoseconds.

Lets examine a real SMP example to illustrate some of these limitations. Sun's Enterprise 6000 SMP processor has a backplane that is clocked at 83 MHz with 500 nanosecond worst case latency. The peak transfer rate of the backplane is 2600 Mbytes/second with a sustained transfer rate of 2500

Mbytes/second. Sun's backplane is packet switched that allows multiple transactions to be outstanding on the backplane at the same time. This leads to the high sustained to peak transfer rate ratio when compared to more traditional circuit-switched backplanes such as VME designs. A single Enterprise 6000 CPU, however, is able to sustain 400 Mbytes/second transfer rates to a single memory bank. Thus, if all CPUs needed to access memory at their peak rate, the backplane could not sustain more than 2500/400 = 6.25 CPUs. In practice, it would be nearly impossible to design a program that drove all CPUs to access memory at peak rates continuously. In addition, each CPU has a local cache of up to 4 Mbytes which further reduces CPU to memory bandwidth. As a result, the Enterprise 6000 shows nearly linear scalability on many benchmarks all the way up to its maximum of 30 CPUs. Other than using a correctly multithreaded application, therefore, there are few software architecture considerations to take into account when using an SMP hardware architecture.

MPP

An MPP, or massively parallel processor, typically has several hundred or more CPUs, each with local memory instead of shared memory. CPUs are interconnected to one or more adjacent processors with high-speed interfaces. A CPU wishing to access the memory of another processor must do so by requesting the access through that processor. Typically, MPP architectures have special message passing interfaces that are tuned to provide high inter-CPU bandwidth. For applications that can be partitioned so that all memory access is local to a given CPU, MPP architectures scale excellently. This, however, requires careful consideration in your software design. MPP architectures are thus well suited to certain classes of scientific problems but generally are not good choices for general commercial computing. A sample MPP architecture is shown in Figure 16-7.

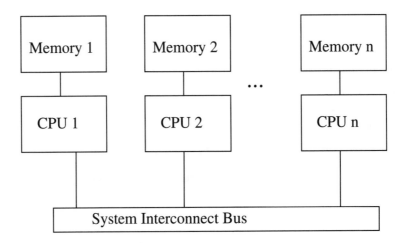

Figure 16–7   MPP Architecture

Another variant of the MPP architecture are so called MPP-SMP hybrid designs such as IBM's SP2. The SP2 is an MPP architecture that consists of multiple RS-6000 nodes with a high speed interconnect between nodes. Each RS-6000 node in the SP2 is actually an SMP architecture with up to 8 CPUs. A much larger class of problems can be partitioned so as to fit within an 8 CPU node and these will scale well on an architecture such as the SP2. If the problem requires more than 8 CPUs, memory access must then take place over the system interconnect, which runs much slower than the Gbyte speed of single backplane systems. If you are planning on using such a hardware architecture, you should pay close attention to your software architecture to allow for application partitioning. If you cannot predict the memory access patterns of you application in advance, such as in a large data warehouse with ad-hoc queries, then you will have a much harder time scaling your application.

NUMA

While a NUMA, or non-uniform memory access, hardware architecture is fundamentally a bad architecture from a computer science perspective, the physical limits of SMP designs are leading all vendors to investigate NUMA or NUMA-like hardware architectures. NUMA architectures were envisioned on the basis that as CPU and backplane speeds increase, physical packaging limitations will limit shared memory SMP designs to fewer and fewer nodes. Even as backplane and cache technologies improve, an SMP system supporting 32 CPUs at 300 MHz in 1998 might only support 24 CPUs at 600 MHz in 2000 and 18 CPUs at 1200 MHz in 2002. To continue building servers whose performance scales with CPU speeds, some sort of NUMA architecture becomes a fundamental requirement by around the year 2000.

An early adopter of NUMA technology is Sequent, with their NUMA-Q architecture. Sequent uses a building block of quad Intel Pentium CPUs, hence the NUMA-Q name. These four CPUs are basically arranged in an SMP architecture. A total of 8 nodes, or 32 CPUs are supported in a fully populated system. The local memory on each node acts as a large cache for the node, and thus a 32 CPU system can be supported with a slower backplane than would be required with a 32 CPU SMP design. The NUMA-Q implementation, for instance, supports a 500 Mbyte/second system bus local to each quad, with a 1.6 Gbyte/second interconnect between quads. Special cache coherency algorithms allow all memory to be accessed in a shared fashion, although there is a significantly higher latency, up to eight times longer, to access memory outside the local quad node. NUMA-Q architecture will thus support standard multithreaded code as long as the application is partitioned such that enough memory accesses are local to each node to offset the higher latency of off-node accesses. Until more industry experience is gained with NUMA architectures and with NUMA cache coherency, the best suggestion is to either partition your software architecture more closely to how you would in an MPP system or to carefully prototype and benchmark your application to ensure anticipated NUMA performance is realized.

Clustering

Another way to extend system performance is to cluster servers together so that, at least at some levels, they appear as one resource to an application.

Compared to MPP or NUMA architectures, clustered nodes typically are more loosely coupled and have lower bandwidth/higher latency interconnects than nodes in an MPP or NUMA system. Since cluster nodes are more loosely coupled, they generally provide greater levels of high availability and fault tolerance than non-clustered systems. One of the earliest examples of a mainstream clustered architecture was the DEC VMS Cluster. Today, the two primary cluster architectures being implemented are the Microsoft "Wolfpack" cluster and Sun's "Full Moon" cluster. Except for specialized parallel database applications such as Oracle's Parallel Database Server, clusters require that the software architecture clearly separate applications running on one cluster node from another. Both vendors, however, have announced roadmaps moving toward a single operating system image running over all nodes in the cluster. When such capability is reached in several years, the differences between MPP, NUMA, SMP, and clusters will be further blurred.

Highly Available and Fault-Tolerant Systems

While closely related, there is a big difference in hardware architecture between highly available and fault-tolerant systems. A highly available system architecture minimizes service interruption, typically by providing IP address failover to a redundant host in the event of a system failure. Fault-tolerant systems employ hardware component redundancy within a host with a system to allow for non-stop operation even in the presence of a hardware failure. Stratus and Tandem are examples of vendors with fault-tolerant system architectures. In their designs, two or more CPUs execute in lock-step fashion, executing the same instructions each memory cycle. Specialized hardware compares the results and disables any CPU or other component upon detection of a failure. Failure recovery time is typically less than a second. Highly available system architectures do not operate redundant hardware in lock-step at the CPU level, but rather provide for redundancy at the system level.

Most highly available architectures rely on IP failover techniques to minimize service interruption in the event of system failures. A typical high availability system architecture is shown in Figure 16-8. This system is based on the concept of physical and logical hosts. In such a system, each logical host typically runs its own set of applications on top of a physical host. A heartbeat signal is exchanged between the two or more physical hosts, usually once a second or more. Should any host stop responding to the heartbeat signal, the assigned failover host will take over control of the failed host's disks and restart all applications on the new host. The host will then takeover the IP address of the failed host and resume responding to client requests. The typical failover time for such a system is on the order of several minutes. The client impact of a failover will depend on whether the application is stateful or stateless. In a stateless application such as NFS file serving or web page serving, clients may see an application timeout, but will otherwise resume normal operation after the failover action completes. Stateful or connection oriented applications will typically require the client application to restart or otherwise reconnect to the server.

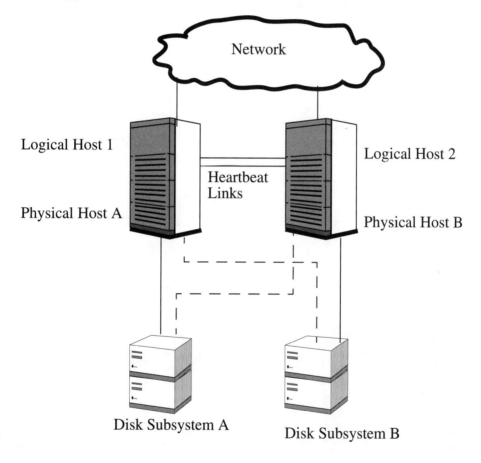

Figure 16–8   Sample High Availability Architecture

Relationship of Hardware to OS and Compiler Design

As illustrated by the many hardware architectures presented in this chapter, hardware, both at the system level and at the CPU level, is becoming ever more complicated. To build a fast overall system it is no longer sufficient to have the fastest CPU. The operating system must also take advantage of the features provided by the CPU and vice versa. That is one of the reasons Microsoft has so many engineers working on-site at Intel and Intel has so many engineers working on-site at Microsoft. Companies that develop their own CPU architectures and operating systems, such as Sun Microsystems with their SPARC CPU architecture and Solaris operating system, also place hardware and OS engineers together on the same project team when designing a new CPU. Compiler writers also work in parallel with CPU and OS designers to make architecture tradeoffs at design time. For instance, instruction reordering was a new CPU optimization technique that SPARC designers considered adding to the UltraSPARC 1 CPU. This feature ended up being left out of the UltraSPARC 1, at the benefit of other functionality, when compiler writers convinced the hardware team they could more efficiently reorder instructions in the compiler. As system architectures continue to get more complicated, you should consider the potential performance improvement of selecting vendors who have a close relationship among their product's hardware, OS, and compiler design teams.

17

Component-Based Software Development

Every software developer knows that it is easier to write ten 100 line programs than to write a single 1,000 line program. Furthermore, any software development manager knows it is easier to manage the development of ten 100 line programs than a single 1,000 line program. Of course the problem is that most stand-alone software programs being written today require much more than 100 or even 1,000 lines of code to implement their required functionality. Breaking a monolithic 1,000 line program into ten 100 line programs, however, can be a slow, expensive task. If fact, if you were to try and break a typical 1,000 line C or FORTRAN program into ten parts, each part would end up being significantly larger than 100 lines. The extra code would be required to coordinate sharing of control and data between the different programs. Component-based software development attempts to address this problem by taking the reverse approach. Rather than build large monolithic applications, developers build a portable, reusable code base of small components.

A component is simply a reusable software object packaged in some sort binary, class, library, or similar form. Components are then combined, along with new code, to create a new application. Usually, components are used in some sort of component framework, such as ActiveX or JavaBeans, which specifies the interfaces each component should include to allow builder tools to access and modify the component in a standard way.

261

There are many business advantages to be gained by using a component-based software development methodology. First, because you can start with a library of pre-built components, it becomes simpler and quicker to attack new market opportunities. In large development organizations, components will bring new opportunities for joint development, as components facilitate the sharing and reuse of code. Components also create an opportunity for developers to sell smaller packages of software, or component libraries.

If you are going to facilitate the building of large programs out of small components, you need a framework to work in. A component framework provides a standard way of defining and manipulating components as well as standard ways of communicating between components when they are combined together. There are two popular component frameworks in use today, Java-Beans and ActiveX. We start this chapter by discussing the history of components that led to these two models. The JavaBeans component model is then used to further illustrate the concepts of component-based software development.

The History of Components

Component-based software development began long before the popularity of JavaBeans and ActiveX. Apple is generally credited with the first commercial implementation of component-based software with its Macintosh "Publish and Subscribe" technology developed in the early 1990s. Publish and Subscribe was Apple's technology for embedding one component, such as a spreadsheet, into another, such as a word processor document. Several years later, Microsoft released their own version of this technology, dubbed Object Linking and Embedding, or OLE. OLE was built on top of Microsoft's Common Object Model, or COM. COM was originally intended to be an object model for stand-alone PCs and did not incorporate any support for networking between hosts. As Microsoft started to support more and more networking, it extended the basic COM model to a distributed one, called DCOM. Today, OLE and DCOM are both part of the broader ActiveX family of Microsoft technologies. Additional information on DCOM, including its relationship to CORBA, is provided in Chapter 21.

One limitation of ActiveX is that today it is generally only available on Microsoft Windows platforms. JavaBeans, by contrast, is a component technology based on the Java language. JavaBeans extends Java's write-once run-anywhere technology to create a true cross-platform component model.

JavaBeans components can be incorporated into either applets or stand-alone applications. While regular JavaBeans can be used to build server-side applications, many such programs typically require additional functionality including persistence and a notion of transactions. The JavaBeans API, therefore, has been extended with the Enterprise JavaBeans API. Enterprise JavaBeans includes persistance, transactions, and other functionality common to many server-side applications. Regardless which component model you choose, a number of vendors, including Microsoft and Sun, have two way bridges that allow JavaBeans components to be used in ActiveX frameworks and vice versa.

Components versus Object-Oriented Technology

Components do not necessarily have to be object-oriented and object-oriented software may be written without any components. Lets step back and examine the structure of a program to see how this can be true.

Early applications often consisted of a single large function. FORTRAN programmers were especially notorious for writing huge single-function programs whose control flow consisted entirely of goto statements and the occasional if statement. Such programs were fondly referred to as spaghetti code because if you drew lines following the goto statements to their target, the result would look much like a tangled bowl of spaghetti. As the science of computer programming evolved, structured programming concepts were introduced. Languages like C contain goto statements mainly for compatibility with FORTRAN and most C programming and style guides strongly discourage their use. As object-oriented technologies became more popular, new languages such as C++ and Java were developed to simplify development of object-oriented software.

An object-oriented C++ program, however, can be just as monolithic as a non object-oriented C program. Object-orientation does not imply components. Going in the other direction, components are more likely to be object-oriented than not. JavaBeans components are, by definition, written in Java and therefore bear some flavor of object-orientation. ActiveX components can be developed in several languages, including Java, C++, and Visual Basic for which Microsoft has developed ActiveX bindings. In either case, the use of an object-oriented language does not guarantee that good object-oriented design methods were used to create the application. What all this emphasizes is that there is no substitute for good design. Take some programmers who don't understand object-oriented technology and ask them to develop an application with JavaBeans, and you will probably still get a monolithic application using JavaBeans as little more than replacements for functions in a structured programming language. Start with a good object-oriented architect who understands JavaBeans and can partition a problem into its basic components and object classes, and the end result will be much more likely to turn out as intended.

Role of Visual Programming in Component Software

Visual programming is the use of graphical development tools to generate code. Traditionally, graphical development tools have been used primarily to generate the user interface of an application. The application logic still needs to be developed by hand. While a JavaBean may certainly implement a user interface component, say a 3 D bar chart, it may just as well implement a scientific function like a fast fourier transform. Visual development tools that support JavaBeans, such as Imprise's JBuilder, Sun's Java Workshop, and Symantec's Visual Cafe (see Chapter 15 for more info on these tools), allow you to graphically manipulate JavaBeans, modify their parameters, and combine them into new JavaBeans.

Component Development Using JavaBeans

JavaBeans is a platform-neutral, component architecture for the Java application environment. The JavaBeans specification defines a set of standard component software APIs for the Java platform. The specification was developed by Sun with a number of leading industry partners and was then refined based on broad general input from developers, customers, and end users during a public review period. While the interactive development tools mentioned above support JavaBeans development, you do not need one of these tools to start developing your own JavaBeans. All you need to write a JavaBean is the Beans Development Kit (BDK) and the Java Development Kit (JDK, version 1.1 or higher). Both the BDK and JDK are available for free download from Sun's Java web site at http://java.sun.com.

A JavaBeans component can be part of both Java applets and Java applications. Because JavaBeans is part of the core JDK 1.1 capability, any JDK 1.1 compliant browser or tool implicitly supports JavaBeans. JavaBean components are generally referred to simply as "Beans." Development tools that support beans usually have some sort of palette or toolbox that lets you view the beans in a particular directory or set. Using the Introspection capability defined in the JavaBeans API, the builder tool can look inside beans and learn their characteristics and parameters. This allows the builder tool to create customization forms for each bean. For instance, a bar chart bean might allow you to set the number of bars and their color. This information would be displayed on the bean's customization form by the builder tool for the developer to edit.

Besides learning about the parameters of a bean that can be modified, Introspection also determines the methods exported and the events generated or handled by a bean. Introspection relies on the core Java reflection API to discover these bean features. This is possible based in part on the design patterns and naming conventions followed by beans. For instance, the "get" preface to a method always specifies an exported parameter and the "set" preface to a method always specifies a settable parameter. In addition to naming conventions, beans can have a related bean information class that defines parameter, method, and event information.

The bean features exposed during introspection can be customized by the developer using standard forms, called property sheets, that are generated by builder tools. Beans with more complicated features may define their own more sophisticated bean customizers.

Beans use events to communicate with other beans. A bean that wants to receive events registers its interest with the bean that generates the event. Builder tools can examine a bean and determine which events that bean can send and which it can receive. Persistence enables beans to save their state, and restore that state later. JavaBeans uses Java Object Serialization to support persistence.

18

Performance Optimization Techniques

No matter how fast systems become, many software applications continue to exceed the performance capabilities of the system they are hosted on at some point during their life cycle. There are two possible solutions to this problem. One is to purchase additional hardware. The other is to optimize the software. Each method has cost and schedule implications. Often, both additional hardware purchases and software optimizations are required. This chapter provides some general performance optimization guidelines that are applicable no matter which vendor's hardware or OS you are using. The examples presented, however, are specific to Sun's Solaris operating environment.

How Much Performance Do You Need?

Performance of software applications can often be very subjective. An application that provides a two second response may be sufficiently fast to meet all driving business requirements of the task at hand. In addition, the application may be meeting all user expectations, as subjective as they might be. However, place a user in front of the same exact system with a one second response time and after several days any effort to use the slower system will probably be rated as unacceptable. In both cases, all business requirements, except perhaps subjective end user ratings, are equally met. The question is, do you now need to provide one second response time for all users?

As in the above example, the most important step to identifying performance problems is to have a well-defined benchmark of system performance to use as a reference. Given such a benchmark, future perceived performance problems can be compared against the benchmark metric to help determine if they are truly problems or changes in performance, versus subjective differences. Once you determine there truly is a performance problem, the next step is to identify the bottlenecks.

How to Identify Bottlenecks

Given a high enough load, any software application will start to exhaust some hardware capacity of the system. Hardware bottlenecks can generally be categorized as CPU, memory, disk, or network capacity limits. Lets examine each of these further, starting with the most common bottlenecks.

Disk Bottlenecks

Relatively speaking, disk I/O is the most overused system resource. Not only will an application read and write data from the disk, so to will the operating system. All modern operating systems employ "virtual memory" techniques. Virtual memory works by moving data from physical memory to a special disk area reserved for use as "virtual memory," also called swap space. Thus many disk bottlenecks may actually be memory bottlenecks in disguise. These will be saved for later discussion. The best way to architect your software application with respect to disk sizing is to recognize the performance and capacity attributes of disks and allow for the correct amount of each.

Every disk drive has a raw data capacity. Calculating capacity is generally the easiest part of disk sizing. However, remember that a 9 Gbyte disk may not give you 9 Gbytes of usable storage. For starters, the operating system may reserve up to 10% of a disk drive for file system use. Secondly, a RAID file system layout will tack on another 20% to 100% overhead depending on the type of striping, parity, or mirroring used.

Every disk drive also has a throughput capacity and is connected to a controller with its own throughput capacity. Consider a modern disk drive with a

5 Mbyte/second throughput. An Ultra-SCSI controller is rated at 40 Mbytes a second and can physically connect up to 15 disk drives. A 40 Mbyte/second controller, obviously, cannot handle 15*5 = 75 Mbytes/second, which is what would be generated by 15 drives all running at full throughput. If your application is data intensive and requires high throughput, then you need to closely consider the number and type of both disk drives and controllers.

Another factor limiting disk performance is the number of random I/O operations a disk can perform per second. This is controlled by a combination of the disk platter RPM speed and the disk read/write head seek time. Applications such as online transaction processing typically stress a disk's I/O operations per second capacity long before total storage capacity or throughput capacity are reached.

While performance attributes of SCSI disk drives is fairly well understood, newer technologies such as FC-AL (fiber channel arbitrated loop) introduce their own unique performance variables into the equation. For instance, one of the reasons for implementing FC-AL technology is that the throughput is more than twice as fast (100 Mbyte/second) than Ultra-SCSI. Another benefit of FC-AL technology is that the fiber channel loops are not limited to Ultra-SCSI's 15 drives. FC-AL hubs and switches allow even greater numbers of drives to be connected in various combinations. It very quickly becomes simple to build disk subsystems that are so complex they are very difficult to diagnose once a performance problem arises.

In sizing disk requirements for your application, you therefore need to consider total storage capacity requirements, total throughput requirements, and total I/O operation capacity. Generally speaking, the larger a disk the greater its cost per I/O operation and the smaller a disk the greater its cost per megabyte of capacity. You will need to consider both when selecting the disk subsystem for your application.

CPU Bottlenecks

In purely CPU-intensive applications, CPU bottlenecks are easy to identify. On larger multiprocessor systems, however, CPU bottlenecks may not always be as readily identifiable. Most operating systems further break down CPU time into user application time, operating system time, wait time, and idle time. If a system is routinely spending more than 20% of its time executing the operating system, there may very well be another software bottleneck. On a multiprocessor system this will typically be a result of resource contention issues caused by multithreaded code. Similarly, large amounts of wait time are probably the result of a multithreading bottleneck either in an application or in the operating system. As opposed to idle time when the CPU has no jobs to run, wait time is measured as the time when a CPU has jobs to run but cannot run any because it is waiting for a shared resource that is currently allocated by another CPU. Chapter 19 on multithreading further explains these kinds of bottlenecks.

Memory Bottlenecks

Memory bottlenecks are often the hardest local problems to detect. One reason is because modern virtual memory systems will use memory as a cache and will keep data in memory as long as possible. Simply monitoring how much free memory a system has will tell you very little about its memory utilization. To correctly determine if a system has enough memory requires at least a basic understanding of the underlying operating system's virtual memory, paging, and swapping algorithms.

Network Bottlenecks

In today's network-centric environments, a system's network interface can easily be a cause of application performance issues. Consider that on most platforms, a single CPU can drive a 100 Mbit/sec network interface card at full speed. On larger, multi-CPU systems, therefore, either faster interfaces or more interfaces are often required. Assuming your network infrastructure can handle it, a faster network interface card such as gigabit ethernet or OC-12 (622 Mbit/sec) ATM may solve a network bottleneck. However, many corporate networks do not yet support such standards. Another approach is to spread the network load out among multiple network interface cards. This often works well on server applications that are serving multiple clients. There are two basic ways to utilize multiple network interface cards in a single server. The first method is simply to use subnetting in your network and connect a single network interface card to each subnet. If you need all the network capacity between hosts on a single network, trunking is another solution. In trunking, multiple network interface cards are assigned a single IP address and the operating system handles the interleaving of data between network interface cards. Trunking is also referred to as "fast ether channel" technology by Cisco.

19

Multithreaded Programming

As discussed in Chapter 16, a number of different multiprocessor hardware platforms are in widespread production use today. Traditional software design, however, is based on processes containing a single set of instructions designed to execute in a serial order. Such so-called single-threaded software cannot take advantage of more than one CPU at a time to increase execution speed and performance. By contrast, multithreaded code is designed to contain multiple sequences of instructions that can execute in parallel. Besides using multiprocessors more efficiently to increase application performance, multithreading can also lead to improved program structure when correctly implemented. For example, system-oriented tasks like event handling, garbage collection, rendering, and animation updates can be cleanly factored into separate threads, away from your core application logic. This chapter introduces you to multithreading concepts and discusses how to design and debug multithreaded programs. The chapter finishes by providing a set of guidelines for multithreaded programming.

Multithreading Defined

There are at least two ways to take advantage of more than one CPU in a multiprocessor system. The first way is to run multiple applications, or multiple copies of the same application. Often, however, one desires to utilize a multiprocessor system to increase the performance of a single application, such as a DBMS or a large scientific program. To do so requires that the program itself be multithreaded, allowing it to be broken up into multiple sequences of instructions that can execute in parallel.

A software developer has three basic options to create a multithreaded program. First, an automatic parallelizing compiler can be used with existing non-threaded source code. Automatic parallelizing works best with simply structured languages such as FORTRAN and with scientific code. Scientific code tends to have large numbers of loops with many iterations and no data dependencies. Such code can be easily multithreaded by a compiler. For instance, consider the code segment:

```
void makeSums()
{

    int i;
    double a[100], b[100], c[100];
    double sum1[100], sum2[100];

    /* initialize a, b, and c arrays */
    ...

    for (i = 0; i < 100; i++){

        sum1[i] = a[i] + b[i];
        sum2[i] = b[i] + c[i];

    }

}
```

Assuming each addition takes one time unit to execute, the above code could execute in 200 time units. Since there are no data dependencies in this code, it could be re-written by a compiler into two sub-functions or threads that could execute independently as follows:

```
/* global variables */
double a[100], b[100], c[100];
double sum1[100], sum2[100];

void makeSums()
{
    /* initialize a, b, and c arrays */
    ...

    thread_create(thread1);
    thread_create(thread2);

}


void thread1()
    int i;

    for (i = 0; i < 100; i++){
        sum1[i] = a[i] + b[i];
    }

}

/* Function thread2 */
void thread2()
{
    int i;

    for (i = 0; i < 100; i++){
        sum2[i] = b[i] + c[i];
    }

}
```

Assume there are two CPUs available to execute the code. The program will now execute in 100 time units, plus any overhead needed to start up the threads.

The second way a developer can create multithreaded code is to insert compiler directives into the source code, manually identifying which loops and other sections of code are candidates for multithreading. This can be useful if the code is structured such that the compiler cannot automatically parallelize the code.

The third method, which generally has the highest performance payback, is to design multithreaded code. As with many of the concepts presented in this book, multithreading has the greatest advantage if it is considered early in the design stage versus trying to retrofit threads into a non-concurrent program.

Two important concepts to understand when discussing multithreading code are those of concurrency and parallelism. Concurrency exists when at least two threads are in progress at the same time. This may occur even in a single CPU system. For instance, one thread might be accepting input from the user interface while another thread is updating the database and waiting for a response from the database server. Because of concurrency, multithreaded code often executes faster even on single CPU systems. Parallelism arises when at least two threads are executing at the same time on a multi-CPU system. On a multi-CPU system, a multithreaded program can take advantage of both concurrency and multithreading.

The Posix multithreading standard defines a two-level threads model as illustrated in Figure 19-1. User level (also called application level) threads are managed by the threads library and operate in user address space rather than kernel (OS) address space. Threads that execute kernel code and system calls are referred to as lightweight processes. The operating system maps user level threads to lightweight processes at execution time. Threads can be either bound or unbound. A bound thread is permanently attached to a lightweight process. An unbound thread attaches and detaches itself from a lightweight process in the operating system's lightweight process pool as necessary. Unbound threads use fewer dedicated OS resources and have a quicker start up time as they attach to an existing lightweight process. Bound threads have a longer start up time and use more OS resources, especially if a new lightweight process must be created for the bound thread. Once initialized, however, a bound thread can provide quicker response and thus may be appropriate for a time sensitive or realtime application. As shown in Table 19-1, creating both bound and unbound threads is significantly faster than creating a new process.

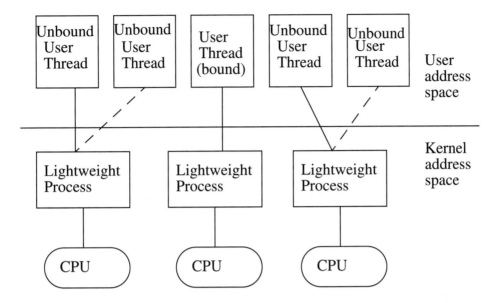

Figure 19–1   Posix Two-Level Threads Model

Table 19–1   Thread Creation Times, Solaris 2.6, 200 MHz Ultra 1

Operation	Time (Milliseconds)	Ratio
Create unbound thread	100	1
Create unbound thread	150	1.5
Create bound thread and new LWP	400	4.0
Create new process with fork()	5000	50

Synchronization Objects

There are four basic synchronization mechanisms supported by Posix threads and most other threading models. These are the mutual exclusion lock, condition variables, semaphores, and reader/writer locks. A brief discussion of each synchronization object and where you might want to use them follows. The function calls presented are all from the Solaris threads library. Most Posix based multithreading libraries will use the identical, or at least very similar, functions.

The most basic synchronization primitive for multithreaded programming is the mutual exclusion lock. This is the most efficient mechanism in terms of both memory utilization and execution time. A mutual exclusion lock is used to serialize access to a resource but before using it you must initialize it with the

```
mutex_init()
```

function. When a thread is ready to access a critical section, you use the

```
mutex_lock()
```

function to acquire the lock. This blocks the thread if the mutex is already locked by another process. To avoid "spinning" on a locked mutex, you can also test the state of a mutex with the

```
mutex_trylock()
```

call. After completing the critical section, you must call

```
mutex_unlock()
```

to release the lock. Finally, when you will no longer need the mutex lock you should call

```
mutex_destroy()
```

to free the lock.

When you are using multiple mutex locks, one of the things you need to avoid is the potential for deadlock. Deadlock occurs when two threads end up waiting for each other to release a lock. Here is a simple example of a deadlock situation.

```
void thread1()
{
    mutex_lock(m1)
    /* use resource m1 */
    ...
        mutex_lock(m2)
        /* use resources m1 and m2 */
        ...
        mutex_unlock(m2)

    mutex_unlock(m1)
}
```

```
void thread2()
{
    mutex_lock(m2)
    /* use resource 2 */
    ...
        mutex_lock(m1)
        /* use resources m1 and m2 */
        ...
        mutex_unlock(m1)

    mutex_unlock(m2)
}
```

In the above example, if thread 1 acquires the mutex lock m1, then thread 2 acquires the mutex lock m2 before thread 1 does, each thread will block, waiting for the other mutex lock to be released. Thread 1 will not release lock m1 until it can acquire lock m2. Thread 2 will not release lock m2 until it can acquire lock m1. In this case, we have a deadlock and neither thread will ever complete.

The simplest way to avoid this type of deadlock is to make sure threads locking multiple mutexes always do so in the same order. This technique is called lock hierarchies. The Unix lock_lint tool can be used to detect deadlocks of this kind. If it is not possible to use lock hierarchies, then the programmer must use the mutex_trylock() function to detect a possible deadlock and manually release any locks it holds and retry the operation.

The next most efficient synchronization primitive is the condition variable. A condition variable is used to block on a change of state. You use a condition lock to block threads until a particular condition is true. Commonly, condition variables are used to implement monitors. Before using a condition lock, you must first initialize it with the

cond_init()

call. Afterwards, a call to

cond_wait()

will block until the specified condition is true. You use the

cond_signal()

call to unblock a specific thread. Other condition variable calls include

cond_timedwait()

to block until a specified event,

cond_broadcast()

to unblock all threads and

```
cond_destroy()
```

to destroy a condition variable when you are finished with it.

Another synchronization object is the semaphore. Semaphores use more memory than condition variables, however, they are easier to use in many instances. Conceptually, a semaphore is a non-negative integer count. Semaphores are typically used to coordinate access to resources, with the semaphore count initialized to the number of free resources. Threads increment the count as resources are added and decrement it as they are removed. When the semaphore count reaches 0, it indicates that no more resources are available. A semaphore is initialized with:

```
sema_init()
```

You increment a semaphore with

```
sema_post()
```

and decrement it with

```
sema_trywait()
```

Once you are done using a semaphore, you destroy it with

```
sema_destroy()
```

The most complex thread synchronization mechanism is the reader/writer lock. A reader/writer lock is useful for resources whose contents are searched more often than they are changed. A reader/writer lock allows simultaneous read access by many threads while restricting write access to only one thread at a time.

A reader/writer lock is initialized with the

```
rwlock_init()
```

call. A thread acquires a read lock with the

```
rw_rdlock()
```

call. This call will succeed as long as the lock is not already being held by a writer thread using the

```
rw_wrlock()
```

call. When any thread holds the lock for reading, other threads can also acquire the lock for reading but must wait to acquire the lock for writing. Writer starvation is avoided because once a thread is waiting on a write lock, no further read locks will succeed until the write lock has been successfully acquired and released.

To unlock either a read or write lock, the

```
rw_unlock()
```

call is used. Once a programmer is completely finished using a reader/writer lock, it should be destroyed with

```
rwlock_destroy()
```

20

Developing for the Web

The widespread deployment of web browsers from corporate PCs to home computers to whole new classes of portable devices such as set-top boxes and PDAs has not failed to catch the attention of software developers. While the "point and click" user interface of web browsers provides a new standard for ease of use, the back-end systems behind those web pages can be more complicated than ever. This chapter describes the basic operation of web browsers and servers and the use of Java applets to add real application functionality to web pages. Several different techniques for web server development, including CGI programming and Java applets, are then discussed.

Web Browsers and Servers

Web browsers were originally developed to display static text and graphics stored on servers. The web browser to web server relationship is similar to many other types of client-server systems, although no other system has ever seen such universal standardization. The most common text formatting standard used on the web is HTML, the HyperText Markup Language. The basic structure of a HTML document is text with formatting commands denoted between the <> brackets. For instance, a simple HTML page would be:

281

```
<html>
<head>
<title> A Sample Page </title>
</head>
<body>
This is my first web page.
</body>
</html>
```

The web page above contains two main parts, a header section and a body section. In the header section is a title. The title is displayed in the top window header by most web browsers. The body contains the actual text of the page. The above file would then be stored in the document directory of a web server.

Basic communication between a web browser and a web server is done using HTTP, the HyperText Transfer Protocol. A web user specifies the web page to load by entering a URL, or Universal Resource Locator into the Location field of web browser. For instance, to access the Sun Microsystems home page, you would enter the URL:

```
http://sun.com
```

During the first few years of widespread web usage, many companies adopted the www.company-name.com convention. Recently, many companies have re-programmed their DNS service to allow their home page to be referenced without the "www" preface, as shown in the URL for Sun's home page above.

A complete URL follows the following syntax:

```
protocol://server name:port number/directory/subdirectory/
filename
```

This is much more complicated than the typical URL of the form "sun.com" or "www.sun.com" common to most people. This is because much of the URL information defaults to set values if not specified. Some default values include:

- protocol: http:
- port number: 80

- directory/subdirectory/filename: default provided by server when not specified, typically defaulting to the file "index.html" in the top level web server document directory

Let's examine exactly what happens when you type in a URL such as "sun.com" into your web browser. First of all, your browser defaults the protocol type to "http" if no protocol was specified. The browser then attempts to make an HTTP connection to the host sun.com. This will involve looking up the actual IP address of the sun.com hostname. The IP address lookup will typically involve a Domain Name Server (DNS) transaction, or at least a name lookup to some system that ultimately is fed by a DNS server. The requested file, in this case blank, is passed to the web server as part of the HTTP request.

The web server accepts the HTTP connection and returns the text of the specified file. If no file is requested, the default "home page" file of the web server is returned. The web browser then receives the HTML file and formats it for display.

The original developers of the HTTP and HTML protocols had cross-platform portability in mind as a key requirement. Because of this, they did not attempt to specify any image format into HTML. Instead, they included in HTML the ability to include arbitrary image types using the "img" tag. An example of a how this is done is shown below.

```
<html>
<head>
<title> Sample Page With Graphics </title>
<body>
This page includes a sample graphic image below.
<img src="my-picture.jpg">
</body>
</html>
```

The special <img> tag tells the web browser that besides the text, a separate image file needs to be retrieved and displayed on the page. The image file type is identified by the.jpg extension. Most web browsers, regardless of platform, understand how to display at least gif and jpeg image files.

Proxy Web Servers

The HTTP protocol originally required a direct TCP/IP connection between the web browser and the web server. This architecture did not work well with many corporate network architectures that employed firewalls between their internal and external networks. This led to the development of proxy web servers. Most web browsers allow the user to specify an optional proxy server. A proxy server is simply an intermediate server that acts as a relay between client browsers on an internal network and external web servers as shown in Figure 20-1.

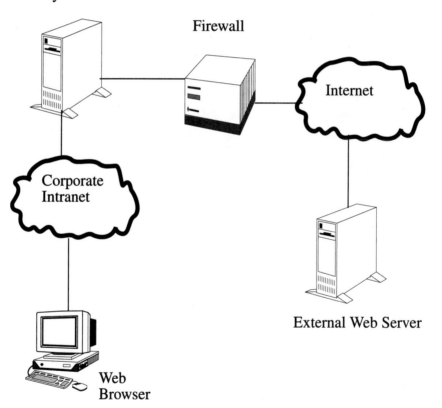

Figure 20–1 Proxy Web Server Architecture

Such a connection is more secure because a direct TCP/IP connection is never made between the client browser and the web server. All connections are "proxied" by the proxy server. Most proxy servers also have a caching capability. A caching server can greatly reduce your required bandwidth. Lets say your company does not use any proxy server and in a given day 100 users download the sun.com home page, which is about 50,000 bytes. That would be a total of 5 Mbytes of data transferred. A caching proxy server would store the sun.com home page the first time it was accessed and serve subsequent requests out of this local cache until such time as the sun.com page was updated. The total bandwidth required is now reduced to 50,000 bytes, plus any overhead to check that the page had not been updated, typically just a few bytes per access. Other functions, such as content filtering, are often also implemented in proxy servers because they provide a convenient single point of control versus the difficulty of trying to control every client browser.

CGI Programming

As web usage expanded, developers began wanting to use web browsers to do more than simply display static text and graphics. The web provided the perfect platform for accessing other applications on the web server from the browser interface. Just like browser developers did not want to create new image types for HTML, web server developers did not want to embed any and all possible server side functionality into the web server. For instance, many excellent database programs existed prior to the web and no one saw any need to add this functionality to web server programs. Thus CGI, the Common Gateway Interface, was born. CGI specifies a mechanism for a web page to invoke an arbitrary program on the web server. A common use of this is to use a form interface to input data into a database. Figure 20-2 looks at how this is done.

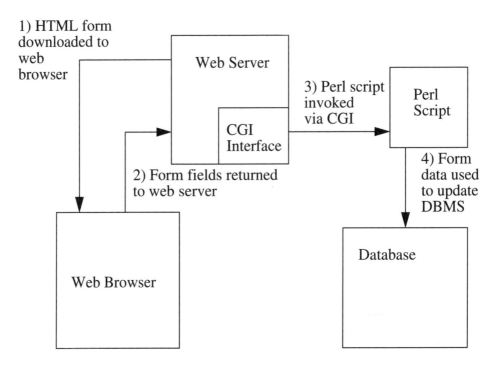

1) HTML form downloaded to web browser

Web Server

3) Perl script invoked via CGI

Perl Script

CGI Interface

2) Form fields returned to web server

4) Form data used to update DBMS

Web Browser

Database

Figure 20–2 Web Form to Database via CGI

CGI programs can be written in any language. The Perl scripting language and C are probably the two most popular CGI programming languages. When the user enters the "submit" button on the form, the information contained in the form is passed, via HTTP, to the web server, along with the name of the CGI program to execute. The web server then starts up a new process to execute the specified program (a Perl script, in the example figure) and passes the form data to the program. The Perl script performs any necessary field validity checking or other preprocessing and then opens up a SQL connection to the database. The Perl program can then provide any desired response to the user by returning an HTML stream, through the web server, to the web browser.

CGI programming was a simple second generation mechanism for adding new functionality to web-based programs and for integrating back-end databases or other existing programs. This simplicity, however, comes with a performance penalty. CGI usually requires a new process to be spawned for each task to be performed. Especially when handling hundreds or thousands of tasks a minute, this becomes inefficient. Initially, these inefficiencies were handled by web server vendors who each developed their own proprietary APIs. Today, the Java Servlet API provides a common mechanism for expanding web server functionality via new Java applications, called Servlets.

Java Applets

Java applets are small Java applications that are downloaded and executed by a web browser. One common use of Java applets is to perform client-side forms processing. Consider the form parsing performed by the Perl script in the above CGI example. If the script finds an error in the form, it must then return the error message to the user. By writing the form input processing in Java and executing it directly in the web browser, user input errors can be identified as they are made, leading to much simpler user interaction and interface design. The use of Java applications is, of course, not at all limited to client-side programming. Today, over fifty percent of the commercial Java programming being done is for server-side applications. Much like a Java applet executes in the web browser, modern web servers include the functionality to execute Java servlets, another type of small Java application. Many other server side applications are also being developed using the Enterprise JavaBeans component technology.

Enterprise JavaBeans

Enterprise JavaBeans (EJB) is a server-side distributed component model for the Java platform. EJB is a different technology from JavaBeans. Building distributed enterprise applications is difficult and introduces new challenges not present in many client-side applications. Developers need to support transactions, resource pooling, security, threading, persistence, remote access, and lifecycle issues. This results in system programming at the expense of business logic. With EJB, developers can focus on the business logic of applications without having to become specialists in system programming.

There are four parts to an EJB component:

1. home interface - how the component is found or created

2. remote interface - how the component is called

3. deployment descriptor - how the component is controlled

4. EJB class - business logic to execute

An EJB server provides the "plumbing" required to make an EJB component work, including:

1. remote access

2. transaction management

3. authentication and authorization

4. resource pooling

5. concurrent service for multiple clients

6. clustering and high availability

There are currently two lifecycle models defined by EJB:

1. session EJB, based on a client session which can be either

- stateless

- stateful

2. entity EJB, based on a persistent data store, which can have either

- bean managed state

- server managed state

Work is also underway to define a message driven EJB model for use in message-based application architectures. An example of how EJB would be used in a web-centric architecture is shown in Figure 20-3. A user would access an application is this environment through a standard web browser. The web browser might contain either plain HTML, or an applet built with Java-Beans. The web browser would communicate with a web server using the HTTP protocol. The web server would use either Java Server Pages (JSP) or Java servlets to dynamically generate HTML for the browser and then communicate with an EJB on the application server via RMI/IIOP. The EJB would then execute the business logic of the application, fetching or storing data in a back-end DBMS via JDBC.

Other Java Enterprise APIs

Enterprise JavaBeans will most often be deployed in conjunction with one or more Java Enterprise APIs including Java Servlets, Java Server Pages (JSP), Java Messaging Service (JMS), and Java Naming and Directory (JNDI). These APIs are briefly described below.

Java Servlet API

The Java Servlet API defines a consistent mechanism for extending the functionality of a web server with Java application code. The easiest way to describe Java Servlets is as applets that run on a web server, without a user interface. Several popular web servers, including servers from Netscape and Sun now implement the Java servlet API.

JavaServer Pages (JSP)

JavaServer Pages defines a facility for server-side scripting. By allowing access to server-side components from web pages, JSP separates the presentation of dynamic content from the generation of that content. Several popular web servers, including servers from Netscape and Sun, now implement JavaServer Pages.

Java Messaging Service (JMS) API

The Java Messaging Service provides a flexible and reliable messaging service implemented in Java. With JMS, developers can implement multiple messaging schemes requiring:

- publish and subscribe metaphors
- reliable queues
- guaranteed deliver

Java Naming and Directory (JNDI) API

The Java Naming and Directory API provides Java applications with a unified directory interface allowing access to multiple naming and directory services, including:

- LDAP
- NIS
- NIS+
- DNS
- file system naming

By using the JNDI interface, Java developers do not tie their applications to any single directory service. Instead, JNDI-enabled applications are portable, with seamless connectivity to a wide variety of heterogeneous enterprise naming and directory services.

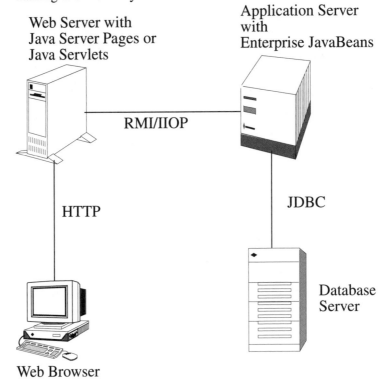

Web Server with
Java Server Pages or
Java Servlets

Application Server
with
Enterprise JavaBeans

RMI/IIOP

JDBC

HTTP

Database
Server

Web Browser

Figure 20–3   Example EJB Architecture

Distributed Applications with CORBA, RMI, and DCOM

For years, software developers have struggled to write distributed applications that take advantage of computing resources independent of their physical location in a network. Unlike client-server applications connecting a single server and a single client, truly distributed applications may utilize dozens of servers spread across a network to deliver a business computing function to a client desktop. Traditionally, writing distributed applications in a heterogeneous environment meant hand coding all the required inter-process communications interfaces, server start up routines, naming services, and other required support facilities. Couple these difficulties with the object-oriented paradigm usually used for distributed applications and you have yourself a very difficult problem indeed.

Luckily for developers, the need for standardized distributed object-oriented application development models drove the development of standards. The Object Management Group (OMG), a consortium of over 800 companies representing the entire spectrum of the computer industry, is today the leading standards body in the distributed objects arena. The Common Object Request Broker Architecture (CORBA) standard developed by the Object Management Group is perhaps one of the most important and all-encompassing standards in the industry for distributed objects. Of course no area in the software industry has a single standard and the distributed object area is no exception. The primary competing object model is Microsoft's Distributed Component Object Model (DCOM). While this chapter will focus on introducing the reader to developing distributed applications with CORBA, it does include a section comparing CORBA with DCOM.

While CORBA is a relatively new and rapidly evolving technology, its origins date back to the early 1990s and predates newer computing models such as the World-Wide Web. Rather than replace CORBA, however, the web has served as a catalyst to spread the adoption of enterprise wide applications utilizing both web and CORBA technologies. Many software developers believe that the day is not far away when users will, by pointing and clicking on their web browser, be able to complete complicated business functions distributed across a corporation or even the Internet on CORBA compliant application servers. Such a scenario is already possible using the Internet Inter-ORB Protocol (IIOP) which is part of the CORBA 2.0 specification. In doing so, CORBA thus has the potential to subsume every other form of existing client/server middleware.

Distributed Objects Using CORBA

CORBA objects are distributed chunks of code that can live anywhere on a network. These objects are packaged as binary components that can be accessed by clients regardless of the programming language, compiler, operating system, or underlying hardware architecture used. What makes such a heterogeneous environment work transparently is CORBA's Interface Definition Language (IDL). Every CORBA object has an interface defined by IDL. The CORBA IDL is purely declarative; it specifies interfaces and not implementations. At present, CORBA IDL bindings have been written for C, C++, Ada, Smalltalk, COBOL, and most recently, Java. This means a COBOL programmer, with absolutely no knowledge of Java, can take advantage of the services provided by a Java object executing on a server halfway across the world. What makes this all possible are CORBA-compliant Object Request Brokers (ORBs) communicating via the CORBA Internet Inter-ORB Protocol (IIOP). Figure 21-1 shows how this works.

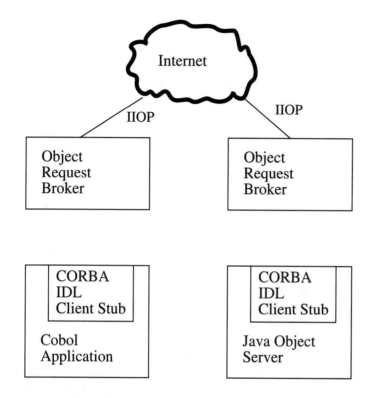

Figure 21–1 IIOP Enables Multi-Language Application Support

One of the keys to the Object Management Group's success has been that it produces only CORBA specifications, not implementations. Any vendor is able to join OMG and create his or her own CORBA implementations. These implementations are all based on the Object Management architecture. There are four main components to this architecture:

1. An Object Request Broker, which implements the CORBA communication bus

2. CORBA Services, which define system level object frameworks that extend this bus

3. CORBA Facilities, which define vertical and horizontal application frameworks used by CORBA objects

4. CORBA Application Objects – business objects and applications using the CORBA facilities and CORBA services

A CORBA Object Request Broker is similar to traditional Remote Procedure Call (RPC) mechanisms in that both create a communication channel between two software objects. However, this is where the similarities end. With a remote procedure call, a client program simply calls a specific function on a remote host. Following an object-oriented paradigm, an ORB is used to invoke a method within a specific object, typically on a remote host. Different object classes may respond to the same method invocation differently because of object polymorphism. In addition, CORBA ORBs provide an entire layer of additional services over and above the basic communication services provided by a remote procedure call mechanism. Here are some of the additional middleware services provided by CORBA ORBs.

- *Static and dynamic method invocations.* RPCs allow only static (pre-compiled) method invocations. An ORB allows clients to dynamically determine the methods callable on a remote object and the parameters necessary to invoke these methods.

- *High-level language bindings.* CORBA IDL bindings are available for C, C++, COBOL, Ada, Smalltalk, and Java. A client does not need to know, and in fact does not care, what language the server is written in. The CORBA IDL compiler creates the necessary code to translate method calls and parameters between the native language and a neutral intermediate format.

- *A self-describing interface repository.* Everything in a CORBA ORB is self-describing and kept in a public repository.

- *Local/remote transparency.* A CORBA client invokes server calls on a remote server exactly as it would on a local server. In fact, the client does not typically know if the server is local or remote.

- *Built-in security and transactions.* CORBA services provide such commonly required services as security and a transaction capability.

- *Polymorphic messaging.* The same method, sent to two different types of server objects, may have entirely different results. This type of polymorphism is a basic capability expected by most object-oriented systems.

- *Coexistence with existing systems.* Not only does CORBA provide different high level language bindings, it co-exists and interoperates with other object systems such as DCOM and Java.

CORBA Services

Every CORBA implementation provides a set of standard services packaged with IDL specified interfaces. These services are used, for instance, to create objects, name objects, and introduce them into the CORBA environment. The Object Management Group has specified fifteen standard CORBA services as of the CORBA 2.0 specification.

1. The Life Cycle Service defines operations for creating, deleting, moving, and copying CORBA components.

2. The Persistence Service defines a common interface for storing objects using a variety of underlying data stores including flat files, relational databases, and object databases.

3. The Naming Service defines a mechanism to locate objects by name. It supports interfaces to the most common existing name service protocols including X.500, DCE (from the OSF), NIS+ (from Sun), NDS (from Novell), and the internet standard LDAP.

4. The Event Service defines an "event channel" that allows objects to dynamically register or unregister for specific events. The event channel collects and distributes events among objects without requiring these objects to have any pre-determined knowledge about themselves.

5. The Concurrency Control Service defines a lock manager for use by either threads or transactions.

6. The Transaction Service defines a two-phase commit mechanism for use by objects.

7. The Relationship Service defines a mechanism for objects which know nothing about each other to create dynamic associations among themselves, allowing for referential integrity, object containment tracking, or other types of linkages as might be required by an object.

8. The Externalization Service defines a stream-like mechanism for object I/O.

9. The Query Service defines an object query mechanism. It is based on a combination of the SQL3 specification and the Object Query Language (OQL) of the Object Database Management Group.

10. The Licensing Service defines a mechanism for object licensing and metering, including support for various licensing schemes included per site, per node, per session, or per instance creation.

11. The Properties Service defines a mechanism for associating dynamic named values with any object.

12. The Time Service defines a time synchronization mechanism along with support for defining and managing time-triggered events.

13. The Security Service defines a framework for distributed object security. This includes authentication, access control lists, confidentiality, and non-repudiation.

14. The Trader Service defines a mechanism for objects to publicize their services and bid for jobs.

15. The Collection Service defines a mechanism for creating and manipulating common types of collections.

CORBA Facilities

CORBA Facilities form the next level of the OMG's Object Management architecture. Think of CORBA Facilities as groupings of CORBA objects organized into IDL-defined frameworks. There are two categories of CORBA Facilities, horizontal facilities and vertical facilities. These frameworks are intended to form an architecture upon which CORBA objects can effectively collaborate to perform some business function. To date, the common facilities being defined include mobile agents, data interchange, workflow, firewalls, business object frameworks, and internationalization. Further definition of these common frameworks will be included in the CORBA 3.0 specification.

CORBA Application Objects

Application objects are the business objects and applications that make up the final component of the OMG's Object Management architecture. Application objects are intended to describe application-independent concepts such as customers, orders, competitors, money, or payments. These business objects are intended to provide a development tool and application independent way of defining re-usable objects. The CORBA 3.0 specification will include additional work on the definition of application objects. This is one of the areas of CORBA technology that is most actively evolving. As this book goes to press, work is underway to link the definition of CORBA

Application Objects to JavaBeans and Enterprise JavaBeans to provide a standard component model across both Java and CORBA.

A CORBA Client-Server Example

Perhaps the best way to illustrate the workings of a CORBA object is to walk through the interactions between a CORBA Client and a CORBA Server. Lets start by looking at the client side of the application.

An application invokes a CORBA object by calling a client-side IDL stub. This stub acts as a static interface to a remote object's services. Client (and server) IDL stubs are precompiled by an IDL compiler. A client has a separate IDL stub for each interface it invokes on the server. To the client, the IDL stub acts like a local procedure call. The calling program has no notion that it may be invoking a service on a physically remote object. The IDL stub performs an operation called marshaling. Marshaling encodes and decodes the method being invoked and its parameters so that it can be passed transparently over networks between clients and servers created using different languages, different compilers, and even different host operating systems and hardware platforms.

An application may also use CORBA's Dynamic Invocation Interface (DII) to discover at run time additional object methods that it may want to invoke. The dynamic invocation interface uses a standard API for looking up metadata used to define the server's interface, generating the parameters, issuing the remote object call, and getting back the results.

The application may also use CORBA's Interface Repository APIs to obtain and possibly modify the description of any registered CORBA object, including the methods supported and their parameters. This runtime distributed database acts as a dynamic metadata repository for the ORB. Every object that lives in the ORB is self-describing using information contained in the interface repository.

Finally, a client application can make use of the ORB Interface to perform local services that may be needed by the application. Such services include things like converting object references to text strings and vice versa. For purposes of identification, every CORBA object has a globally unique repository ID. This ID is a string consisting of a three level name hierarchy that is globally unique across any ORB, independent of the vendor or physical location of the object.

Once a client side stub is invoked, the method information travels over the ORB (and possibly between ORBs using the IIOP) to a server object. A description of what happens on the server follows.

The client call is sent to a Server IDL Stub, also referred to as a skeleton. The skeleton provides static interfaces for a service provided by the server. A separate skeleton is created for each exported server service by an IDL compiler. Just like on the client side, the IDL compiler hides all the specifics of data marshaling and network protocols from the application programmer.

The Dynamic Skeleton Interface (DSI) is the server counterpart to the Dynamic Invocation Interface (DII) on the client. The DSI provides a runtime binding mechanism for incoming method calls that do not have IDL-based skeletons. This is done by examining the parameter values of the incoming message and determining the target object and method.

An Object Adapter provides the runtime environment for instantiating server objects, passing requests to them, and assigning them object IDs. The Object Adapter also is responsible for registering the classes it supports and their runtime instances with the Implementation Repository. In the current CORBA 2.0 specification, each ORB must support a Basic Object Adapter (BOA). The upcoming CORBA 3.0 specification also includes a portable version of the BOA, called the Portable Object Adapter (POA).

The Implementation Repository provides a runtime repository of information for every class a server supports, all instantiated objects, and their object IDs. The Implementation Repository is also used to store other administrative data such as security information and debugging information.

DCOM Objects

The only major vendor to not adopt CORBA as its distributed object model is Microsoft. The Microsoft answer to CORBA is its Distributed Component Object Model, or DCOM. While DCOM has many similarities to CORBA, it has some very basic differences. This section does not attempt to provide a complete description of DCOM. Rather, it compares and contrasts DCOM and CORBA using CORBA terminology.

There has been much inter-mixing of the terms COM, DCOM, and ActiveX in computer literature. Here is a quick summary of the differences between these terms. The technological infrastructure, or foundation, for DCOM is Microsoft's Component Object Model (COM). DCOM is COM with distribution support. ActiveX objects are simply self registering COM components. For purposes of this section, we will focus on the term DCOM.

Like CORBA, DCOM separates the object interface from its implementation. All DCOM interfaces are declared using an Interface Definition Language. Unfortunately, the Microsoft IDL is not compatible with CORBA IDL. Another major difference between the two is that DCOM does not support IDL-specified multiple inheritance. DCOM does, however, support multiple interfaces. DCOM reuse can thus be achieved by encapsulating the interfaces of inner components and representing them to a client.

Hard-core object-oriented programmers will claim that DCOM's lack of multiple inheritance disqualifies it as a true object-oriented model. Furthermore, DCOM interfaces do not have any state and cannot be instantiated to create a unique object with a unique object reference. A DCOM interface is thus really just a group of related functions. While DCOM clients are given a pointer to access the functions in an interface, this pointer is not related to state information. Therefore a DCOM client cannot reconnect to exactly the same object instance with the same state at a later time. It can only reconnect to an interface pointer of the same class. This means that DCOM is not well suited to implementing applications requiring stateful connections. Stateful connections are often desirable when communicating over noisy or error-prone channels such as the Internet.

To compensate for its lack of persistent objects, DCOM implements "Monikers." A DCOM moniker allows a transient, stateless, DCOM object to be associated with a persistent alias name for another object. Monikers can thus provide aliases for such objects as distributed filenames, database queries, or a paragraph in a document. A moniker is really a patch for DCOM's lack of support for object identifiers. Like many of DCOM's drawbacks, the need for monikers is due to DCOM's origins in COM, which was not originally a distributed object model.

DCOM implements local/remote transparency of server locations through its Service Control Manager. Unlike CORBA, in which server location is totally transparent, DCOM defines three different types of servers: in-process, local, or remote. An in-process server executes in the same address space as the client. In Microsoft Windows this is implemented as a dynamic link library (DLL). Local servers execute in a separate address space from the client but are local to the same machine. Microsoft Windows implements local servers in their own executable (.exe) file. DCOM uses a Lightweight RPC (LRPC) mechanism to communicate between clients and local servers. Finally, remote servers execute on a remote machine. DCOM clients use a remote procedure call-like mechanism to communicate between clients and remote servers.

On top of its other limitations, DCOM is primarily a Microsoft-only solution. At least one, third party non-Windows implementation of DCOM has been completed, but one would be hard pressed to find any widespread DCOM implementation outside of a Microsoft platform. With all its limitations, why would one consider using DCOM? Basically, because Microsoft uses DCOM for everything it is doing today with objects. DCOM is included with Windows NT 4.0 and Windows 98 and can be installed on Windows 95. DCOM is the foundation for Microsoft's Internet component strategy, often referred to as ActiveX. Microsoft has also based its Microsoft Transaction Server (MTS), also known as Viper, on DCOM as the component coordinator for transactional services. Microsoft's Visual J++ development tool for Java includes Java language bindings for DCOM and tightly integrates the two. If you are developing for a pure Microsoft client environment, are not concerned with high-end server scalability beyond that offered by Windows NT, and are not concerned with Internet standards and cross-platform interoperability, then DCOM is indeed a very attractive solution.

Distributed Java Applications with RMI

Version 1.1 of the Java Development Kit (JDK) introduced the Remote Method Invocation (RMI) API to support remote method invocations on objects across Java virtual machines. RMI provides new Java interfaces to find remote objects, load them, and then run them securely. One can think of RMI as a mini-CORBA for Java. RMI was never intended to compete against CORBA, as DCOM does, but rather to offer a subset of CORBA functionality for pure Java environments. Because it offers a small subset of the CORBA functionality, RMI can be much easier to learn than CORBA for new developers. RMI fills a definite need, as many applications have a simple requirement for remote method invocation without all the functionality of CORBA. On the other hand, larger, more complicated distributed systems developers might just do very well to take the plunge and use CORBA.

To help compare CORBA and RMI, let's examine the steps you would follow to create an RMI client and server.

For the Server:

1. Define a remote interface. A remote interface always extends the java.rmi.Remote interface and must throw a java.rmi.RemoteException.
2. Implement the remote interface. By extending the java.rmi.UnicastRemoteObject class, you create the server class that implements your remote interface.
3. Compile the server class. This is done using any Java compiler.
4. Run the stub compiler, rmic. The rmic compiler creates client and server stubs for your remote class from your server's .class file.
5. Start the RMI registry on your server. The RMI registry implements a non-persistent naming service for RMI servers. Only one RMI registry per server machine is required.
6. Start your server objects. You must load your server classes and then create instances of remote objects.
7. Register your remote objects with the registry. Each instance of a server object must be registered using the java.rmi.Naming class.

For the Client:

1. Write the client code. The java.rmi.Naming class is used to locate a remote server object. Methods are invoked on this remote object using the client stubs created by rmic.
2. Compile the client code with any Java compiler.
3. Start the client.

In the future, there will be greater convergence between RMI and CORBA. RMI enhancements included in the JDK 1.2 release include support for persistent object references and support for remote object activation. Sun also has announced plans to provide a version of RMI that works over the IIOP transport. This will provide RMI with built-in support for propagation of transactions, ORB-based firewall support (as opposed to the current HTTP tunneling), and interoperability with objects written in other languages via the RMI/IDL subset.

A Sneak Peak at Jini Technology

Forward-looking companies are always trying to re-invent themselves before someone else does, especially in the software industry. After developing the C programming language, AT&T developed C++. After Windows 95 introduced millions of PC users to new desktop metaphors like the "My Computer" and "Network Neighborhood" icons, Windows 98 changed the default interface paradigm from the familiar Windows desktop to a browser interface based on Internet Explorer. Many of the software trends in recent years have been propelled forward at breakneck speeds by the rapid adoption of the Internet and its underlying technologies such as TCP/IP, HTML, and the Java platform. With over three years having passed since the introduction of Java technology by Sun Microsystems, one can only wonder what the Sun research labs have been working on for a follow-on. In the recent summer of 1998, Sun's Vice President of Research, Bill Joy, broke three years of silence to talk about Sun's R&D project to develop Jini technology.

Jini is not a new software language or hardware technology. In fact, Jini is based on Sun's Java platform. What Jini does is dramatically expand the power of Java technology to allow spontaneous networking for a wide variety of hardware and software. Jini allows people to use networked devices and services as simply as they would use a phone today. Think about it. You can unplug your home phone today and plug it in at your friend's home without any doubt that you would get a dial tone and be able to make a call. Can you say the same about plugging in your laptop and being able to use your friend's printer? The very terms "plug and play" have been associated with a PC-centric paradigm, plugging new devices into your PC. Jini tech-

nology expands on "plug and play" to define a new metaphor of "plug and participate" from a network viewpoint based on network dial tone.

Because Jini takes advantage of Java technology, it can be easily recognized by the more than one million Java programmers in the world. Jini consists of a small amount of Java code, packaged as Java class libraries, and some conventions used to create a "federation" of Java virtual machines. Today, Jini technology could be applied to the 100 million+ Java virtual machines running on every type of computer as we know it. Now think again about Jini technology enabling several billion[1] Java virtual machines inside printers, disk drives, cell phones, PDAs, virtually any microprocessor-powered device with some sort of network port. Jini technology allows all devices in a network to be dynamically connected to share information and perform tasks. Just as HTML is about to become a universal document format,[2] Jini technology promises to provide a universal resource sharing over network dial tone. This chapter provides a sneak peak at the infrastructure components and distributed programming model of the Jini platform.

Jini Infrastructure

The Jini infrastructure provides a universal mechanism for devices and software to connect to and register with a network. In the past, networks had fundamentally different ways of dealing with hardware devices and software, so it may seem strange at first to consider the two in the same fashion. For instance, hardware interconnects are typically described by a physical or link level protocol such as Ethernet or SCSI. Software interconnects are typically described by application level protocols, often unique to the programming language being used. Jini infrastructure, however, takes a fundamentally different approach and considers both hardware devices and software as network citizens who are both consumers of and possibly providers of network services. The first Jini infrastructure element is called *Discovery and Join*. Discovery and Join solves the difficult problem of how a device or application registers itself with the network for the first time with

---

1.Sun estimates that by the year 2000, the semiconductor industry will produce 10 billion microprocessors per year, with roughly 25% or 2.5 billion of these capable of running a Java virtual machine.
2.Microsoft has announced that the Office 2000 product suite will use HTML as the default file format.

no prior knowledge of the network. The second Jini infrastructure element is called *Lookup*. Lookup is a sort of bulletin board for all services on the network.

Discover and Join

Today, plugging a new computer into a network is a major system administration task. In most TCP/IP networks, the system administrator must obtain the ethernet address of the device being added (a hexadecimal number like 8:0:20:1f:10:a) and assign that device an IP address (of the form 129.9.200.1). The network naming service must then be updated to assign a host name (like computer1) to the IP address. The Internet standard naming service commonly used to do this is the domain name service, or DNS. In many large corporations, DNS updates are only distributed once a day and it thus can take up to 24 hours after a new device is registered for it to be fully recognized on the network. This does not even start to address the ability of the new computer to access and run applications over the network. In some networks, the Dynamic Host Configuration Protocol (DHCP) is used to dynamically assign IP addresses on the fly to new hosts as they are plugged into specific networks. However, both DHCP and the evolving dynamic DNS protocols still require significant setup and configuration to be done ahead of time on both the name server and the client host. In order to expand the ability to participate in networks from roughly 100 million PCs today to the several billion microprocessor powered devices expected to be Java capable in a few years, a more spontaneous method of networking is required. In Jini technology, this is called discover and join.

Jini's discover and join protocol allows both devices and applications to join a network without either the device (application) or the network having to know anything about the other in advance. Here is how discovery works:

When a Jini enabled device is plugged into a network, it sends out a 512 byte multicast discovery packet on a well-known multicast port. Among other information, this packet contains a reference back to itself. The IP multicast protocol is used instead of a broadcast protocol for several reasons. Traditional naming services typically use a broadcast protocol because they assume that a name server is present on the local subnet. Most routers are configured to not pass broadcast packets to avoid quickly flooding networks with broadcast traffic. In addition, naming services like DNS predate the widespread usage of multicast protocols. Multicast packets, rather than being received by every host, are only received by hosts configured to listen on the particular multicast address being used. This significantly cuts down on network overhead. Like broadcast packets, however, the sender need only send out a single copy of the multicast packets to be received by many hosts.

The Jini lookup service listens on the multicast port. When the Discovery packet is received, Lookup uses the device's interface to pass an interface to itself back to the plugged-in device or application.

At this point, the new device or application can communicate with the Lookup service and vice versa. The first thing the device or application does is upload all its characteristics to the Jini Lookup. The process of uploading characteristics is the Join part of Discovery and Join.

Lookup

The Jini Lookup functions as a network bulletin board and clearinghouse for all services on the network. Unlike DNS which only contains IP addresses and their corresponding host names, Lookup stores pointers to all the services available on the network and also the actual code and/or pointers to the code for these services.

As an example of Lookup, let's examine how a printer would be added to a network using Jini technology. When the printer was first plugged into the network, it would load a printer driver, or an interface to the driver, into Lookup. When a client wants to use the printer, the driver and driver interface would get downloaded from the Lookup onto the client. In this way, clients do not need to be loaded in advance. Of course what makes all this work in a simplified fashion is the power of Java's write-once-run-anywhere model. The Java printer driver is guaranteed to work on any client with a Java Virtual Machine. Without Java technology, trying to store all the possible different printer drivers on the Lookup would be next to impossible.

The printer might also load other attributes into the Lookup. For instance, the printer might store attributes describing that it is a color printer and supports duplex printing, along with the print speed. Besides attributes, the printer could also load value added services into the Lookup. One example would be to store wizards that would run on the client and help with printer set up.

Because all networks may not contain a Lookup, a Peer Lookup capability is also defined. When a client desiring a service cannot find a Lookup on the network, it can register by sending out the same Discovery and Join packets a Lookup would use to request any service providers (this is what a Lookup does when it first is plugged into a network). Service providers would thus register with the client as though it were a Lookup. Peer Lookup obviously makes the most sense to implement when there is a very low density of Jini devices in a network. As more and more Jini capable devices are added to a network, it makes sense to implement a dedicated Lookup function.

Distributed Programming

It is envisioned that Jini technology will be used to build a wide variety of distributed systems. To facilitate this, Jini distributed programming adds functionality to the core Java platform for three types of distributed programming operations: leasing, distributed events, and distributed transactions. Each of these is defined below.

Leasing

In distributed systems, the concept of leasing is analogous to leasing a car. When you lease a car, you negotiate a certain amount of time to use the car. When the lease expires, you return the car, never having to worry about it again. Similarly, the leasing company does not need to worry about keeping records on you after you return the car (except, of course, for future marketing purposes). With 2.5 billion Java capable devices, naming services like today's DNS would quickly be overwhelmed and ad hoc distributed programming would not be possible. Jini objects, therefore, negotiate leases with each other that dictate how long they wish to use, or offer for use, a particular service. This negotiation takes place during the Discovery and Join process. Before a lease expires, a device must re-negotiate the lease or its connection becomes no longer valid. This solves the problem of distributed garbage collection on Lookup tables.

Distributed Events

In a single computer, the operating system can guarantee that events will be received in the same sequence as they were sent. In a distributed environment, however, events can possibly be received out of order or perhaps never received at all. To facilitate distributed events in a Java environment, Jini technology includes a Java API for facilitating distributed events. This API defines a event number and sequence for each distributed event. By comparing sequence numbers, the receiving party can thus determine if an event was received out of order or lost.

Distributed Transactions

Distributed transactions are nothing new to computer science. Mainframe software such as IBM's CICS and client-server software such as BEA's Tuxedo have provided transaction services such as two-phase commit for many years. In a distributed Java environment, however, sometimes what is required is a very lightweight two-phase commit. Simply put, a two-phase commit assures that all events in a distributed transaction occur before the transaction is actually committed. Furthermore, in a Jini environment, two-phase commit functionality must be provided without pre-loading specific transaction handling software. This is done in Jini via another simple Java API.

The Jini distributed transaction API enables any Jini object to start up a transaction manager that manages two-phase commit for its transactions. Every object that needs to participate in the transaction discovers the transaction manager via Discovery and Join and then registers with the transaction manager. In any transaction, if one of the participating objects does not complete an event in the transaction, this information is then communicated back to the transaction manager. The transaction manager then tells all the participating objects to roll back to the last well-known state in the transaction.

Millennium versus Jini

A good reality check for the viability of publicly announced research projects such as Jini is to look for other companies pursuing similar projects. While it has not been publicized much by Microsoft, if you dig several layers deep into the Microsoft Research web pages there is talk of a project dubbed Millennium, which promises "a new self-organizing, self-tuning distributed system" where "any code fragment might run anywhere, any data object might live anywhere." In fact, since the public announcement of Jini, Microsoft has made some attempts to compare Millennium with Jini. Marketing talk aside, there are some very fundamental differences. Communication in Jini is based on the Java RMI (remote method invocation) API. Interestingly enough, the Java RMI classes are part of the core Java specification that Microsoft has chosen not to implement in some versions of its Java Virtual Machine (and is one of the factors in Sun's license infringement lawsuit against Microsoft). At present, there is not enough publicly available material on Millennium to complete a thorough comparison between the two. It's hard to believe, however, that Microsoft would give in at this point and base Millennium on the Java RMI specification. However, given that by the year 2000 interoperability between CORBA and DCOM will have been suitably addressed for most developers (via various vendors' uni and multi-directional bridges), don't be surprised to see Millennium versus Jini to become one of the new defacto standards battlegrounds.

Software Development Frequently Asked Questions

Over the last fifteen years, we have met with thousands of software developers working on hundreds of projects ranging in size from simple ten line Java applets written by one developer in an evening to complex three million line software systems developed by hundreds of developers over many years. During this time, certain questions stand out as those that are asked again and again by every type of organization. We have gathered these into our very own Frequently Asked Questions list. Following the structure of our book, this FAQ starts with a section on general questions, followed by sections on people, process, and technology related questions.

General Questions

1. What percentage of software development projects are successful?

When you consider all project success factors, including budget, schedule, functionality, performance, and user satisfaction, twenty percent or less of software development projects are completely successful. Of course this does not imply that only twenty percent of software development projects are ever completed. There are many projects that complete either over budget, not as originally scheduled, or missing some functionality or performance goal.

2. What is the primary reason so few software development projects complete successfully?

While it's impossible to pinpoint a single reason so few software development projects complete successfully, most project failures can be traced to early phases in the software life cycle. Typically, unsuccessful software development projects either have not accurately defined their requirements or have not successfully translated these requirements into a successful software architecture.

3. We all know the role metrics play in the infrastructure (i.e., online system availability, etc.). What metrics do you need for a successful software development project?

Unfortunately, software development metrics are not as easy to define as typical data center operations metrics. We specifically caution against using single point metrics such as lines of code to benchmark a development project. Chapter 12 provides more information on software metrics and their relation to productivity and quality. That chapter introduces the McCabe metrics, which we believe are some of the more useful software metrics.

People Related Questions

1. What is the key to successfully managing software developers?

Give them a manager who understands what they want to do and how they want to do it. There is no one less motivated to the success of your project than a developer who feels he or she is being asked to do something the wrong way by a manager who doesn't understand the technology to begin with.

2. Should I centralize or decentralize my applications development group?

Centralized application development groups are often criticized as being too unresponsive to departmental needs. Decentralized application development groups may not be large enough to support the wide range of software specialists needed for modern development projects. In addition, decentralized organizations may also lead to duplicate functionality. A good compromise is to centralize enterprise-wide applications development (payroll, finance, etc.) while letting each large department maintain its own decentralized development group for department-specific applications. "Big" architecture decisions, those that affect any development group, should be made by a centralized architecture team.

3. Should I outsource my applications development?

For starters, don't outsource your software architecture. This is so crucial to development and tied to business knowledge that it should be kept in-house. You should consider outsourcing to fill peak development demands or specific specialties when it is not economical to maintain an in-house staff for these needs.

4. How much training should my developers get each year?

This, of course, varies considerably with the skill of your developers and the complexity of the software you are developing. Organizations consistently ranked at the highest levels of the software capability maturity model (see Chapter 8) allocate up to 25% of a developer's time for both formal and informal training.

5. Do good software developers make good software architects or software development managers?

Not necessarily. Some developers who are very good at writing code may never have an interest in becoming software architects or software development managers. One of the biggest mistakes you can make is to try and turn a great developer into a software architect or software development manager when they have no real interest nor the proper training and skills to do the job.

6. Does a software development manager need to have hands-on software development experience?

In general, the best software development managers started their careers as software developers.

7. What are the main qualifications when hiring a senior developer?

When hiring a senior developer, excellent technical skills are simply a minimum bar for consideration. We look to senior developers to be the role models and "goto" persons for the rest of a project team. Some of the main qualifications we look for include:

- initiative

- dedication
- flexibility
- respect

If we had to name a single technical skill we look for it would be knowledge of object-oriented technology. By this we mean not simply being able to write code in an object-oriented language like Java, but truly understanding the concepts of object-oriented architecture, design, and development.

8. Should you try to breed developers internally as well as utilize external recruitment efforts?

The lack of a strong educational foundation in the basics of computer science, reasoning, and problem solving is one of the most common reasons for poor developer performance. For this reason we do not typically try to breed developers internally from employees that do not have such a foundation. However, we absolutely do transition developers of one type, say Mainframe/COBOL programmers, to developers of another type, e.g., Java programmers. We do this because an experienced developers business and domain knowledge, along with his or her "corporate memory" or culture, and educational foundation in computer science easily outweigh the advantages of most external candidates who might have the exact technology experience required.

9. How would you structure the organization for proper skills development for young programmers?

Having proper training processes in place is just as important a process for the long-term success of a development organization as is requirements management or configuration management. Each developer, from most junior to most senior, has specific training goals set as part of his or her annual review. In addition, junior developers are given "mentors" when they come on board to help them adjust to the company work environment. Besides spending time with their mentor, all junior programmers or ones new to the organization are given a goal of spending two hours a week meeting with developers, managers, or other employees outside of their immediate work group. This gives them a chance to informally learn from a wider range of people. Finally, in areas were we have two-person offices, we always try to pair a junior and more senior developer in the same office.

10. How long does it take to train a mainframe COBOL programmer to learn C, Java, or C++?

It depends on how fast they want to learn. One of the ways we select COBOL programmers to transition to web-centric environments is by their level of external interest in the subject. A COBOL programmer who still doesn't use the web regularly and has never requested to take any C or Java programming probably doesn't make a good candidate to transition. Given a good candidate, we find most COBOL programmers can learn the syntax of C or Java with two weeks of formal training and another few weeks of on-the-job training. Learning the syntax of C++ takes about twice as long. However, simply knowing the syntax of C++ or Java doesn't mean a programmer is ready to take on object-oriented design tasks. Once a COBOL programmer has mastered the syntax of C++ or Java, we find it takes another month of formal training and at least four months of on-the-job training, for a total of six months, to master object-oriented programming technology. To become a good object-oriented architect takes at least another year.

11. In all client/server environments the communication between Applications Development and Production Support is horrendous, and that is putting it nicely. What would you recommend?

The best way to get Applications Development and Production Support to communicate is to get the two groups talking early in the design phase of a project. This is one of the key reasons we developed the Web-Centric Production Acceptance process described in Chapter 13 of this book.

12. In many companies the Database Administration group reports into Applications Development, in others they report into the operations group, and yet others their reporting is split between both. What would you recommend?

Database administration is closely tied to database design, as many database tuning operations will impact the design of the application and vice versa. We recommend, however, that day-to-day database administration functions be part of the operations group. You should, however, have database designers with hands-on database administration experience as part of your applications development group. For starters, this will help you develop database schemas that are easier to tune for maximum performance and stability. Secondly, this will help your database designers communicate with a common vocabulary with the database administrators who are part of the operations group.

13. What is the role of the architecture function within Applications Development?

The architecture function with Applications Development should set the high-level application standards that will be used by all enterprise-wide applications in your organization.

14. How would you structure the architecture function in the organization?

Chapter 6 describes several different ways to structure the architecture function. We generally suggest that you have a small group responsible for setting enterprise-wide application architectures for the entire corporation. Individual systems or projects, however, should have the architecture function integrated into the project team.

Process Related Questions

1. What are the key processes to implement for software development?

Ultimately, one of the most important processes to implement for software development is one of process management. This is not circular reasoning. The most successful software development organizations have an organizational focus on development processes and their constant improvement. Other key processes, as defined in Chapter 10, include:

- requirements management
- configuration management
- peer code reviews
- training processes
- production acceptance

2. How would you establish a Test/QA environment?

Before the complete answer, a quick reminder from Chapter 6. While we certainly recommend a QA environment, we never recommend a unique QA function or department. QA is every developers responsibility and having a separate QA function just tends to relieve developers of their daily responsibility for quality assurance.

We generally recommend at least three completely separate environments for an application:

- the development environment
- the QA environment
- the production environment

- and perhaps even a fourth separate test environment

By environment we mean at least a separate version of the operating system, application, database, and disk storage. Some application vendors, such as SAP, specifically require customers to implement separate environments for development, QA, and production. SAP does customers a big favor by not supporting anyone who does not. While it is tempting to save costs by mixing development environments with QA or production, it is definitely not a good idea. It is simply too easy for one function to have an impact on another when they are intermixed within the same environment. There are, however, ways to save costs without deploying three copies of every hardware component. Consider some of these approaches.

- Not every environment needs to be sized the same. QA, for instance, may require much fewer hardware resources than production.

- Remember that each environment is likely to have time-phased requirements. For instance, the full production environment is not needed on day one of development. However, avoid the mistake of assuming your development hardware will simply transition to production once an application is ready to deploy. For starters, some development hardware is typically required for ongoing application maintenance. Secondly, especially on projects lasting a year or more, development hardware may very well be outdated by the time the application is ready for deployment.

- Consider using a hardware environment with dynamic system domains, such as Sun's Enterprise 10000 server. Dynamic system domains allow system resources to be dynamically reallocated among development, QA, and production environments on the fly, allowing you to size for the maximum concurrent usage of all environments. This will always be less costly than sizing for the sum of the maximum usage of all environments as peak loads on each environment will be time-staggered.

3. **How would you handle stress testing in this world of networked computing?**

Stress testing of web-centric applications is much more difficult than for traditional stand-alone or client-server applications. The only real way to completely stress test a web-centric application is to use an end-to-end application performance testing tool such as Pegasus from Ganymede Software. This tool and others are described in Chapter 15, Software Development Tools.

4. I just ran the program yesterday and it worked fine, why can't I get it to work today?

Processes that ensure a repeatable test environment and a stable production environment are crucial to the success of any software development project. If program results are different, then either the program changed, the program inputs changed, or the environment changed. A well run test or production environment will prevent a program from being updated without properly notifying any affected parties. Change logs will ensure any changes are easy to track and back-out if necessary. Program inputs, especially from user inputs are more subjective and subject to non-repeatability unless some sort of input event capture and scripting is done. The most difficult condition to keep non-variable in a complex test or production system is the environment. Environmental conditions outside of the user's control or notice, such as network load or CPU load may produce different results if the software has not taken the possibility of these environmental variables into account during program design.

5. My new software project is starting next month. I have budgeted for a headcount of 25 developers. Should I bring them all aboard the first month?

Absolutely not. The most important part of any software project is the system design phase. Before you have any developers writing code, you want to have your system design and software architecture firmly in place. This is the task of your software architects. Even the largest software development projects rarely call for more than three software architects and throwing more people at the problem early on will only hamper the effort by making communication more difficult. Of course this is not to say that in an iterative development environment you won't have one group of developers writing prototype code while the architects design the final system.

Technology Related Questions

1. How much longer can Moore's Law continue to hold true?

Moore's Law is based on the observation made in 1965 by Gordon Moore, co-founder of Intel. Moore observed that the number of transistors per square inch on an integrated circuit had doubled every year since the integrated circuit was invented. He also predicted that this trend would continue for the foreseeable future. Today, nearly 35 years after Moore's initial observation, CPU density, along with CPU speed and processing power, continue to double every twelve to eighteen months. Most experts, including Moore himself, expect Moore's Law to hold for at least another two decades.

2. What is the best Interactive Development Environment (IDE) for developing software?

We don't really have a single favorite IDE – it really depends on what sort of code you are trying to write and in what environment. For general purpose IDEs, two favorite tools are Sun's Java Workshop for developing in a Solaris environment and Symantic's Visual Cafe for Java for developing in a Windows environment. For C or C++ environments, both companies have sister tools with similar names. Imprise's JBuilder would be our pick for Windows development where the application had a large amount of database connectivity. Finally, if there was a large amount of legacy Unix/X-Windows code, we would choose UIM/X because of its excellent X-Windows to Java conversion utility. Additional information on these and other development tools is provided in Chapter 15.

3. How long does it take to learn Java?

Java was designed from the ground up with simplicity in mind. A week of training is typically sufficient for a C or C++ developer to get started with Java programming. Programmers whose experience is limited to less-similar languages such as COBOL or FORTRAN will usually take longer to learn Java and several weeks training will probably be required. In either case, learning Java syntax is much simpler than learning object-oriented design, the subject of the next question.

4. How long does it take to learn object-oriented design?

You will gain only a small fraction of the benefits of an object-oriented language such as Java if your software architects and designers do not understand object-oriented design principals. It takes between six and eighteen months for a good procedural developer to become a good object-oriented software architect, and time alone is no guarantee.

5. Shouldn't I wait for Java technology to mature before I start considering it for large software development projects?

As with any new technology, Java is climbing the maturity curve and may not be suited today for every large software project you will undertake. However, the explosion of the Internet has caused Java to mature much faster than it would have otherwise done so. If you are not at least considering Java today for your enterprise-wide applications, you are probably hopelessly behind your competitors who are already figuring out how best to use and benefit from Java technology.

6. How fast is a real-time operating system?

While there is no precise definition, a typical real-time operating system is able to respond to interrupt signals with a worst case latency of fifty microseconds or less. General purpose operating systems, such as Windows NT or Unix may have an interrupt latency up to five hundred microseconds or more. For a typical computer operation, it may not matter if the computer responds within fifty or five hundred microseconds. However, many classes of control systems, ranging from telephone switches to modern anti-lock brake systems, require interrupt signals to be processed within precise deterministic time periods or an essential process – i.e., stopping a car – will not function properly.

7. Can a RAID-5 disk configuration contain more than (fewer than) five disks?

Yes. Most RAID-5 systems support as few as three disks (two data plus one parity) in a stripe and as many as several dozen or more. A five disk stripe is one of the more common configurations as it minimizes the data overhead while retaining plenty of space for parity information while not overtaxing log disks.

See Chapter 16 for a more complete description of RAID disk systems.

8. Doesn't a RAID 0+1 (mirrored) system cost twice as much as a RAID-5 system?

No. Assuming a five way stripe, a RAID-5 system already uses 20% more disk than a system of stand-alone disks. The additional cost overhead to move to a RAID 0+1 system is thus only $1.2 / 2 = 60\%$. These figures are for disk costs only, and do not include any additional controller costs.

9. Which tools would you recommend for source/version control?

A source/version control tool is a basic requirement of successful software development projects. Nevertheless, we continue to see many software development projects well underway without any such tool in use. So for starters, the first recommended tool is any tool that you have. Most Unix operating systems come with a bundled version of either SCCS (source code control system) or RCS (revision control system). Either provide all the functionality necessary to implement a basic source/version control system. The second recommended source/version control tool is the one, if any, that comes with your Integrated Development Environment (IDE). Many IDEs come bundled with some sort of source/version control tool. The only warning here is that you get what you pay for. Bundled source/version control tools may be stripped down versions of other products or may be simple afterthoughts to meet a check box on a marketing brochure. For instance, some IDEs have source/version control tools that, while integrated into the IDEs graphical user interface, do not have command line equivalents. Anyone who has ever handled configuration management for a large project knows that this is almost impossible with command line interaction that can be called from automated build (and other types of) scripts. One of the most innovative source/version control tools, and our favorite, is JavaSafe, from Sun's Java Products Division.

Despite its name, JavaSafe is not just for managing Java code. JavaSafe can be used for managing C, C++, Perl, HTML, or almost any other type of file. JavaSafe has two components: a server based on Sun's Java Webserver, and a client that can be run stand-alone or within a web browser. Both components can be used locally by a single developer on a single workstation. In contrast, the server and client components can be distributed across an Intranet or even the Internet providing unparalleled support for distributed developer teams. More information on JavaSafe can be found at http://java.sun.com/products/javasafe/.

10. Which tools would you recommend for software stress testing?

Stress testing is a critical component of the Web-Centric Production Acceptance (WCPA) process described in Chapter 13. One of my favorite quick and easy tricks for stress testing web servers is the Lynx text-only web browser. Lynx is commonly available at freeware sites over the Internet. One of the little known features of Lynx is that it has a command line interface. It is trivial to write a simple script to call Lynx in a loop. Once you download a copy of Lynx, just run "lynx -h" for help in determining the appropriate command line options. Be sure to set the lynx cache to 0 or you will be defeating the purpose of your web testing. If you want something a little fancier to stress test your web server, WebLoad, from Radview Corporation (http://www.radview.com) is my favorite commercial web server stress testing tool. It does cost more than Lynx, but it's worth the cost.

Most stress testing, however, requires more than the simple process defined above. One of my favorite application level stress testing tools is Jtest from Parasoft (http://www.parasoft.com). Parasoft also has a complete line of testing tools for C and C++ code.

At the enterprise level, stress testing really needs to go one step further than simple application or web server stress testing. Ganymede Software's Pegasus tool (http://www.ganymedesoftware.com) is one of the few stress testing tools available that performs complete end-to-end performance analysis and stress testing of web-centric and client-server applications.

11. What is a JavaBean?

JavaBeans are reusable software components written in Java. A more complete description of JavaBeans can be found in Chapter 17. Using an Integrated Development Environment such as Symantec Cafe, Imprise JBuilder, or Sun's Workshop for Java (see Chapter 15), you can customize JavaBeans parameters and visually manipulate them to create Java applets or standalone Java applications.

12. What is the difference between a Java applet and a JavaBean?

JavaBeans are designed to be easily reused and visually manipulated by JavaBean aware development tools. The JavaBeans API endows a JavaBean with specific component functionality, including:

- introspection: allows a development tool to analyze a JavaBean and determine its properties
- customization: allows a developer to customize a JavaBean by modifying the properties that have been discovered by introspection
- events: allows a JavaBean to communicate with other JavaBeans and connect together to form a processing tree
- persistence: enables developers to save customized JavaBeans for further reuse

Software History and Trivia Questions

1. Did Intel develop the first integrated circuit?

No. Credit for developing the first integrated circuit is generally given to Jack Kilby, who developed a working integrated circuit in 1958 while at Texas Instruments.

2. Was BASIC developed at Microsoft?

No. The BASIC language (Beginners All-purpose Symbolic Instruction Code) was developed by John Kennedy and Thomas Kurtz of Dartmouth in 1964.

3. How did the Ada language get its name?

Ada was named after Ada Augusta, Countess of Lovelace, who in 1842 translated Luigi Menabrea's pamphlet on the Charles Babbage's Analytical Engine, adding her own commentary.

4. How did the C language get its name?

C was so named because the prototype language that was its predecessor was called "B."

5. When was C developed?

C was developed in 1972 by Brian Kernighan and Dennis Ritchie of Bell Labs.

6. When was C++ developed?

C++ was developed in 1983 by Bjarne Stroustrup of AT&T.

7. Was C++ the first object-oriented language?

No. Simula, developed in 1967 by Ole-Johan Dahl and Kristen Nygaard of the Norwegian Computing Centre, is generally considered as the first object-oriented language.

Java Coding Standard Template

Introduction

This appendix is not meant to be a stand-alone coding standard – it simply describes some of the things you would want to put in your own Java coding standard. You should use this template as the basis for your own standard and tailor it to meet the requirements of your particular development organization.

This sample standard borrows heavily from the *Java Style Guide*, initially an internal Sun paper by Achut Reddy and now available in its complete form on the Sun home page at http://sun.com. We wish to thank Mr. Reddy for his permission to use this style guide as a basis for the sample Java coding template presented herein.

The importance and benefits of a consistent coding style are well known. A consistent style:

- improves the readability, and therefore the maintainability of code
- facilitates sharing of code among different programmers;
- allows easier development of automated tools to assist in program development, including tools that automatically format code using these style guidelines;

- makes it easier to conduct code reviews, another software engineering process with well-known benefits. In turn, a practice of regular code reviews can help enforce a consistent style; and

- saves development time, once the guidelines are learned, by allowing programmers to focus on the semantics of the code, rather than spend time trying to determine what particular format is appropriate for a given situation.

However, no standard is meant to be rigidly enforced without exception. This document does not cover all possible situations. Experience and informed judgment should be used wherever doubt exists. Consistency of coding style is more important than using a particular style.

Source Files

On file-based host implementations of Java, the compilation unit is a Java source file. A Java source file should contain only one public class or interface definition, although it may also contain any number of non-public support classes or interfaces. Source files should be kept to less than 2,000 lines. Files longer than this become difficult to manage and maintain. Exceeding this limit is a good indication that the classes or interfaces should probably be broken up into smaller, more manageable units.

For all but the most trivial projects, source files should be kept under a version management system (such as SCCS in Unix).

Source File Naming

You should always follow a common naming convention for program source files. In Java, most compilers enforce a source file naming convention of the form:

```
ClassOrInterfaceName.java
```

where `ClassOrInterfaceName` is exactly the name of the public class or interface defined in the program file. The file name suffix is always .java except on systems that support only three-character extensions; on such systems, the suffix is .jav.

Source File Organization

You should always follow a standard organization within a program source file. In Java, one possible format would be:

1. file identifiers

2. file comments

3. package declaration

4. import declarations

5. one or more class/interface declarations

If you are using a version control tool based on SCCS, you can automatically generate much of the file identifiers by embedding SCCS ID strings. Some commonly used SCCS ID strings keywords include:

```
%W%: module version
%E%: date
```

Every source file should contain a package declaration. Omitting the package declaration causes the types to be part of an unnamed package, with implementation-defined semantics.

Example:

```
package java.lang;
```

Import statements should start in column 1, and a single space should separate the keyword import from the type name. Import statements should be grouped together by package name. A single blank line may be used to separate groups of import statements. Within groups, import statements should be sorted lexically.

Wildcard type-import-on-demand declarations (e.g., import java.util.*;) should not be used; use fully qualified type names instead. Specifically listing packages being imported makes their use clear to future readers of the program and also prevents someone later adding a new unexpected class to a file that conflicts with another type you are using.

Following the import sections are one or more class declarations and/or interface declarations, collectively referred to simply as type declarations. The number of type declarations per file should be kept small. There should be at most one public type declaration per file. The public type, if any, should be the first type declaration in the file.

Naming Conventions

The naming conventions specified here apply only to Java code written in the basic ASCII character set. Terms such as "upper-case" are obviously meaningless for some Unicode character sets.

Package Naming

Generally, package names should use only lowercase letters and digits, and no underscore. Examples:

```
java.lang
java.awt.image
dinosaur.theropod.velociraptor
```

An exception to this rule is when using the unique package prefix scheme for packages that will be widely distributed. In this scheme, a unique prefix is constructed by using the components of the Internet domain name of the host site in reverse order. The first component (top-level Internet domain) is all upper-case, and the remaining components of the prefix are in whatever case they are conventionally written in. Example:

```
COM.Sun.sunsoft.tools.graphics
```

Class/Interface Naming

All type names (classes and interfaces) should use the InfixCaps style. Start with an upper-case letter, and capitalize the first letter of any subsequent word in the name, as well as any letters that are part of an acronym. All other characters in the name are lowercase. Do not use underscores to separate words. Class names should be nouns or noun phrases. Interface names depend on the salient purpose of the interface. If the purpose is primarily to endow an object with a particular capability, then the name should be an adjective (ending in -able or -ible if possible) that describes the capability, e.g., Searchable, Sortable, NetworkAccessible. Otherwise use nouns or noun phrases.

Field Naming

Names of non-constant fields (reference types or non-final primitive types) should use the infixCaps style. Start with a lowercase letter, and capitalize the first letter of any subsequent word in the name, as well as any letters that are part of an acronym. All other characters in the name are lowercase. Do not use underscores to separate words. The names should be nouns or noun phrases. Examples:

```
boolean resizable;
char    recordDelimiter;
```

Names of constant fields (final, primitive type fields) should be all upper-case, with underscores separating words. Remember that all interface fields are inherently final. Examples:

```
MIN_VALUE, MAX_BUFFER_SIZE, OPTIONS_FILE_NAME
```

One-character field names should be avoided except for temporary and looping variables. In these cases, use:

```
b for a byte
c for a char
d for a double
e for an Exception object
f for a float
g for a Graphics object
i, j, k, m, n for integers
p, q, r, s for String objects
```

An exception is where a strong convention for the one-character name exists, such as x and y for screen coordinates.

Avoid the character l ("el") in non-word variable names because it is hard to distinguish it from 1 ("one") on some printers and displays.

Method Naming

Method names should use the infixCaps style. Start with a lowercase letter, and capitalize the first letter of any subsequent word in the name, as well as any letters that are part of an acronym. All other characters in the name are lowercase. Do not use underscores to separate words. Note that this is identical to the naming convention for non-constant fields; however, it should always be easy to distinguish the two from context. Method names should be verbs or verb phrases. Examples:

```
// GOOD method names:
```

```
showStatus(), drawCircle(), addLayoutComponent()
```

```
// BAD method names:
mouseButton()
// noun phrase; doesn't describe function
```

```
DrawCircle()
// starts with upper-case letter
```

```
add_layout_component()
// underscores
```

A method to get or set some property of the class should be called getProperty() or setProperty(), respectively, where Property is the name of the property. Examples:

```
getHeight(), setHeight()
```

A method to test some boolean property of the class should be called isProperty(), where Property is the name of the property. Examples:

```
isResizable(), isVisible()
```

Statement Label Naming

Statement labels can be targets of break or continue statements. They should be all lowercase, with words separated by underscores. Example:

```
for (int i = 0; i < n; i++) {
    search: {
        for (int j = 0; j < n/2; j++) {
            if (node[j].name == name)
                break search;
        }
        for (int j = n/2; j < n; j++) {
            if (node[j].name == name)
                break search;
        }
    } //search
}
```

White Space Usage

Blank Lines

Blank lines can improve readability by grouping sections of the code that are logically related. A blank line should also be used in the following places:

1. after the copyright block comment, package declaration, and import section;
2. between class declarations;
3. between method declarations;
4. between the last field declaration and the first method declaration in a class; and
5. before a block or single-line comment, unless it is the first line in a block.

Blank Spaces

A single blank space (not tab) should be used:

1. between a keyword and its opening parenthesis. This applies to the following keywords: catch, for, if, switch, synchronized while. It does not apply to the keywords super and this;
2. after any keyword that takes an argument. Example: return true;
3. between two adjacent keywords;
4. between a keyword or closing parenthesis, and an opening brace "{";
5. before and after binary operators except .(dot);
6. after a comma in a list; and
7. after the semicolons in a for statement, e.g.:

```
for (expr1; expr2; expr3) {.
```

Blanks should not be used:

1. between a method name and its opening parenthesis;
2. before or after a .(dot) operator;
3. between a unary operator and its operand;

4. Between a cast and the expression being casted;

5. After an opening parenthesis or before a closing parenthesis; and

6. After an opening square bracket [or before a closing square bracket].

Examples:

```
a += c[i + j] + (int)d + foo(bar(i + j), e);
a = (a + b) / (c * d);
if (((x + y) > (z + w)) || (a != (b + 3))) {
    return foo.distance(x, y);
}
```

Do not use special characters like form-feeds or backspaces.

Indentation

Line indentation is always 4 spaces, for all indentation levels.

The construction of the indentation may include tabs as well as spaces in order to reduce the file size; however, you may not change the hard tab settings to accomplish this. Hard tabs must be set every 8 spaces.

Continuation Lines

Lines should be limited to 80 columns (but not necessarily 80 bytes, for non-English languages). Lines longer than 80 columns should be broken into one or more continuation lines, as needed. All the continuation lines should be aligned, and indented from the first line of the statement. The amount of the indentation depends on the type of statement.

If the statement must be broken in the middle of a parenthesized expression, such as for compound statements, or for the parameter list in a method invocation or declaration, the next line should be aligned with the first character to the right of the first unmatched left parenthesis in the previous line. In all other cases, the continuation lines should be indented by a full standard indentation (4 spaces). If a class or method declaration has one or more continuation lines, then a single blank line should immediately follow the opening brace.

Examples:

```
if (long_logical_test_1 || long_logical_test_2 ||
    long_logical_test_3) {
    statements;
}


function(long_expression1, long_expression2,
         long_expression3, long_expression4,
         long_expression5, long_expression6);
```

A continuation line should never start with a binary operator. Never break a line where normally no white space appears, such as between a method name and its opening parenthesis, or between an array name and its opening square bracket. Never break a line just before an opening brace {. Examples:

```
// WRONG
while (long_expression1 || long_expression2
       || long_expression3)
{
}

// RIGHT
while (long_expression1 || long_expression2 ||
       long_expression3) {
}
```

Comments

Java supports three kinds of comments: documentation, block, and single-line. These are described separately in the subsequent sections below. Here are some general guidelines for comment usage.

- Comments should help a reader understand the purpose of the code. They should guide the reader through the flow of the program, focusing especially on areas that might be confusing or obscure. Avoid comments that are obvious from the code, as in this famously bad comment example:

    ```
    i = i + 1;        // Add one to i
    ```
- Remember that misleading comments are worse than no comments at all.
- Avoid putting any information into comments that is likely to become out-of-date.

- Avoid enclosing comments in boxes drawn with asterisks or other fancy typography.
- Temporary comments that are expected to be changed or removed later should be marked with the special tag "XXX:" so that they can easily be found afterward. Ideally, all temporary comments should have been removed by the time a program is ready to be shipped.

Example:

```
// XXX: Change to call sort() when the bugs are fixed
list->mySort();
```

Documentation Comments

Java has support for special comments documenting types (classes and interfaces), fields (variables), constructors, and methods, hereafter referred to collectively as declared entities. The javadoc program can then be used to automatically extract these comments and generate formatted HTML pages.

A documentation comment should immediately precede the declared entity, with no blank lines in between. The first line of the comment should be simply the characters /** with no other text on the line, and should be aligned with the following declared entity. Subsequent lines consist of an asterisk, followed by a single space, followed by comment text, and aligned with the first asterisk of the first line. The first sentence of the comment text is special, and should be a self-contained summary sentence. A sentence is defined as text up to the first period that is followed by a space, tab, or newline. Subsequent sentences further describe the declared entity.

The comment text can include embedded HTML tags for better formatting, with the exceptions of the following tags: <H1>, <H2>, <H3>, <H4>, <H5>, <H6>, <HR>.

Following the comment text are the documentation tag lines. A documentation comment should include all the tags that are appropriate for the declared entity.

Class and interface comments can use the @version, @author, and @see tags, in that order. If there are multiple authors, use a separate @author tag for each one. Required tags: none.

Constructor comments can use the @param, @exception, and @see tags, in that order. Required tags: one @param tag for each parameter, and one @exception tag for each exception thrown.

Method comments can use the @param, @return, @exception, and @see tags, in that order. Required tags: one @param tag for each parameter, one @return tag if the return type is not void, and one @exception tag for each exception thrown.

Variable comments can use only the @see tag. Required tags: none.

A documentation comment ends with the characters */. It is also acceptable to end the comment with the characters **/ to aid in visual identification of the documentation comment.

Block Comments

A regular block comment is a traditional "C-style" comment. It starts with the characters /* and ends with the characters */.

A block comment is always used for the copyright/ID comment at the beginning of each source file. It is also used to "comment out" several lines of code. Since block comments do not nest, their use in other parts of the source code would make it difficult to comment out code. Hence, the use of block comments other than for the copyright/ID comment and commenting out code is strongly discouraged.

Single-line Comments

A single-line comment consists of the characters // followed by comment text. There is always a single space between the // and the comment text. A single line comment must be at the same indentation level as the code that follows it. More than one single-line comment can be grouped together to make a larger comment; however, if the number of lines is very large, consider using a block comment instead. A single-line comment or comment group should always be preceded by a blank line, unless it is the first line in a block. If the comment applies to a group of several following statements, then the comment or comment group should also be followed by a blank line. If it applies only to the next statement (which may be a compound statement), then do not follow it with a blank line. Example:

```
// Traverse the linked list, searching for a match
for (Node node = head; node.next != null; node = node.next) {
```

Single-line comments can also be used as trailing comments. Trailing comments are similar to single-line comments except they appear on the same line as the code they describe. At least one space should separate that last non-white space character in the statement and the trailing comment. If more than one trailing comment appears in a block of code, they should all be aligned to the same column. Example:

```
if (!isVisible())
    return;                     // nothing to do

length++;                       // reserve space for null term.
```

Avoid the assembly language style of commenting every line of executable code with a trailing comment.

Classes

A class declaration looks like the following. Elements in square brackets [] are optional.

```
[ClassModifiers] class ClassName [Inheritances] {
    ClassBody
}
```

ClassModifiers are any combination of the following keywords, in this order:

```
public abstract final
```

Inheritances are any combination of the following phrases, in this order:

```
extends SuperClass
implements Interfaces
```

SuperClass is the name of a superclass. Interfaces is the name of an interface, or a comma-separated list of interfaces. If more than one interface is given, then they should be sorted in lexical order.

A class declaration always starts in column 1. All of the above elements of the class declaration up to and including the opening brace { should appear on a single line (unless it is necessary to break it up into continuation lines if it exceeds the allowable line length). The ClassBody is indented by the standard indentation of four spaces. The closing brace } appears on its own line in column 1. There should not be a semicolon following the closing brace. If the class declaration has one or more continuation lines, then a single blank line should immediately follow the opening brace.

Class Body Organization

The body of a class declaration should be organized in the following order:

1. class variable field declarations
2. instance variable field declarations
3. constructor declarations
4. class method declarations
5. instance method declarations

These three elements – fields, constructors, and methods are collectively referred to as "members."

Member Access Levels

There are four access levels for class members in Java: public, protected, default, and private, in order of decreasing accessibility. A member should be given the lowest access level that is appropriate for the member. For example, a member that is never accessed outside the class should be set to private access.

Members Comments

All public members must be preceded by a documentation comment. Protected and default access members may have a documentation comment as well, at the programmer's discretion. Private fields should not have a documentation comment. However, all fields that do not have documentation comments should have single-line comments describing them, if their function is not obvious from the name.

Class and Instance Variable Field Declarations

Class variable field declarations, if any, come first. Class variables are those fields that have the keyword "static" in their declarations. Instance variable field declarations, if any, come next. Instance variables are those that do not have the keyword "static" in their declarations. A field declaration looks like the following. Elements in square brackets [] are optional.

```
[Field Modifiers] Type FieldName [= Initializer];
```

Field Modifiers are any legal combination of the following keywords, in this order:

```
public
protected
private
static
final
transient
volatile
```

Always put field declarations on a separate line; do not group them together on a single line:

```
static private int useCount, index;      // WRONG
static private int useCount;             // RIGHT
static private int index;                // RIGHT
```

A field that is never changed after initialization should be declared final. This not only serves as useful documentation to the reader, but also allows the compiler to generate more efficient code.

Constructor Declarations

Constructor declarations, if any, come after any field declarations. All of the elements of the constructor declaration up to and including the opening brace { should appear on a single line (unless it is necessary to break it up into continuation lines if it exceeds the allowable line length). Example:

```
/**
 * Constructs a new empty FooBar.
 */
public FooBar() {
    value = new char[0];
}
```

If there is more than one constructor, sort them lexically by formal parameter list, with constructors having more parameters always coming after those with fewer parameters. This implies that a constructor with no arguments (if it exists) is always the first one.

Class and Instance Method Declarations

Class method declarations, if any, come next. Class methods are those that have the keyword "static" in their declarations. Instance method declarations, if any, come next. Instance methods are those which do not have the keyword "static" in their declarations. All of the elements of a method declaration up to and including the opening brace { should appear on a single line (unless it is necessary to break it up into continuation lines if it exceeds the allowable line length). A method declaration looks like the following. Elements in square brackets [] are optional.

```
[Method Modifiers] Type MethodName(Parameters) [throws
Exceptions] {
```

Method Modifiers are any combination of the following phrases, in this order:

```
public
protected
private
abstract
static
final
synchronized
native
```

Exceptions is the name of an exception, or a comma-separated list of exceptions. If more than one exception is given, then they should be sorted in lexical order.

A method that will never be overridden by a subclass should be declared final. This allows the compiler to generate more efficient code. Methods that are private, or declared in a class that is final, are implicitly final; however, in these cases, the method should still be explicitly declared final for clarity.

Methods are sorted in lexical order, with one exception: if there is a finalize() method, it should be the very last method declaration in the class. This makes it easy to quickly see whether a class has a finalize() method or not. If possible, a finalize() method should call super.finalize() as the last action it performs. If the method declaration has one or more continuation lines, then a single blank line should immediately follow the opening brace.

Interfaces

Interfaces follows a similar style to classes. An interface declaration looks like the following. Elements in square brackets [] are optional.

```
[public] interface InterfaceName [extends SuperInterfaces] {
        InterfaceBody
}
```

SuperInterfaces is the name of an interface, or a comma-separated list of interfaces. If more than one interface is given, then they should be sorted in lexical order.

An interface declaration always starts in column 1. All of the above elements of the interface declaration up to and include the opening brace { should appear on a single line (unless it is necessary to break it up into continuation lines if it exceeds the allowable line length). The InterfaceBody is indented by the standard indentation of four spaces. The closing brace } appears on its own line in column 1. There should not be a semicolon following the closing brace.

All interfaces are inherently abstract; do not explicitly include this keyword in the declaration of an interface.

All interface methods are inherently abstract; do not explicitly include this keyword in the declaration of an interface method.

Interface Body Organization

The body of an interface declaration should be organized in the following order:

1. interface constant field declarations
2. interface method declarations

The declaration styles of interface fields and methods are identical to the styles for class fields and methods.

Statements

Simple Statements

Assignment and Expression Statements

Each line should contain at most one statement. For example,

```
a = b + c; count++;      // WRONG
```

```
        a = b + c;              // RIGHT
        count++;                // RIGHT
```

Local Variable Declarations

Generally, local variable declarations should be on separate lines; however, an exception is allowed for temporary variables that do not require initializers. For example,

```
        int i, j = 4, k;        // WRONG
        int i, k;               // acceptable
        int j = 4;
```

Compound Statements

Compound statements are statements that contain a statement block enclosed in {} braces. All compound statements follow the same braces style; namely, the style commonly known as the "K & R" braces style. This includes class and method declarations. This style is specified below.

1. The opening left brace is at the end of the line beginning the compound statement.
2. The closing right brace is alone on a line, indented to the same column as the beginning of the compound statement.
3. The statements inside the enclosed braces are indented one more level than the compound statement.

In cases where the language allows it, the braces may be omitted in the following situations:

1. The statement block consists of the null statement ";".
2. The statement block consists of a single simple (not compound) statement that fits on a single line.

The rules on how to format particular statements are described below.

if Statement

```
        if (condition) {
            statements;
        }
```

```
if (condition) {
    statements;
} else {
    statements;
}

if (condition) {
    statements;
} else if (condition) {
    statements;
} else {
    statements;
}
```

for Statement

```
for (initialization; condition; update) {
    statements;
}
```

while Statement

```
while (condition) {
    statements;
}
```

do-while Statement

```
do {
    statements;
} while (condition);
```

switch Statement

```
switch (condition) {
case 1:
case 2:
    statements;
    break;
case 3:
    statements;
    break;
default:
    statements;
    break;
```

```
    }
```

try Statement

```
try {
    statements;
} catch (exception-declaration) {
    statements;
} finally {
    statements;
}
```

synchronized Statement

```
synchronized (expression) {
    statements;
}
```

Labeled Statements

Labeled statements should always be enclosed in braces { }. The label itself should be indented to the normal indentation level, followed by a colon, single space, and opening brace. The closing brace should have a trailing comment on the same line with the label repeated:

```
statement-label: {
} // statement-label
```

Sample Internal Support Agreement (ISA)

Root Authority

Root access will be given to Mr. A and Ms. B to support servers AD0001 and AD0002. Mr. A and Ms. B are to support/backup each other (i.e., during illness/vacation). If they're both unavailable, contact Technical Support (within the Data Center).

All changes to root will be audited to provide a trace of activity from the root user. The following activities are to be done by Technical Support upon request:

- kernel changes
- disk reconfigurations
- modifying the root user environment
- installation of any binary into the system directory structure
- modification to any network-related configuration files
- manipulation/modification of any system daemon that is run as root
- changes to the /etc/rc* files

The following (but not limited to these) activities may be done by the Applications Development root owners:

- change /etc/exports for mount directories
- change /etc/vfstab
- add users/groups

Server Availability Hours

- 00:00 - 23:59 Mon, Tue, Wed, Thu, and Sun
- 00:00 - 23:00 Fri
- 03:01 - 23:59 Sat
- 20:00 - 23:59 (once a month for system maintenance/upgrade/testing; all will be posted through Change Control)

Backups

- Full system backups start at 23:00 every Friday; total downtime is 4 hours.
- Incremental backups start at 20:00 (approximately 30 min. Mon-Thr)

Support Responsibility

Table <V>–4 Support Responsibilities

Services	Groups	Types of Services	Hours
System Software	Technical Support	Solaris, Sybase; installation, upgrade, maintenance	00:00-23:59 Mon-Fri

Table <V>–4 Support Responsibilities

Services	Groups	Types of Services	Hours
System Hardware	Desktop Support	Server and workstation, installation and maintenance	00:00-23:59 Mon-Fri
Applications	Applications Development	Setup application, run demos, project file access	08:00-18:00 Mon-Fri

Function of Each Server

Server: AD00001

This server will be the primary development machine to carry the more CPU- intensive workload. Free temporary disk space is available on this machine via Unix automount. Disk quota will be set up for each project. Disk space availability will be determined by the scope of the project.

Configuration Details

- Solaris 2.6
- DNS and NIS slave server host name, IP address, aliases
- Data base server. For example: /export/sybase
- Free hog disk space via automount. For example: /export/common

Server: AD0002

This machine will be used as the Pre-Production server.

- Solaris 2.6
- Project files, data, databases. For example: /export/hrproj
- Clients personal files. For example: /home/username
- Support SPARC clients

Special Requests

These are different categories of special requests and their estimated completion times. These changes include investigating whether the proposed change affects other applications on the server. Technical Support will notify the requester if the request takes longer than the estimated completion time.

Table D–1   Special Request Response Times

Request Type	Response Time
Emergency backups and restores	4 hours
File maintenance	8 hours
Change /etc/dfs/dfstab for mount directories	8 hours
Change /etc/vfstab	8 hours
Add users/groups	8 hours
Solaris kernel changes	5 working days
Database changes	5 working days
Hardware configuration changes	5 working days

How This Book Was Written

Given that this book is about software development and includes many sections on hardware, we thought some readers might be interested in what software and hardware was used to write this book. As with all good software, we will start by discussing the requirements. At the request of the series editor, all drafts had to be done in Microsoft Word. Of course this turned out to be somewhat of a dilemma for primary author Hamilton, who was one of the few people in the computer industry who didn't own a Windows PC. As with all difficult software challenges, however, an answer was found.

At home, where Hamilton wrote most of this book, he used a Power Macintosh 7500/100. Happily, he says, his daughter's school still uses Macintosh computers instead of Windows PCs and thus their home computer was a Mac. Given that today's ads are full of the latest 450 MHz PCs, it's amazing what you can still do with a 100 MHz Mac. Thanks to Steve Jobs' and Bill Gates' recent agreements, the latest version of Microsoft Office actually runs very well on the Mac. The other tool Hamilton used almost daily on the Mac was Netscape, for e-mailing copies of the draft back and forth to all of those who helped to review it, as well as for doing online research.

At work, Hamilton's desktop was a somewhat newer, albeit now over two years old, 200 MHz UltraSPARC desktop running Solaris 2.6. He used this workstation to create all the code segments and most of the various timing numbers listed in this book. Solaris, of course, raised a slightly bigger challenge for editing Microsoft Word documents, not that the author ever did much of that at work. His solution was SoftWindows 95 from Insignia Solutions. SoftWindows lets you run a complete Windows 95 environment on your UltraSPARC desktop; in fact, it even ran Word 7.0 and the complete Office '97 suite. Finally, about halfway through the book, we started using an early release of Sun's PC File Viewer. This tool let the entire Solaris desktop, including the file viewer and mail client recognize (with the correct icons), display, and print Microsoft Word documents (along with about 33 other popular PC file formats). This was useful whenever we wanted to take a quick look at a chapter without having to launch SoftWindows. Things will certainly improve once Office 2000 becomes available with its default HTML file format.

Finally, the completed draft was imported into Adobe's FrameMaker 5.5 desktop publishing tool on a Sun workstation, which was also used for drawing most of the final figures. While this sounds like a lot of work, it really wasn't. Given the wide array of import and export filters available on both Word and FrameMaker, very little extra effort was required to transition back and forth between the two environments.

Bibliography

Arnold, K., and Gosling, J., (1996). *The Java Programming Language*. Addison Wesley.

Boehm, B. (1988). A Spiral Model of Software Development and Enhancement. *IEEE Computer*, May.

Brooks, Jr. F. P., *(1975)*. No Silver Bullet: Essence and Accidents of Software Engineering, *IEEE Computer*, April.

Brooks, Jr. F. P., (1975). *The Mythical Man Month*. Addison Wesley.

Cockcroft, A., (1998). *Sun Performance and Tuning: Java and the Internet, Second Edition*. Prentice-Hall.

Grady, R., (1992). *Practical Software Metrics for Project Management and Process Improvement*. Prentice-Hall.

Kern, H. and Johnson, R., (1994). *Rightsizing The New Enterprise*. Prentice-Hall.

Kern, H., Johnson, R., Galup, S., Horgan, D., (1998). *Building The New Enterprise*. Prentice-Hall.

Kern, H., Johnson, R., Hawkins, M., (1996). *Managing The New Enterprise*. Prentice-Hall.

Kern, H., Johnson, R., Hawkins, M., (1997). *Networking The New Enterprise*. Prentice-Hall.

Kernighan, B. and Ritchie, D. (1988). *The C Programming Language, Second Edition*. Prentice-Hall.

Meyer, D., (1997). *Structural Cybernetics*. NDMA Publishing.

Orfali, R., and Harkey, D., (1998). *Client/Server Programming with JACA and CORBA, Second Edition*. John Wiley & Sons.

Stroustrup, B., (1997). *The C++ Programming Language*. Addison Wesley.

Wong, B., (1997). *Configuration and Capacity Planning For Solaris Servers*. Prentice Hall.

Winston W., (1970). Managing the Development of Large Software Systems: Concepts and Techniques. 1970 WESCON Technical Papers, Western Electronic Show and Convention, Los Angeles, Aug. 25-28.

Glossary

API

Application Programming Interface - a description of the interface, usually presented in terms of the callable functions (or methods) and their parameters, used to program a particular application.

Application Server

A server used in a multi-tier architecture to process programs, typically implementing the business logic functionality of an application.

BLOBS

Binary Large Objects - a database type that allows large binary files to be managed as fields of a database. Usually used for video, audio, or program files.

CGI

Common Gateway Interface - an API used by programmers to invoke other applications (such as databases) from a web server.

DNS

Domain Name Service - the standard hostname directory service on the Internet.

Extranet

An Intranet that includes external organizations or individuals such as suppliers or customers.

Internet Time

The notion of Internet time, also referred to as dog-years on the Internet, was popularized by Marc Andreesen and the early developers of Netscape's first web browser. To meet competitive pressures, Netscape's developers were forced to work schedules that were at least seven times more compressed than regular schedules.

Intranet

An information system internal to an enterprise that follows the Internet web based metaphor. Intranets are most commonly used for distributing internal manuals, procedures, and other online documents; for distributing web-centric applications; and for enterprise-wide office applications such as electronic mail, calendar, and workflow.

Index

debugger 47, 228
Dennis Ritchie 199
Developer 2000 220
disassembler 228
Discovery and Join 304
DMZ 187
DNA 67
DNS 190, 282, 290, 307
DOS 23
Dr. Barry Boehm 34

E

Edsger Diijkstra 201
EJB 287
emacs 226
EMC 249
ENIAC 233
Enterprise JavaBeans 203
enterprise resource planning 59
ERP 61
Essential complexity 169
Ethernet 304
Extranet 185

F

FC-AL 251, 269
FDDI 247
fields 43
firewall 180, 301
FORTRAN 28, 143, 201, 204, 261, 272
Full Moon 258

G

Ganymede Software 224
garbage collection 206
Gary Oing 139
Gemstone Systems 222
GemStone/J 222
GIS 57
Global Positioning System 27

global variable 40
Grady Booch 48

H

Halstead metrics 168
Help Desk 184
High Performance Computing 139
HotJava 203
HP/UX 213
HTML 56, 64, 213, 225, 281, 303
HTTP 180, 283
HTTP proxy 180

I

IBM 50, 141, 181, 201, 216, 256
IDE 86, 211
IDL 292
IEEE Computer 34
IIOP 292
ILOG 219
implementation inheritance 45
Imprise 215
Information Technology Association of
    America 72
infrastructure 25
interface inheritance 45
Internet 26, 123, 142, 159, 162, 214
intranet 214
Introspection 265
ISA 185
ISP 190
Ivar Jacobson 48

J

Jaguar 223
James Gosling 180, 203
Java 42, 72, 94, 97, 138, 202, 306
Java ACES 139
Java Development Kit 17
Java Messaging Service 289